BASIC LETTER & MEMO WRITING

FOURTH EDITION

Susie H. VanHuss, Ph. D.
Professor and Program
Director of Management
University of South Carolina
Columbia, South Carolina

JOIN US ON THE INTERNET
WWW: http://www.thomson.com
EMAIL: findit@kiosk.thomson.com   A service of I(T)P®

South-Western Educational Publishing
an International Thomson Publishing company I(T)P®

Cincinnati • Albany, NY • Belmont, CA • Bonn • Boston • Detroit • Johannesburg • London • Madrid
Melbourne • Mexico City • New York • Paris • Singapore • Tokyo • Toronto • Washington

Vice President of Publishing	Peter McBride
Editional Coach	Penny Shank
Production Coordinator	Patricia M. Boies
Manufacturing Coordinator	Kathy Hampton
Marketing Manager	Mark Linton
Marketing Coordinator	Tricia Allen
Cover Design	Lou Ann Thesing

Copyright © 1998

by SOUTH-WESTERN EDUCATIONAL PUBLISHING

Cincinnati, OH

ISBN: 0-538-67516-0

2 3 4 5 6 7 8 9 C1 05 04 03 02 01 00 99 98

Printed in the United States of America

I**T**P®

International Thomson Publishing

South-Western Educational Publishing is an ITP Company. The ITP logo is a registered trademark used herein under license by South-Western Educational Publishing.

CONTENTS

CHAPTER 8 COLLABORATIVE AND TEAM WRITING

CHAPTER 9 GOODWILL AND PERSONAL BUSINESS MESSAGES

CHAPTER 10 EMPLOYMENT COMMUNICATIONS

APPENDICES

PREFACE

LEARN TO WRITE EFFECTIVELY

Success in your educational endeavors and in your career requires the ability to communicate effectively in writing. *Basic Letter and Memo Writing, 4th edition,* helps you to become a more effective writer by showing you how to:

- enhance and adapt your basic writing to meet the needs of the reader and the particular situation
- employ good strategies for solving business problems
- learn and use effective editing techniques
- develop information management skills and use technology effectively to facilitate writing and production of messages
- become more aware of cultural diversity and the importance of the global marketplace

APPLY CRITICAL THINKING TO THE WRITING PROCESS

Effective writing incorporates many subskills, such as analyzing, visualizing, and decision making. Many of these subskills have been identified in a national survey called the SCANS Report (Secretary's Commission on Achieving Necessary Skills) as skills critical for success in the workplace. These subskills are emphasized in *Basic Letter and Memo Writing*. The chart on pages x–xii shows how the SCANS skills are incorporated into each chapter.

The reason for producing a document often determines the specific subskills that will be needed to make the document effective. Basic documents require you to communicate ideas clearly, concisely, and accurately using appropriate language. More complex documents require you to acquire information from on-line or traditional sources, analyze and evaluate that information, and interpret it before you can prepare the document. These subskills focus on creative thinking, decision making, and problem solving. Preparing the document may require you to simplify the material by illustrating it with charts, graphs, and other symbols to enable the reader to comprehend the material. You will have an opportunity to develop and apply all of these skills as you work through the applications in *Basic Letter and Memo Writing*.

MASTER BASIC WRITING PRINCIPLES AND PRODUCE HIGH QUALITY BUSINESS COMMUNICATIONS

Basic Letter and Memo Writing's combination problem-solving and writing strategy (model) approach makes it easy to learn the process of planning and writing effective messages. You will produce high-quality results early in the learning experience. You will begin by mastering basic principles and then applying those principles to basic documents before progressing to more complex business documents.

A simple to complex approach is used to achieve these results. The first two chapters of the text are designed to introduce and teach basic writing principles. The remaining eight chapters show how to apply those basic principles to specific writing situations.

Chapter 1—Style, Process, and Product: Focuses on communication from the perspective of the organization, the employee, and the recipient. It distinguishes between learning the process of writing and developing good results. The chapter illustrates and analyzes writing styles and focuses on adapting style to meet the needs of the reader and the situation.

Chapter 2—Ten Guides for Effective Writing: Presents and illustrates basic writing principles, including: writing for the reader, presenting ideas clearly, using concrete language, formatting documents carefully, and editing and proofreading.

Chapter 3—Positive Letters and Memos: Shows you how to analyze situations, and anticipate the manner in which the reader is likely to react to a message. The examples illustrate appropriate styles and strategies for situations in which the reader is likely to respond in a neutral or positive way.

Chapter 4—Negative Letters and Memos: Focuses on situations in which the reader is likely to be displeased and to respond to the situation in an unfavorable manner. It also addresses mixed-news situations that elicit both favorable and unfavorable reactions. Effective examples of direct and indirect strategies are provided.

Chapter 5—Persuasive Letters and Memos: Focuses on factors that influence persuasion. Ethical issues in persuasion are highlighted and brainstorming techniques are presented to help generate creative ideas.

Chapter 6—Letter and Memo Reports: Focuses on messages used for decision making. This chapter gives you experience analyzing, organizing, formatting, and conveying information in an objective, systematic manner.

Chapter 7—Form Letters and Memos: Explains the need for efficiency, as well as effectiveness in preparing documents. The text covers four types of forms—complete forms, variable forms, form paragraphs, and guide forms.

Chapter 8—Collaborative and Team Writing: Emphasizes the need to work effectively in teams and presents strategies for team writing.

Chapter 9—Goodwill and Personal Business Messages: Focuses on the need to build goodwill and presents strategies for writing thank you, congratulatory, and special occasion messages. Sympathy messages are also discussed.

Chapter 10—Employment Communications: Addresses employment both from the perspective of the employer and the employee. Major emphasis is placed on applicant tracking systems and electronic résumés. Traditional employment communications are also discussed. You can use this chapter to facilitate your job search after you have completed chapters 1 through 5.

BROADEN YOUR AWARENESS THROUGH KEY FEATURES

- Global and Technological Connections—Each chapter features a discussion of global and technological issues as they relate to business communication. For example:

  Using technology to create, process, and transmit documents
  Cultural diversity and global competitiveness

Using technology to prepare form messages
Groupwriting
Automating the employment process

- Internet: The SuperHighway of Communications—Each chapter provides information about using the Internet. For example:

Guides for Preparing Electronic Mail Messages
Security of Electronic Communications
Netiquette
Electronic Distribution of Documents
Using the Internet in Your Job Search

- Miscommunications—A look at the lighter side of communications.
- Heritage Corporation Case Study Applications—Each chapter ends with a case study assignment which places students in the role of an employee of the Heritage Corporation.

Real-world business assignments include:

Prepare for a brainstorming session on new product development
Prepare meeting notes
Search the Internet for information
Brainstorm content for an international training video
Prepare a report with recommendations on video content
Research training guide materials
Write a memo reporting on team development project
Research and report on using the Internet in international recruiting and employment activities

SIMPLIFY LEARNING WITH EASY-TO-FOLLOW CHAPTER ORGANIZATION

Each chapter includes:

- Performance goals—competencies that you will develop by studying the materials carefully and completing the applications
- Overview—a preview of the contents of the chapter
- Discussion and illustrations of the topic
- Features

Global or Technological Connections
Internet: The Superhighway of Communications
Miscommunications

- Applications—In addition to the on-going Heritage case study, there are applications for reviewing the basic writing principles, applying the content of the chapter, editing documents, and performing a self-assessment. The applications in Chapters 1 and 2 vary slightly from those in Chapters 3 through 10. Chapter 1 contains three applications.

1A applies the content of the chapter.
1B is a self-assessment that you can use to determine if you have mastered the content of the chapter.
1C introduces you to Heritage Productions, a case study that continues with applications in every chapter.

- Chapter 2 contains four applications.

  2A applies the content of the chapter.
  2B is an editing and language arts checkpoint.
  2C is a self-assessment.
  2D is the Heritage Productions case study.

- Chapters 3 through 10 contain five applications.

  Application A reviews the basic writing principles.
  Application B is an editing and language arts checkpoint.
  Application C applies the content of the chapter.
  Application D is a self-assessment.
  Application E is the Heritage Productions case study.

DEVELOP YOUR ON-LINE EDITING SKILLS

A template diskette is available for use with this text. The template diskette contains the editing exercises and can also be used with word processing software for drafting, editing, and revising documents. You are encouraged to prepare communications at the computer and to use on-line reference tools with all applications.

APPRECIATION

The author and publisher wish to thank the teachers who used the previous editions of this text and provided suggestions for improving the 4th edition. Special thanks to the following for reviewing the manuscript.

Kimberly S. Wilson
Business Education Instructor
Greene County Career Center,
Xenia, Ohio

Donna Hardin
Clinton County Mentor Teacher
Clinton County Educational Services Center,
Wilmington, Ohio

Susie H. VanHuss

WORK SKILLS CRITICAL FOR CAREER SUCCESS

Basic Letter and Memo Writing	Foundation Skills			Workplace Competencies				
	Basic Skills	Thinking Skills	Personal Qualities	Resources	Information	Interpersonal	Systems	Technology
Chapter 1								
Content	✓	✓	✓	✓	✓	✓	✓	✓
Application 1A	✓	✓	✓		✓	✓	✓	
Application 1B	✓	✓			✓	✓	✓	✓
Application 1C	✓	✓	✓		✓	✓		
Chapter 2								
Content	✓	✓	✓		✓	✓		✓
Application 2A	✓	✓	✓		✓	✓		
Application 2B	✓	✓						✓
Application 2C	✓	✓		✓	✓	✓		
Application 2D	✓	✓			✓			
Chapter 3								
Content	✓	✓	✓		✓	✓	✓	✓
Application 3A	✓	✓						✓
Application 3B	✓	✓						✓
Application 3C	✓	✓		✓	✓			✓
Application 3D	✓	✓						✓
Application 3E		✓			✓	✓		✓
Chapter 4								
Content	✓	✓	✓		✓	✓	✓	✓
Application 4A	✓	✓				✓		
Application 4B	✓	✓						✓
Application 4C	✓	✓	✓			✓		✓
Application 4D	✓	✓	✓		✓	✓		✓
Application 4E	✓	✓	✓	✓	✓	✓		✓

WORK SKILLS CRITICAL FOR CAREER SUCCESS

Basic Letter and Memo Writing	Foundation Skills			Workplace Competencies				
	Basic Skills	Thinking Skills	Personal Qualities	Resources	Information	Interpersonal	Systems	Technology
Chapter 5								
Content	✓		✓		✓		✓	✓
Application 5A	✓			✓	✓			✓
Application 5B	✓	✓						
Application 5C	✓	✓		✓	✓	✓		✓
Application 5D	✓	✓	✓		✓	✓		✓
Application 5E	✓	✓	✓		✓	✓		✓
Chapter 6								
Content	✓	✓			✓	✓		✓
Application 6A	✓	✓			✓			
Application 6B	✓	✓	✓		✓	✓		✓
Application 6C	✓	✓			✓			✓
Application 6D	✓	✓		✓	✓			✓
Application 6E	✓	✓		✓	✓	✓		
Chapter 7								
Content	✓	✓		✓	✓	✓	✓	✓
Application 7A	✓	✓						
Application 7B	✓							✓
Application 7C	✓				✓		✓	
Application 7D	✓				✓			✓
Application 7E	✓	✓			✓	✓		✓
Chapter 8								
Content	✓	✓	✓	✓	✓	✓	✓	✓
Application 8A	✓	✓					✓	
Application 8B	✓	✓						
Application 8C	✓	✓	✓	✓	✓		✓	✓
Application 8D	✓	✓	✓		✓	✓		✓
Application 8E	✓	✓	✓		✓	✓		✓

WORK SKILLS CRITICAL FOR CAREER SUCCESS

Basic Letter and Memo Writing	Foundation Skills			Workplace Competencies				
	Basic Skills	Thinking Skills	Personal Qualities	Resources	Information	Interpersonal	Systems	Technology
Chapter 9								
Content	✓	✓	✓		✓	✓		✓
Application 9A	✓					✓		✓
Application 9B	✓							✓
Application 9C	✓	✓	✓		✓	✓		✓
Application 9D	✓	✓	✓		✓	✓		✓
Application 9E	✓	✓	✓	✓	✓	✓		✓
Chapter 10								
Content	✓	✓	✓	✓	✓	✓	✓	✓
Application 10A	✓							
Application 10B	✓							✓
Application 10C	✓	✓	✓		✓	✓		✓
Application 10D	✓	✓	✓		✓	✓	✓	✓
Application 10E	✓	✓	✓		✓	✓	✓	✓

STYLE, PROCESS, AND PRODUCT

Performance Goals

After you complete Chapter 1, you should be able to
- ❏ *Compare modes of communicating and select the best mode for a specific situation*
- ❏ *Assess styles of writing*
- ❏ *Develop a plan for improving your writing style*
- ❏ *Become more comfortable with the process of writing*
- ❏ *Assess the factors that influence your writing*

OVERVIEW

Chapter 1 focuses on communication from several different perspectives:

- The role of communication in the success of an organization.
- The role of communication in the career development of an employee.
- The impact of communication on the recipient.

Viewing communication from these three different perspectives makes it essential to analyze factors such as the importance of communications, the volume and type of communication, the tools used to facilitate communication, the development of employees to be effective communicators, and the importance of stylistic elements. Effective communication is the ultimate goal. Chapter 1 and the chapters that follow focus on ways to achieve excellence in communication.

Effective communication is not an automatic happening; it results from
- ■ *strong desire*
- ■ *persistent effort*
- ■ *wise choice*
- ■ *knowledge*
- ■ *masterful execution*

THE ORGANIZATION'S PERSPECTIVE

Communication is a critical component of every facet of an organization's operation. Today's information-based economy requires a growing number of white-collar workers to manage and process the information critical to the success of their businesses. When things go as planned, effective communication is often taken for granted; however, when things go awry, most people label poor communication or lack of communication as the culprit.

Organizations communicate orally, in writing, and nonverbally. Selecting the best mode of communication requires careful analysis of the situation and

Organizations include businesses, governmental agencies, professional firms or associations, clubs, nonprofit groups, and so on.

the objectives to be accomplished by the communication. Many factors influence the decision to use one mode of communication over another, such as the:

- anticipated response of the recipient to the way in which information is communicated
- sensitivity of the situation
- the speed required
- the need for documentation
- destination (internal or external) of the communication and the accessibility of the recipient
- the costs involved

Selecting the mode or combination of modes of communication may be the most significant factor in determining the outcome of a communication.
(Your instructor may direct you to complete Application 1A, page 13 at this time.)

For example, many people prefer to transmit sensitive information in a person-to-person setting. Electronic mail, on the other hand, is generally considered informal and impersonal; therefore, it would not be a good alternative for sending sensitive information. Complex information, information needed for future reference, and situations that require documentation should be put in writing.

Often, combining modes of communication works better than using a single mode of communication. Most organizations confirm telephone conversations in writing to preserve a record of the information transmitted. A short electronic voice message or written message may alert a recipient to expect detailed information about a particular topic or event. This textbook focuses on situations requiring written communications exclusively or in combination with other modes of communication.

TYPE AND VOLUME OF COMMUNICATIONS

Some organizations require far more written communications than do other types of organizations. However, virtually every organization has extensive need to put ideas in writing and to share them with others within and external to the organization.

Storing information in an on-line database that can be accessed directly by anyone needing that information creates a new paradigm for transmitting information internally.

Internal communications. A large majority of communications generated within an organization stay within the organization. Forms, memos, reports, newsletters, electronic mail, and other documents are all used for internal mail. Storing information in an on-line database so that any employee who needs the information can access it directly is becoming the newest mode of transmitting internal information.

External communications. Clients, customers, suppliers, and a host of other individuals and businesses receive external communications. These types of communications include letters, reports, newsletters, proposals, forms, and numerous other documents.

A significant portion of every worker's day is spent communicating—the product of that time and effort is a tremendous volume of communications.

Often one business transaction triggers numerous communications. A business that is applying for a loan to build a new office building may generate hundreds of external and internal documents. The internal documents may focus on the needs of various work groups, specifications for facilities, and logistical factors. External communications may focus on obtaining cost information from a variety of sources to determine the amount of money to be borrowed and on pursuing sources of funding. The financial institution that receives the loan application may, in turn, generate 50 or more internal and external communications in processing the loan.

COST AND QUALITY OF COMMUNICATIONS

Organizations spend significant amounts of money on written communications. The cost of a communication varies dramatically depending on a number of factors, such as

- who produced the document
- where the document is produced
- how the document is produced
- what type of document is produced

A document produced by a senior executive costs more than a document produced by a customer service representative. An electronic message that takes only two or three minutes to compose and transmit costs less than a formal letter. Complex documents cost less than simple straightforward documents. Estimates of the average cost of a letter or memo range from $15 upward.

The same factors that impact costs often impact quality. Organizations tend to be very cost conscious. However, most organizations place quality before cost. They are unwilling to sacrifice quality to obtain cost savings.

The costs of communicating effectively may be very high—but not nearly as high as the cost of not communicating effectively.

THE EMPLOYEE'S PERSPECTIVE

The ability to communicate effectively in writing is one of the skills needed for success in every career. The individual who has developed the ability to communicate effectively in writing has a very marketable skill that will facilitate career growth within an organization and that is transferable to other organizations.

Effective writing incorporates many subskills that are emphasized in this textbook. The reason for producing a document often determines the subskills that a writer needs to prepare an effective document. Most documents require the writer to communicate ideas clearly, accurately, and concisely using appropriate language. However, numerous situations require the writer to have many subskills beyond just basic writing skills.

Lifetime employability requires, among other things, the ability to write effectively.

- A document designed primarily to communicate information may require the writer to acquire the information, evaluate it, organize the information, and interpret it in order to communicate that information effectively.
- A document designed to convey a way to solve a problem requires a different set of subskills that may focus on creative thinking, decision making, and problem solving.
- A document designed to persuade someone to do something that the individual would not normally elect to do may require a totally different set of subskills such as using emotional and logical appeals.
- Writing documents that contain complex information often requires the writer to be able to illustrate information with graphs, charts, and other symbols to enhance the recipient's ability to comprehend the information in the document.

Basic writing skills are prerequisite to producing effective written documents; other skills include
- *thinking and analytical skills*
- *reading skills*
- *interpersonal skills*
- *information management skills*
- *the ability to use technology effectively*

THE RECIPIENT'S PERSPECTIVE

Far too many documents are written from the perspective of the writer rather than from the perspective of the person receiving the document. A key fact to remember is that the writer already knows and understands the information that needs to be communicated. The recipient lacks that information. Therefore, anything that can be done to enhance the recipient's understanding of the information should take precedence over the preferences of the writer.

THE PROCESS OF WRITING

The difference between mediocre and good writing often rests in the time and effort spent editing and refining documents.

People generally think of writing only as a product and devote relatively little thought to the process of developing an effective product. In their minds, a communication is either effective or not effective. Thinking of writing as a process is important because any process can be learned.

Good writers tend to have several qualities in common. First, they have a strong desire to write effectively. Second, they recognize that many subskills—such as the ability to think logically, to apply basic principles of communication, and to use language appropriately—are involved in writing. Third, they realize that effective writing generally is not achieved in the first attempt. Good writing is usually the product of revising and editing to achieve the desired results. Fourth, good writers work hard at improving their writing skills. They develop the subskills needed, and they revise and edit documents until the final product is effective.

Fortunately, the more that writers work at improving their writing skills, the easier writing becomes. Once writers have mastered the basic skills and have gained experience in the process of writing and revising, they are able to produce high-quality documents in less time and with less effort. The actual process, or the way in which people write, varies dramatically.

USING A FREE-FORM APPROACH

Some writers like to put their thoughts down on paper quickly as those thoughts occur. Then they go back and organize their thoughts and add substance to provide a first draft. Then they revise and edit the draft to produce the desired result.

USING A STRUCTURED APPROACH

Other writers prefer to use a more structured approach to writing. Usually they follow a very systematic approach of planning a communication, collecting all the information needed to write the communication, organizing the information, preparing a detailed outline, preparing a draft, reviewing the draft to determine its effectiveness, and then revising and editing the document.

USING A COMBINED APPROACH

Many writers use an approach that combines or modifies features of the two extremes just presented. Usually this approach consists of planning the document, having at least a mental outline, preparing the draft, revising the draft, and editing and proofreading to ensure that the communication is effective.

SELECTING AN APPROACH

No one best approach for writing exists. Always select an approach that is natural and easy for you to use.

The process that will work best for you depends on the basic skills that you bring to the task, the amount of experience you have in writing, and the way that you are most comfortable writing. The key is to select a process that focuses on writing in a way that is natural and easy for you. You may want to start by using a very structured approach. As your writing skills improve and as you gain more experience, you can combine and eliminate some of the steps in the process.

STYLE

Style refers to a pattern of observable behaviors or characteristics. Style is reflected in the choice of clothing, in the way hair is worn, in the interactions between people, and in the way people speak and write. Each individual has a unique or preferred style.

Communication always involves more than one person. The preferred style of a speaker may not match the style preferences of a listener. The writing style that one individual prefers to use may not be compatible with the style of the reader. To be effective, the style that an individual uses often has to be adapted to meet the needs and preferences of other people.

Style must also be appropriate for the situation. For example, a person who is writing a congratulatory note to an individual who received a promotion and a note of sympathy to an individual who lost a family member should not use the same style for both situations.

The degree of formality in a situation also influences the style that is appropriate. An analogy can be made between dress and writing style. You would probably be very uncomfortable if you attended a formal banquet in a jogging suit. Your jogging suit may be very stylish, of the very best quality, and may cost more than the formal attire worn by other individuals, but it would not be appropriate for the occasion. Likewise, you would probably be very uncomfortable going on a picnic in formal banquet attire.

Think about the invitations that might be written to attend the formal banquet and the picnic. Would the same style of writing be appropriate to invite guests to a formal banquet and to a picnic? To be effective, writing style as well as dress must be appropriate for the specific situation.

The following pages illustrate three very different writing styles for answering the same letter. First read the letter that was received (shown on page 6) and must be answered. Analyze it carefully, paying particular attention to the writer's style and to the situation involved. Then read the three alternative responses that illustrate different styles used to answer the letter.

The key to using style effectively in written communications is to adapt the style of the writer to accommodate the needs of the reader and the situation.

Letter Received

The Vista Development Foundation
1385 Gervais Street ▪ Columbia, SC 29201-9473
E-Mail SAPIENZA@VDF.COM ▪ (803) 555-0187
FAX (803) 555-0193

October 15, 19—

Mr. Mark Elkins, President
Elkins and Associates
1284 Hampton Ridge Road
Columbia, SC 29209-4753

Dear Mr. Elkins

You have made many contributions to the development of our community
while a member and former president of the Builders Association. You
helped to organize the volunteers who worked on many projects that we
can now point to with great pride in our community. On the Youth
Recreation Complex, you served as coordinator and project overseer. That
project today is a model for what can be done when caring citizens work
together to improve the community for all our citizens.

As you probably read in the newspaper, the new Vista Development Master
Plan has been approved by all the parties involved and is ready to become
a reality. The Vista Development Foundation is now constituting an
advisory board to coordinate all the individual building projects involved.
The Vista Advisory Board will review bid specifications, evaluate all bids
that are received, select the winning bid, and provide oversight during
development to ensure that all projects adhere strictly to the Master Plan.
We invite you to serve as a member of the Vista Advisory Board and to
help ensure the successful completion of the project.

Please let me know within the next two weeks that you will be able to
assist us in this important endeavor. We truly need your guidance.

Sincerely

Angela Sapienza
Executive Director

pr

Why is it important to analyze the style of a message you receive? _____

_____

_____

Reply: Style 1

Elkins and Associates
1284 Hampton Ridge Road
Columbia, SC 29209-4753
(803) 555-0144 ■ FAX (803) 555-0166

October 20, 19—

Ms. Angela Sapienza, Executive Director
The Vista Development Foundation
1385 Gervais Street
Columbia, SC 29201-9473

Dear Ms. Sapienza

Thank you for your most kind and generous letter with a gracious
invitation to serve on the Vista Advisory Board. Nothing would please me
more than to be able to serve our wonderful community once again as it
moves forward with the extremely ambitious and exciting plans to develop
the Vista area. However, I am unable to do so at this time.

Our business has increased significantly, and I have made major
commitments of my time to building projects scheduled over the next two
years. Therefore, I would be unable to devote either the quality or the
quantity of time that this most worthy project deserves. In fact, one of the
projects we have on the drawing board may potentially be a candidate for a
site in the Vista Development area.

Again, thank you for the most complimentary remarks about my
community service and your confidence in my ability to serve on this
prestigious advisory board. Please call on me again sometime in the future
if I can be of service. You may be assured that I will give future requests
from you serious consideration with the expectation that I will be in a
position to reply affirmatively.

Sincerely

Mark Elkins
President

sr

*Read all three responses and
compare the styles before you
complete the questions at the
bottom of each page.*

*After you have read the three
letters, try to determine why
you prefer one style over the
others.*

How do you react to this style? ❑ Favorably ❑ Unfavorably ❑ Neutral

What did you like about the style? _____

_____

What did you dislike about the style? _____

_____

Reply: Style 2

Read all three responses and compare the styles before you complete the questions at the bottom of each page.

After you have read the three letters, try to determine why you prefer one style over the others.

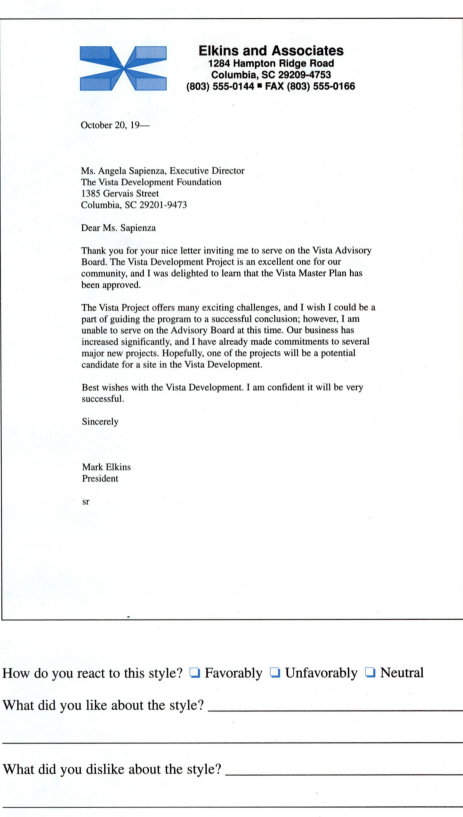

Elkins and Associates
1284 Hampton Ridge Road
Columbia, SC 29209-4753
(803) 555-0144 ◼ FAX (803) 555-0166

October 20, 19—

Ms. Angela Sapienza, Executive Director
The Vista Development Foundation
1385 Gervais Street
Columbia, SC 29201-9473

Dear Ms. Sapienza

Thank you for your nice letter inviting me to serve on the Vista Advisory Board. The Vista Development Project is an excellent one for our community, and I was delighted to learn that the Vista Master Plan has been approved.

The Vista Project offers many exciting challenges, and I wish I could be a part of guiding the program to a successful conclusion; however, I am unable to serve on the Advisory Board at this time. Our business has increased significantly, and I have already made commitments to several major new projects. Hopefully, one of the projects will be a potential candidate for a site in the Vista Development.

Best wishes with the Vista Development. I am confident it will be very successful.

Sincerely

Mark Elkins
President

sr

How do you react to this style? ❑ Favorably ❑ Unfavorably ❑ Neutral

What did you like about the style? _____

_____

What did you dislike about the style? _____

_____

Reply: Style 3

Elkins and Associates
1284 Hampton Ridge Road
Columbia, SC 29209-4753
(803) 555-0144 ■ FAX (803) 555-0166

October 20, 19—

Ms. Angela Sapienza, Executive Director
The Vista Development Foundation
1385 Gervais Street
Columbia, SC 29201-9473

Dear Angela

Thanks for a neat letter. Sure wish I could help you by serving on the Vista
Advisory Board, but I can't.

Our business is zipping, and I can barely keep it on course with all the
activities that are going on now.

Good luck with the project. Hope it is a huge success.

Sincerely

Mark Elkins
President

sr

Read all three responses and compare the styles before you complete the questions at the bottom of each page.

After you have read the three letters, try to determine why you prefer one style over the others.

How do you react to this style? ❏ Favorably ❏ Unfavorably ❏ Neutral

What did you like about the style? _____

_____

What did you dislike about the style? _____

_____

Typical reactions to the letters are noted below. If you disagree, why?
Letter 1: Style is wordy and egotistical.
Letter 2: Style seems to be sincere and appropriate for the situation.
Letter 3: Style seems to be insincere and flippant.

Observation
The content of the three versions is basically the same; however, the style is very different.

The technology used to create, process, and transmit documents affects the cost, quality, and time required to produce and transmit documents.

Technology facilitates the writing and editing of documents—it does not replace good writing.

Technology enhances productivity by enabling writers to produce and transmit high-quality documents more efficiently. It helps lower the cost of producing effective documents.

TECHNOLOGICAL CONNECTIONS

A vast array of technologically advanced tools are available for use in producing and distributing documents. The traditional way of producing documents—handwriting them or dictating them for support staff to produce on a typewriter and distribute through internal mail or the postal service—accounts for a small percentage of all documents produced. The traditional model clearly separated the originator of documents and the producer of documents. Today, multiple models exist. The originator and producer of a document may be the same individual, different individuals, or even a team of writers who jointly originate and produce the document. The way that a document is distributed often depends on the technology used to produce the document.

SUITE OF APPLICATIONS

Today, the bulk of all documents are produced using personal computers and suites of software. The software used for document production is more likely to be a suite of integrated office applications—word processing, spreadsheet, database, and graphic/presentation software—rather than just a word processing package.

Integrated applications. The ability to integrate a variety of software applications and use them to facilitate communication creates a whole new paradigm for document creation, production, and dissemination. Compound documents—documents containing elements or objects from two or more software applications—are produced routinely. These tools, when used appropriately, have the potential to significantly improve document quality and readability as well as streamline the production of documents.

On-line reference tools. Historically, writers depended on a series of hard-copy references, such as a dictionary, thesaurus, and communications handbook. Today, the suite of office applications contains these references on-line for quick and easy use. Although these tools do not replace editing and proofreading, they do assist the writer in editing and proofreading more efficiently.

LASER PRINTERS

The capabilities of laser printers add a new dimension to document design and document production. High-quality resolution, the addition of graphic elements, and the use of color drastically improve the image and readability of documents when principles of good design are applied.

ELECTRONIC DOCUMENT TRANSMISSION

Networks that facilitate the distribution of information create new categories of documents that are used frequently in organizations. These network applications integrate the origination, production, and distribution of documents.

Electronic mail. In most organizations, electronic mail generally refers to short, informal communications that are sent on-line over an intranet (a proprietary or company-owned network). However, it is sometimes used for more extensive documents and with file attachments. Electronic mail has replaced a substantial portion of paper-based internal memos and telephone messages. An electronic message can be transmitted to single or multiple recipients. Electronic messages usually are created and produced by the same individual.

Facsimile. The use of facsimiles (faxes) has revolutionized the distribution of documents. A separate fax machine or a fax modem in a computer can be used to transmit documents to remote locations in a matter of minutes. Through the combined use of scanning and telephone technology, documents containing text, graphs, photographs, and other images can be delivered quickly and inexpensively to recipients worldwide.

Electronic distribution of documents has dramatically altered the speed and cost of delivering documents to remote locations.

THE SUPERHIGHWAY OF COMMUNICATIONS

INTERNET

Organizations and individuals use the Internet for many different applications. Individuals typically use an on-line service to access the Internet. Organizations frequently have intranets (proprietary networks) as well as links to the Internet. Intranets are used primarily for internal communications or for communications with suppliers and customers. The Internet has a variety of uses. It may be used to search for information on a specific topic that a writer is researching, for example, or to publish on-line information that an organization wishes others to be able to access.

The Internet section in each chapter of this text focuses on using the Internet to facilitate communications. Technical information about accessing or using the network is not addressed.

MISCOMMUNICATIONS

Classified ad placed in local newspaper by a day-care center:

Wanted: 4-year-old teacher with
at least one year of experience.
Reference required.
Call 555–0147.

It would have to be a pretty bright youngster to be able to teach at the age of four and already have a year of experience.

Despite good intentions, communications often result in miscommunications, such as chuckles or bloopers, and in other unintended results.

NAMING CONVENTIONS FOR TEXT FILES

The template diskette that accompanies this textbook uses a very simple, straightforward approach for naming files. You are encouraged to use a similar approach when you prepare communications throughout this text. In some cases, such as in this first chapter, it is easier to handwrite the assignments. In other cases, you will find it easier to compose communications at the computer. Use the following conventions for naming your files throughout the textbook.

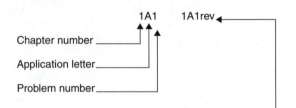

Chapter number, Application letter, Problem number, revised

APPLICATION 1A *Select the Best Communication Mode*

1. An employee who has a good performance record has been late for work several times during the past three weeks, and you must call the situation to the attention of the employee.

____ E-mail	❏ Acceptable	❏ Unacceptable
____ Memo	❏ Acceptable	❏ Unacceptable
____ Telephone call	❏ Acceptable	❏ Unacceptable
____ Personal visit	❏ Acceptable	❏ Unacceptable

2. An employee that you supervise has just received an award from a community service agency for outstanding service, and you want to congratulate the employee.

____ E-mail	❏ Acceptable	❏ Unacceptable
____ Memo	❏ Acceptable	❏ Unacceptable
____ Telephone call	❏ Acceptable	❏ Unacceptable
____ Personal visit	❏ Acceptable	❏ Unacceptable

3. An out-of-state customer recently experienced the death of a spouse, and you wish to express your sympathy. You have a business—not personal— relationship with the customer and have never met the spouse.

____ E-mail	❏ Acceptable	❏ Unacceptable
____ Personal letter	❏ Acceptable	❏ Unacceptable
____ Telephone call	❏ Acceptable	❏ Unacceptable
____ Sympathy card	❏ Acceptable	❏ Unacceptable

Apply the concepts you learned in Chapter 1.

1. *For each situation described, place a check mark in the blank before the **one mode of communication you think would be the very best to convey the information.***
2. *For each alternative mode provided for the situation, check if the mode is acceptable or unacceptable.*
3. *In the space below the mode, indicate why you think the mode would be acceptable or unacceptable.*

4. A customer is considering installing a home elevator that your company sells; the customer has requested specifications for the elevator and has indicated that the information is needed urgently.

____ E-mail	❏ Acceptable	❏ Unacceptable
____ Letter	❏ Acceptable	❏ Unacceptable
____ Telephone call	❏ Acceptable	❏ Unacceptable
____ Fax	❏ Acceptable	❏ Unacceptable

5. A customer requesting a credit limit increase from $5,000 to $10,000 has a bad credit rating, and you cannot grant the increase.

____ E-mail	❏ Acceptable	❏ Unacceptable
____ Letter	❏ Acceptable	❏ Unacceptable
____ Telephone call	❏ Acceptable	❏ Unacceptable

APPLICATION 1B *Self-Assessment*

1. Describe several factors that influence the decision to use one mode of communication rather than another mode.

Chapter 1

Complete the questions to determine if you have mastered the content of Chapter 1.

2. Describe how information stored in an on-line database can affect communications in an organization.

3. Describe what is meant by style and how it affects communications.

4. Describe how technology affects the creation and distribution of documents.

5. Explain how developing the ability to write effective communications can positively impact your career.

APPLICATION 1C *Introduction to Heritage Productions*

Heritage Productions, a well-known producer of educational and training videos, has hired you as a management trainee. Your training program includes rotating through the various departments of Heritage to gain a better perspective of the entire organization. Your role is to assist the manager of each department to which you are assigned, and your title is assistant manager.

Heritage has identified a niche market that it is considering developing. Currently, Heritage has a very successful line of video training programs that supplement EFL (English as a Foreign Language) classes. Heritage is now thinking about developing two new product lines.

1. EFL videos designed for business people who are either preparing to accept a foreign assignment or who do business with individuals in an English-speaking country. These videos differ from the current school line in that the content would be business topics and the videos would be self-paced training programs used at home or in the office.

2. Cross-cultural training videos designed to acquaint business people who are either preparing to accept an assignment in a foreign country or who do business with individuals in a foreign country with the culture of that country.

All managers have been asked to give serious thought to these potential product lines. You will attend a brainstorming session in a few days to address the following topics:

• English is considered the language of business around the world. EFL classes are extremely popular, but in many countries they are hard to access. Would individuals be willing to work on their own to learn English rather than take classes? Would video materials containing business vocabulary and content have an advantage over the general materials that are typically used in EFL classes?

• Is it important for people to understand the culture of other countries in which they are doing business? Why? Can Heritage market these videos?

Give thought to these two questions and in the space on the next page outline key points that you can contribute to the discussion.

TEN GUIDES FOR EFFECTIVE WRITING

Performance Goals

After you complete Chapter 2, you should be able to
- ❏ *Apply the guides for effective writing*
- ❏ *Format letters using a consistent style*
- ❏ *Edit communications more effectively*

OVERVIEW

You can learn to be an effective writer! The first step in the process of becoming a good writer is to learn basic guides for effective writing. A writer with limited experience should follow guides closely. More experienced writers can take a little more latitude in adapting basic guides to accomplish the objectives of a message.

Chapter 2 contains ten sections. One basic guide for effective writing is presented and explained in each section. Examples illustrating the application of the guide are also presented.

A guide is a recommended or suggested way of writing; it is not an inflexible rule that can never be violated.

- Application 2A gives you practice applying the guides. Your instructor may direct you to complete part of the application after studying each guide or to complete all of it after you have studied the ten guides. This application also requires you to review your basic language arts skills because you are expected to write complete and grammatically correct sentences and paragraphs.
- Application 2B contains a document that you must edit. This application is designed to help you improve your editing, proofreading, and basic language arts skills.
- Application 2C contains a self-assessment so that you can determine if you have mastered the content of Chapter 2.
- Application 2D contains your work as a management trainee for Heritage Productions.

GUIDE 1—PLAN MESSAGES CAREFULLY

Planning is the most critical step in writing a message. Think about why you are writing. You do not write just for the sake of writing. You write to accomplish a specific purpose. The purposes of communications vary widely. The

Careful planning is the key to ensuring that a message accomplishes its intended purpose.

purpose might be to provide information, to seek information, to solve a problem, to build good relationships, to persuade a reader to do something, or even to force action. Your message must be designed to accomplish the purpose for writing it.

FOCUS ON ACHIEVING OBJECTIVES

Planning sounds very simple, and the need for careful planning seems to be very obvious. Many writers, however, skip the planning process. They start writing, dictating, or keying the message and try to plan it as they write. Writers who skip the planning process run the risk of creating a message that does not achieve its objective.

Writers who plan as they write also run another risk—the risk of creating a stereotyped message. Stereotyped messages are mundane; they all sound alike. When writers plan while they write, they tend to use the same opening and closing statements. For example, when they answer letters, they may begin all their responses with a statement such as *Thank you for your letter of (insert date)*. They may end all responses with a statement such as *If I can be of further service, please let me know.*

These statements may be good opening and closing statements for certain situations; however, in other instances, they may be terrible opening and closing statements. In a positive situation in which the writer meets the needs of the reader, the opening and closing statements would probably be effective. In a negative situation in which the writer did not meet the needs of the reader, these opening and closing statements would probably not be effective.

THINK THROUGH THE ENTIRE SCENARIO

Planning skills require logical thinking and the ability to solve problems.

Planning is a mental, or thinking, process. It requires that you think through a situation carefully and determine the best way to handle that situation. Effective planning focuses on meeting the objectives of both the reader and the writer.

Think about this example. Put yourself into the position of a sales representative for an oriental rug dealer who has just received an inquiry about a large, high-quality oriental rug. The letter requested information about

- price range
- availability of 14′ × 20′ rugs or larger
- availability of one-of-a-kind and museum-quality pieces
- literature on available oriental rugs

Think carefully about this situation in order to plan the best possible approach for answering this letter.

Brainstorming involves a freewheeling approach to generating as many ideas as possible and delaying critical evaluation of the ideas during the idea generation process.

Use questions to facilitate the thought process. The best way to begin a thinking exercise is to do a little brainstorming. In this example, asking questions provides an excellent way to begin the brainstorming process. Formulate as many questions as you can about the writer, the purpose for writing, and the entire situation. The following list of questions provides a good start for the process of thinking through this particular situation. As you think about the questions, speculate on possible answers to the questions. You may wish to discuss them with the other members of your class. Also try to add questions to the list provided here.

1. Why did the individual request the information?

2. Do you think the individual contacted other rug dealers?

3. What do you know about the individual who requested the information?

4. Do you think the individual is very knowledgeable about the quality and costs of oriental rugs?

5. Does the information requested give you any clues about the lifestyle of the individual?

6. Does the information requested give you any clues about the financial status of the individual?

7. What mental image do you have of the individual?

8. How do you think your competitors would respond to the request for information?

9. What do you have to gain from this situation?

    Add your own questions here:

10. _____

    _____

11. _____

    _____

12. _____

    _____

An effective message meets the needs of both the reader and the writer of a message.

The important point here is that thinking through the situation usually begins with analyzing the reader, but it eventually leads you to consider both the reader's objectives and your own objectives.

PLAN MESSAGES SYSTEMATICALLY

The recommended message planning process consists of five steps. One of the best ways to think about each step is to answer key questions about the process.

You are more likely to hit the target if it is clearly identified.

Determine objectives. The key questions to ask are *What do I expect to accomplish by writing this message?* and *What does the reader expect to accomplish with my message?* Effective planning requires careful consideration of the objectives of both the writer and the reader.

Most writers have a general idea of why they are writing a message. A general idea is a good beginning, but it is not adequate to ensure an effective message. Specific ideas need to be identified. Unless you know exactly what you are trying to communicate, you are not likely to be successful in getting the message across.

Analyze the reader. The key questions to ask are *What information do I have about the reader that will help me understand the reader's needs?* and *Can I visualize the person?*

Knowledge about a reader's occupation or expertise in a particular area is important. This type of information helps you determine if the reader would be familiar with the technical language that relates to a particular area. An engineer could use engineering terminology in communicating with another person who understands engineering terminology. A layperson, however, would not likely understand engineering terminology. Terms that are used by people in a particular industry are known as *jargon*. Jargon is appropriate only for people in that industry who are likely to understand it.

Other factors that could affect the style of a message and, therefore, should be considered are culture, approximate age, gender, rank or position, and the importance of the topic to the individual.

The best psychological approach for presenting information can be selected only after all decisions have been made.

Make decisions. The key question is *What decisions must be communicated in the message?* All decisions should be made prior to writing a letter or memo. In the business world, both information that will be received positively and information that will be received negatively must be communicated. The same writing style is not appropriate for both types of messages.

Start the writing process using a detailed outline until you become more comfortable writing; then move to a very brief outline; finally move to a mental plan.

Collect information. The key questions are *What information is needed to write this message effectively?* and *Is the information available?* Once you have determined the information that you need, you should assemble that information before you start writing. Knowing what you are going to include in a message enables you to organize the material and sequence it in the order that will be most effective in communicating the points you want to make.

(Your instructor may direct you to complete the Guide 1 Application on page 49 at this time.)

Develop the plan. The key question is *Do I have a written outline or at least a mental plan for the entire message?* The entire message should be planned before you begin to write. The beginning and the ending of the message deserve particular attention. Writing a message is simple once the logical analysis has been completed. The only thing left is to ensure that you implement your plan effectively.

GUIDE 2—WRITE FOR THE READER

Always remember that you are writing to communicate to the reader. A good message meets the needs of both the reader and the writer. Most readers expect a message to be logical, helpful, sincere, and courteous. Even messages that contain negative information can meet these expectations.

USE EMPATHY

The best way to adapt a message to meet the needs of the reader is to use empathy. Think of yourself in the position of the reader. If you were the reader rather than the writer of the message, how would you react in the same situation? Would you view the message as logical, helpful, and sincere? The person who receives a message often views it differently than the person who sends that message. A person writing a message may want the reader to do something. The reader, on the other hand, is likely to view the message with a what's-in-it-for-me attitude.

Empathy means placing yourself mentally into the reader's position.

Messages written from an empathetic, considerate point of view are likely to be considered effective by readers. Writing from the viewpoint of the reader is sometimes called the *you attitude*. The you attitude is often misinterpreted to mean that the pronoun *you* should be used frequently and the pronoun *I* should rarely be used. Both pronouns are appropriate and can be used effectively. Overuse of the pronoun *I* makes the writer appear to be self-centered. A common and very obvious overuse of the pronoun *I* is to begin every paragraph with *I*.

Good writers usually try to avoid beginning an entire message and the majority of paragraphs within the message with I.

The pronoun *you* can also be misused. The you attitude is appropriate only when it is used in a sincere and honest manner. The idea is to show respect and a genuine concern for the reader. The attitude is far more important than the pronoun choice.

Compare the following sentences that illustrate writing from the perspective of the writer and writing from the perspective of the reader. The message is essentially the same in each example, but the tone is very different.

> ### WRITER'S PERSPECTIVE
>
> I need printing supplies, and I want you to order them today if possible.
>
> I have a Planning Committee meeting scheduled at 9:30 on Tuesday morning that I cannot attend, and I want you to represent me while I am out of town unless you have something scheduled that can't be canceled.
>
> I reviewed your proposal, and I think it is excellent.

Compare the messages; which would you prefer to receive?

> ### READER'S PERSPECTIVE
>
> Would you please order our printing supplies today if possible.
>
> If your schedule permits, would you please represent me at the Planning Committee meeting at 9:30 on Tuesday morning while I am out of town?
>
> Your proposal is excellent.

USE A COURTEOUS TONE

The concept of courtesy means being polite, kind, and considerate of others. *Please* and *thank you* are words most often associated with the concept of courtesy. Most people appreciate requests that are prefaced with

Every reader deserves courteous treatment; no justification exists for bad manners.

please. They also appreciate being thanked **after** they have done something for someone else. Note the timing of the words—*please* is appropriate before something has been done and *thank you* is appropriate only after something has been done.

Some writers with good intentions make the mistake of thanking people before they grant a request. *Thank you in advance* assumes that the person will do what you are asking, and most people do not like to be taken for granted. It also implies that you do not plan to thank them after they have done something. Rather than thank a person in advance, show gratitude in another way.

Courtesy implies more than just saying please and thank you. Courtesy also includes the tone or manner in which something is said. Sarcasm, lectures, condescending statements, derogatory comments, and crude language offend most readers. Write in a way that respects rather than offends readers.

OFFENSIVE TONE

Report to my office for a short meeting at 2:00 today.

Since you are so late with your report, fax it to me as soon as you finish it.

If you had mailed your July payment on time, your account would have been credited correctly.

COURTEOUS TONE

Please come to my office for a short meeting at 2:00 today.

Please fax your report to me just as soon as you finish it.

Your July payment arrived after your statement was prepared; therefore, the credit does not appear on your August statement.

WRITE IN A FAIR AND UNBIASED MANNER

Use a fair and unbiased style without awkward phrases such as he/she.

Good writers present their ideas using a nondiscriminatory style. Using a fair and unbiased style avoids the possibility of offending the reader. Discrimination in writing occurs in several ways, including using sexist or racist words, using masculine pronouns to refer to both men and women, using words that stereotype women and minorities, and using words that reduce the status of individuals. Often writers use discriminatory language without intending to be discriminatory; they simply do not realize that a problem exists.

DISCRIMINATORY OR AWKWARD STYLE

The girls won more medals at the Olympics than the men did.

If a manager does his job well, he will be promoted.

Did the black judge question the tactics used by the salesman?

If a customer wants to pick up his or her clothes the same day, he or she must bring them in by 8:30 A.M.

> **FAIR AND UNBIASED STYLE**
>
> The women won more medals at the Olympics than the men did.
>
> Managers who do their jobs well will be promoted.
>
> Did the judge question the tactics used by the sales representative?
>
> Customers who wish to pick up their clothes the same day must bring the clothes in by 8:30 A.M.

(Your instructor may direct you to complete the Guide 2 Application on page 53 at this time.)

GUIDE 3—PRESENT IDEAS POSITIVELY

Positive thinking is powerful. You can accomplish far more with a positive attitude than with a negative attitude. In business, circumstances often require you to convey both positive and negative information. Most writers find it easy to convey positive information and very difficult to convey negative information. Rarely is receiving negative news a desirable experience; however, you can make the situation less painful for the reader by using an honest—but positive—writing style.

DISAGREE, BUT DO NOT BE DISAGREEABLE

The ability to disagree without being disagreeable is an art. You may not always agree with an individual to whom you must write, but you do not have to be disagreeable just because you see things from a different perspective. Good writers present their views without offending the reader.

Determining whether the cup is half full or half empty is a matter of attitude.

> **DISAGREEABLE**
>
> The payment plan you proposed is totally ridiculous.
>
> You sold us a worthless piece of junk that you called a projector. Bring us a real projector or refund our money.
>
> **DISAGREE WITHOUT BEING DISAGREEABLE**
>
> The following payment plan builds on your proposed plan and makes it a workable solution.
>
> The projector you sold us continues to malfunction; please replace it with a projector that functions properly.

Disagreeing is often necessary and is acceptable; being disagreeable is neither necessary nor acceptable.

USE POSITIVE IDEAS AND FOCUS ON WHAT CAN BE DONE

Writers with good intentions often use negative statements to present positive ideas. One of the most frequently used sentences to close business letters is *If I can be of further service, please do not hesitate to let me know.* Note that the negative form is used. Why should the reader hesitate to ask you for additional service if it is needed? The intention is good, but the result is not as good. A more effective closing would be *Please let me know if I can be of further service.*

Tells you where you cannot park.

Tells you where you can park.

Good writers tell readers what they can do rather than what they cannot do. Focusing on the negative frequently accomplishes only half the job. It tells you what cannot be done but it leaves out what can be done. A sign prohibiting parking in "this area" only indicates what cannot be done. Drivers are not told where they may park if they desire to do so.

> **NEGATIVE**
>
> Don't forget to mail this letter today.
> Why don't you call your doctor for an appointment?
> Don't smoke in the office.
>
> **POSITIVE**
>
> Please remember to mail this letter today.
> Perhaps, you should call your doctor for an appointment.
> Smoking is permitted only on the outside terrace at the west entrance.

LIMIT THE USE OF NEGATIVE WORDS

Your instructor may direct you to complete the Guide 3 Application on page 55 at this time.

Many words have a negative connotation. Use negative words sparingly. Although it may be necessary to convey a negative message, you should select words that are not excessively strong. The best approach is to focus on the solution rather than the problem. Writing negative messages will be discussed in more detail in Chapter 4.

GUIDE 4—WRITE IN A CLEAR, READABLE STYLE

Clarity means writing so clearly that the message cannot be misinterpreted.

Clarity involves more than writing a message that can be easily understood by the reader. Clarity is achieved when a message is presented in such a way that a reader interprets the message exactly as the writer intended for it to be interpreted. Clarity plays a crucial role in written communications because immediate feedback is not available. In a conversation, a listener who is not sure how to interpret a message usually will ask clarifying questions. That option is not available when written communications are used to convey messages.

The language an individual uses in conversations usually varies significantly from the language used in writing. Conversation language tends to be very informal, and written language is often very stiff and stilted. The objective in written communications is to use a comfortable, conversational tone, but not an overly informal tone.

> **STILTED LANGUAGE**
>
> The above referenced matter was acted upon in an expeditious manner at the Executive Committee meeting yesterday with an affirmative response.
>
> Pursuant to our discussion on Thursday, I evaluated the inventory level and ascertained that it is being maintained according to prescribed guidelines.

CONVERSATIONAL LANGUAGE

The Executive Committee considered and approved your proposal at its meeting yesterday.

After our conversation on Thursday, I checked our inventory levels and found them to be in line with the guides we established.

Simplicity is the key to a conversational tone.

FACTORS INFLUENCING CLARITY

The purpose for writing a message is to communicate ideas to the reader. Therefore, you should do everything possible to ensure that the reader will understand and interpret the ideas in the way that you intended. Good writers write to express an idea clearly; they rarely write primarily for the purpose of impressing the reader. Therefore, they tend to simplify their writing as much as possible. A number of factors influence the clarity and readability of a message.

Write to express ideas clearly—not to impress the reader.

Vocabulary. Word selection is a very important factor that influences clarity. The difficulty of the vocabulary depends on the reader and can be viewed from several different perspectives. The length of words and the number of syllables influence difficulty. Generally, longer words with many syllables are more difficult than shorter words, but this is not always the case. Words such as *agricultural* and *satisfactorily* are long and have many syllables, but the average reader would not have difficulty with these words. *Albeit* (meaning *although*) is a short word with three syllables, but the average reader would find it to be relatively difficult. Familiarity is the difference in those two examples. Most readers are familiar with a*gricultural* and *satisfactorily,* but not with *albeit.*

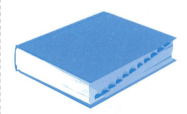

The use of jargon and foreign expressions are vocabulary influences that affect the clarity of messages. Jargon is language that is common within an industry, but not generally known by outsiders. Foreign expressions, such as *proforma* (meaning *as a matter of form*) and *antebellum* (meaning *before the war*) can be a problem to readers who are not familiar with the terms. Acronyms, such as *ASAP* (meaning *as soon as possible*), also influence difficulty because someone who is not extremely familiar with the acronyms has to translate them in the same way that a foreign expression is translated.

The reader should not have to use the dictionary to understand your message.

DIFFICULT VOCABULARY

The recalcitrant, obstreperous students commenced with an interminable dissertation about the eccentricities of the professor.

Distractor analysis performed on the questionable item on the SQT and appropriate decision criteria provided a basis for determining if the response was miskeyed.

We must scrutinize alternative solutions, prioritize and strategize, and develop an appropriate implementation plan.

EASIER VOCABULARY

The noisy, defiant students began a long discussion about the teacher's odd behavior.

The answer choices on a questionable item on the Skills Qualification Test were analyzed to determine if the wrong answer key was used.

We must analyze the situation, determine the best strategy, and put an action plan in place.

Sentence structure and length. Clarity is influenced by sentence structure and length. Short, direct sentences are easier to understand than long involved sentences. Usually a long involved sentence must be read more than once to grasp its meaning.

LONG, INVOLVED SENTENCES

During her tenure of 25 years with the agency, Mary's manager said that she had been absent only a total of 10 days.

If by some fortuitous opportunity you should discover my umbrella, which I appear to have abandoned in your office facility, please give me the courtesy of a telephone call.

SHORT, MORE DIRECT SENTENCES

Mary's manager said that Mary has worked with the agency 25 years and has been absent only 10 days.

I think I left my umbrella in your office. Please call me if you find it.

Note in this example how easily the first sentence could be misinterpreted. Did Mary or Mary's manager have 25 years of tenure with the agency? Was Mary or her manager absent ten days? The sentence is the foundation of all writing. Developing effective sentences is critical to achieving the objectives of a message. Guide 8 provides additional information about structuring sentences effectively.

Paragraph length and structure. The length and structure of paragraphs influence clarity. Long paragraphs are difficult to read and often have to be read more than once to determine the meaning intended. Paragraphs that contain complex material, multiple items, and statistical material deserve special attention.

Multiple items in paragraphs should be itemized to simplify reading and to balance the emphasis given to each item. Graphs, charts, tables, and illustrations should be used to simplify the presentation of complex or statistical information.

COMPLEX PARAGRAPHS

The content of the training program was based on four recurring themes, including developing an ownership mentality, giving good internal customer service results in effective external customer service, working as a team and communicating openly and effectively, and following up on action promised.

The age of our employees includes 9 percent less than 21 years old, 31 percent between 21 and 40 years old, 45 percent between 41 and 65 years old, and 15 percent older than 65.

SIMPLIFIED PARAGRAPHS

The content of the training program was based on four recurring themes:

- Developing an ownership mentality
- Giving good internal customer service results in effective external customer service
- Working as a team and communicating openly and effectively
- Following up on action promised

The age of our employees is shown in the following chart:

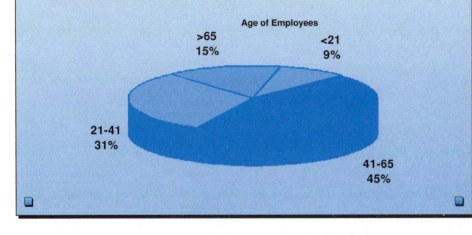

A picture is worth a thousand words.

Although the information in the complex and the simplified paragraphs is the same, the simplified paragraphs are easier to read. Enumerating items makes it easier for the person responding to a message because items can be easily checked off. Checking off items is more difficult when the items are clustered in a paragraph than when they are enumerated. Guide 8 provides additional information on structuring paragraphs effectively.

(Your instructor may direct you to complete the Guide 4 Application on page 57 at this time.)

GUIDE 5—CHECK FOR COMPLETENESS

A complete message is one that contains all the information necessary to meet the objectives of both the writer and the reader. Messages that have been planned and edited carefully will usually contain all essential information. However, not all messages are planned or edited carefully. Incomplete messages often require a second communication. Therefore, you should ensure that a message has all the essential information to avoid the cost, embarrassment, and lost time that often results from incomplete messages.

ANTICIPATE QUESTIONS

A complete message anticipates questions the reader may have and provides answers before the questions are asked.

In addition to presenting the information needed, you should also anticipate questions that the reader may have and provide answers to those questions. Analyze the following situation to determine the essential information that must be provided and the types of questions that can be anticipated from the reader.

> You are coordinating a special function for the high-volume independent agents who sell insurance provided by your company. The Saturday function at Pat's Place, a beach resort near Charleston, includes a two-hour business meeting followed by lunch and an afternoon of recreation including a choice of golf, tennis, or beach activities. The evening includes an appreciation dinner for the agents. Your company will provide hotel accommodations for Saturday night.

ESSENTIAL INFORMATION

- Address, telephone number, and how to get to the resort
- Complete schedule of activities
- Information about who is invited; specified agents and spouses
- Information about the business session and recreational events
- Procedure for handling expenses

ANTICIPATE QUESTIONS

- What type of attire is appropriate for the various functions? How should "casual dress" be interpreted?
- Can reservations be extended? At whose cost? At what amount?
- Are accommodations available for children? How are children's expenses handled?
- What activities include spouses?

A message that anticipates questions readers may have and provides answers to those questions is more effective than a message that assumes readers know the information. A complete message keeps the reader from making assumptions that may prove to be incorrect or even embarrassing. It also saves time for both the writer and the reader by making additional inquiries unnecessary. A writer may not always be able to anticipate all questions that a reader may have; however, the writer who plans carefully will anticipate as many key questions as possible and provide answers to those questions.

ASSUMPTIONS

Assumptions are similar to walking a tightrope—a fine line divides providing too little or too much information.

Assumptions deserve special attention. Assumptions require making judgments. Determining whether the reader knows or does not know the information is a judgment call. If the reader does not know the information and it is omitted, the letter is incomplete. If the reader knows the information and the writer repeats it, the letter is likely to be considered wordy.

In the situation in which agents were invited to an event, two different scenarios probably would occur. Agents who had been invited previously would probably know the answers to most of the anticipated questions. Agents who had not been invited previously would probably not know the answers to the anticipated questions. If the same information is sent to all, the only real choice is to provide more information than some may need.

The best way to ensure that a message is complete is to edit for completeness after the letter has been written but before it has been printed. Ask what information should have been included and then check to see if the message contains the information.

Assuming too little and providing more information than needed serves as a safety net and is better than assuming too much and omitting needed information.

(Your instructor may direct you to complete the Guide 5 Application on page 59 at this time.)

GUIDE 6—USE AN EFFICIENT, ACTION-ORIENTED STYLE

Most business people are busy and would prefer to read only what is necessary. Conciseness is a virtue in business writing. An efficient style, however, should not be confused with a blunt or curt style. Most people expect courtesies and do not consider them to be wordy. An efficient writer strives to get the message across in a considerate manner and with the fewest words possible. Building goodwill should never be sacrificed in the name of efficiency.

Writing in an efficient style means saying everything that needs to be said and nothing more.

Writing in an action-oriented style generally is the preferred style. However, in some situations, an action-oriented style may be a poor style choice. When negative messages are conveyed, an action-oriented style may be interpreted as being too aggressive or too strong. A neutral or less lively style may be more appropriate for conveying negative situations.

In addition to giving a feeling of movement, communications written in an action-oriented style tend to be shorter than communications written in a passive style. Busy people appreciate communications that are condensed. Condensed copy contains all information necessary to achieve the objectives of the message and omits all unnecessary words, phrases, and details.

Writing in an action-oriented style means writing in a strong, lively style that gives a sense of movement.

EFFICIENT WRITING TECHNIQUES

Efficient writing is accomplished in several ways. The technique that is most effective depends on the situation and on the style preferred by both the reader and the writer. Good writers select and use a variety of different techniques depending on the situation.

Use direct style. Information presented in a logical, straightforward manner usually results in efficient writing. Direct style normally takes fewer words to accomplish the objectives than does an indirect style of writing. Direct style generally works best when positive information is being conveyed.

Eliminate repetitive material. Efficient writing eliminates material that has already been presented or that the reader already knows. The writer should be wary of assuming a reader knows certain information and should try to ensure that the reader actually knows the information before eliminating it. Some repetition is useful and even necessary. Repetition can be used effectively to emphasize ideas and to show relationships between material already presented and new material. Unless repetition accomplishes a specific purpose, repetitive information should be eliminated.

Avoid hidden verbs. Verbs are sometimes hidden in noun form. Using a noun form rather than an active verb tends to weaken a sentence and make it wordy.

Writing efficiently generally requires replacing correct—but wordy—elements with shorter elements.

In the sentence *Pat announced that the tour will start at 10:15 a.m.,* the active verb *announced* is used. In the sentence *Pat made the announcement that the tour will start at 10:15 a.m.,* the verb *announced* is changed to a noun form and another verb is added to the sentence.

Compare the following sentences that use a hidden verb form with those that use an active verb form.

HIDDEN VERB FORM

Robert sent Leigh an invitation to the Carolina Cup.

Fred must make a decision on the builder today.

Please let me know if I can be of assistance to you.

Please take all factors into consideration before making a decision on the issue.

ACTIVE VERB FORM

Robert invited Leigh to the Carolina Cup.

Fred must decide on the builder today.

Please let me know if I can assist you.

Please consider all factors before deciding on the issue.

Note the differences in length of the sentences using the hidden verb form and those using the active verb form. Noun forms are correct; they just tend to weaken writing and add words to the sentence.

Replace wordy phrases. Wordy writing often contains phrases for which one word would convey the message adequately. Phrases add variety and should not be eliminated totally. A workable approach consists of substituting a word for the phrase and then evaluating the sentence to see if the change weakened the sentence in any way. The following examples illustrate words that can be used to replace phrases.

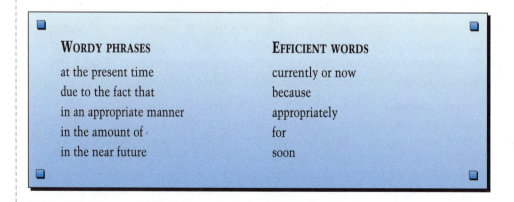

WORDY PHRASES	EFFICIENT WORDS
at the present time	currently or now
due to the fact that	because
in an appropriate manner	appropriately
in the amount of	for
in the near future	soon

Use modifiers and descriptive words when they add variety or contribute to the message in other ways.

Limit the use of modifiers to essential ones. Modifiers should be used when words need to be qualified. Some words, however, should not be qualified; they stand alone. Examples of words that should not be qualified follow.

WORDS THAT STAND ALONE	INAPPROPRIATE MODIFIERS
cooperate	cooperate together
innovation	new innovation
maximum	maximum possible
merge	merge together
repeat	repeat again
revert	revert back

Minimize the use of descriptive words. Descriptive words should be used when they clarify information. Some descriptive words simply occupy space and contribute nothing of value to the sentence. For example, in writing about New York, distinguishing between the city and state is important. Therefore, it may be essential to say *the state of New York* to distinguish it from *the city of New York*. However, in referring to New Orleans, saying *the city of New Orleans* wastes space and adds nothing of value. Note the following examples of words with unnecessary descriptors.

Eliminate modifiers and descriptive words to reduce message length and wordiness.

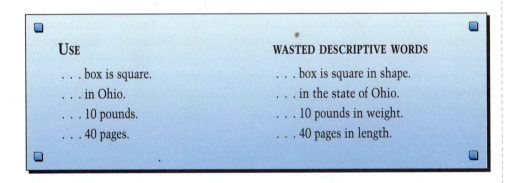

USE	WASTED DESCRIPTIVE WORDS
. . . box is square.	. . . box is square in shape.
. . . in Ohio.	. . . in the state of Ohio.
. . . 10 pounds.	. . . 10 pounds in weight.
. . . 40 pages.	. . . 40 pages in length.

The sentences containing extra descriptive words are correct; the words simply are wasted because the meaning is clear without them. Some additional words may be used to add variety. Overuse of descriptive words creates wordy communications. Limited use may be appropriate.

Use active voice appropriately. Although the active voice condenses copy, using active voice deserves special attention because it influences style, strength, and movement. The key issue is deciding when active voice is appropriate and when passive voice would be a better alternative. Active verbs are used when the subject does the action described by the verb. Passive verbs are used when the subject receives the action. Passive verbs consist of some form of the verb *to be* (*am, are, is, was, were, be, being,* and *been*) and a past participle. Passive statements usually contain a *by* phrase to identify the subject.

Use active voice to convey positive information and give appropriate emphasis to the subject.

Knowing when to use active voice is important. Active voice is used effectively to convey positive information and to show the importance of the subject. Passive voice is used effectively to convey negative information and when the subject is irrelevant. Compare the sentences that follow.

Use passive voice when the subject doing the action is irrelevant and to tone down negative messages.

PASSIVE SENTENCES

The announcement of the Employee of the Year will be made by the Governor.

Mark was presented with the award by the senior senator.

The baby was saved by Eve Young.

✓ The annual report is mailed to stockholders on March 30.
✓ Your check was mailed today.
✓ The watch was broken when the box was opened.

ACTIVE SENTENCES

✓ The Governor will announce the Employee of the Year.
✓ The senior senator presented the award to Mark.
✓ Eve Young saved the baby.

The corporate secretary mails the annual report to stockholders on March 30.

The accounting clerk mailed your check today.

You broke the watch when you opened the box.

(Your instructor may direct you to complete the Guide 6 Application on page 61 at this time.)

Note the checked (✓) sentences. The first three passive sentences are more effective when they are converted to active voice. The sentences are stronger and place appropriate emphasis on the subject. The last three passive sentences are more effective in passive voice than active voice. In the fourth and fifth sentences, who mails the annual report or the check is irrelevant. No one cares who mails it. The last sentence would be far too strong if it were written in active voice. Active voice places blame and would be considered offensive.

GUIDE 7—USE CONCRETE LANGUAGE

Concrete is usually defined as existing in material form. Using concrete language is important in writing because readers can usually relate better to specifics than to generalities. Abstract ideas are often open to interpretation. Specific language takes the guesswork out of reading.

Consider the following scenario. Bill complained that he received a poor raise and was unhappy about it. Jim indicated that he received a very nice raise and that he was pleased. Ironically both employees received identical raises of 5 percent, and Jim's performance evaluation was better than Bill's. This situation points out the confusion that can occur when general language is used. What one individual perceives to be very bad, another may perceive to be very good.

Concrete language is very specific language that conveys precise meaning.

Specific language conveys stronger messages than does general language. Specific language calls attention to and adds emphasis to statements. Therefore, specific language is preferred. However, general language may be more appropriate for handling sensitive or negative situations.

The expression *ASAP* meaning *as soon as possible* deserves special attention in business. Writers use it when they need something immediately. However, readers often interpret the message to mean when I can get around to it. How would you respond if your bills came with an ASAP notice? Would you pay them immediately? *At your earliest convenience* has the same connotation.

Read the following sentences that contain general language. Then interpret the general language in the space provided.

GENERAL LANGUAGE

Jean makes a very good salary. (How much?) _____

Joe bought a substantial number of books. (How many?) _____

Please send me the material as soon as possible. (When?) _____

I need a good supply of forms. (How many?) _____

Pat wears expensive suits. (What's expensive for a suit?) _____

SPECIFIC LANGUAGE

Jean makes an annual salary of $75,000.

Joe bought 20 books.

Please send me the material by May 1.

I need 500 forms.

Pat wears $1,500 suits.

(Your instructor may direct you to complete the Guide 7 Application on page 63 at this time.)

GUIDE 8—USE EFFECTIVE SENTENCE AND PARAGRAPH STRUCTURE

Effective sentences and paragraphs provide the foundation for effective messages. Sentence structure can be used to add variety to writing and to make a message interesting. Effective sentences must be organized appropriately to form effective paragraphs. Messages carefully organized are easier to read and understand. Paragraphs divide material into manageable units of thought.

Good writers pay careful attention to sentence structure and to the way paragraphs are organized.

SENTENCE AND PARAGRAPH LENGTH

The length of sentences and paragraphs directly affects readability. Good sentence length averages about 17 to 20 words, and good paragraph length averages about 4 to 8 lines. The length of individual sentences and paragraphs should vary. You should not count words and lines. Rather, develop a feel for the amount of copy that is appropriate for a sentence or paragraph. If either seems to be too long, restructure the sentence or paragraph.

Long sentences and paragraphs are more difficult to read than are short sentences and paragraphs.

USE SENTENCE STRUCTURE STRATEGICALLY

The three basic types of sentences—simple, compound, and complex—should be used strategically to accomplish objectives.

Simple sentences. A simple sentence presents an idea clearly and emphatically. Thus, to emphasize an idea, use a simple sentence. Conversely, to de-emphasize an idea use a complex sentence. Too many simple sentences result in choppy, dull writing. Use complex and compound sentences to add variety and to break the monotony of simple sentences.

The best sentence structure to use depends on the objective you are trying to achieve.

Compare the following paragraphs. The first paragraph contains only simple sentences. The second paragraph contains a variety of sentences.

SIMPLE SENTENCES

Thank you for sending me the prospectus on the stock. I reviewed it carefully. The investment looks very good. It matches my goals very closely. A significant investment is required. I hope that I will be able to afford it.

VARIETY OF SENTENCES

Thank you for sending me the prospectus on the stock. I reviewed the investment opportunity carefully, and it looks very good. Although a significant investment is required, the program matches my goals very closely. I hope that I will be able to afford it.

Complex sentences. Complex sentence structure is used effectively to present two ideas of unequal importance. The main clause should contain the most important idea, and the dependent clause should contain the least important idea. Both ideas should be related so that the sentence will have unity. Review the following examples of complex sentences that contain unequal ideas.

COMPLEX SENTENCES

Although the atmosphere was very informal, the food was elegant.

The food was well worth the cost even though it was very expensive.

When the food arrived, it was prepared perfectly.

When we are in town, we will come back to this restaurant.

If we hurry, we may be able to make the next movie.

Compound sentences. When you want to present ideas of equal importance, use compound sentence structure. Place each idea in an independent clause joined by a conjunction. Both ideas should be related so that the sentence will have unity. Review the following examples of compound sentences that contain equal ideas.

COMPOUND SENTENCES

The service was delightful, and the prices were reasonable.

Terry bought the brown coat, and Pat bought the black one.

The drive was long, but the beautiful scenery made it worthwhile.

We were strangers, but she welcomed us warmly.

The environment was pleasant, and we were in a happy mood.

STRUCTURE SENTENCES CAREFULLY

Using sentence structure strategically is important, but it is also important that sentences be structured so that they are clear and grammatically correct. Several sentence structure errors that occur frequently are reviewed in this section.

Position words carefully. The position of words in a sentence can change the meaning of a sentence. Keep related words as close together as possible to ensure clarity. Note how position affects clarity in the following sentences.

Sentences structured properly provide the foundation and the building blocks for an effective message.

POSITION CONFUSES

She put the books in the office on a shelf.

He read the book in two hours that was 60 pages long.

Leslie wrote a check to pay for supplies that was for $30.

POSITION CLARIFIES

She put the books on a shelf in the office.

He read the 60-page book in two hours.

Leslie wrote a check for $30 to pay for supplies.

Avoid dangling modifiers. One very common sentence structure error is the use of dangling modifiers. A dangling modifier is a modifier that is incorrectly placed; that is, it modifies the wrong word. Compare the following sentences with dangling modifiers to those that have improved structure.

DANGLING MODIFIERS

If your nose is packed during the surgery, it will be removed in three days.

At maturity, I will pay the note.

At the age of three, Lee taught his son to play the piano.

The first sentence implies that the nose will be removed if it is packed. The second sentence implies that the note will be paid when the individual matures. The third sentence implies that Lee was three years old when he taught his son to play the piano.

Clear writing requires correct grammar and sentence structure.

IMPROVED STRUCTURE

If your nose is packed during the surgery, the packing will be removed in three days.

When the note matures, I will pay it.

Lee taught his three-year-old son to play the piano.

Use parallel structure. Equal, or coordinate, ideas should be expressed in the same form. If one coordinate idea is in an infinitive form, then all coordinate ideas should be in infinitive form. Compare the following examples that have parallel structure and those that do not.

UNPARALLEL STRUCTURE

We like to eat, go swimming, and take a hike.

Our goals include quality products, meeting deadlines, and customer satisfaction.

To use this program:

1. Insert the disk in Drive A and press ENTER.
2. You should then type your password.
3. When the title screen appears, press the escape key.

PARALLEL STRUCTURE

We like to eat, to swim, and to hike.

Our goals include providing quality products, meeting deadlines, and satisfying customers.

To use this program:

1. Insert the disk in Drive A and press ENTER.
2. Type your password next.
3. Press the escape key when the title screen appears.

Avoid the overuse of expletives. Expletives are unneeded words. They take space and contribute nothing to the message. Examples of expletives include, *it is, there is, there are, it was,* and similar words used to begin sentences. Compare the following sentences that contain expletives and the sentences without the expletives.

EXPLETIVES

There is a meeting scheduled at 10:30 A.M. on Monday.

It is important to be at the meeting on time.

There were six reports listed on the agenda.

REVISED TO ELIMINATE EXPLETIVES

A meeting is scheduled at 10:30 A.M. on Monday.

Being at the meeting on time is important.

Six reports were listed on the agenda.

STRUCTURE PARAGRAPHS CAREFULLY

Paragraph structure often determines whether writing is interesting or dull. Unity, coherence, and emphasis are the key concepts that must be considered in developing effective paragraphs.

Unity. A paragraph has unity when all sentences in the paragraph relate to one topic. Limiting the number of sentences in a paragraph helps to ensure unity. The longer the paragraph, the more likely sentences will stray from the main topic. Including a topic sentence helps to build unity. The topic sentence expresses the main idea of the paragraph. All other sentences should develop and support the main idea expressed in the topic sentence.

Topic sentences provide a unifying influence on paragraphs.

Although topic sentences are not required, most good paragraphs do have topic sentences. The placement of topic sentences varies depending on the objective of the paragraph. Normally, topic sentences begin or end paragraphs. Occasionally, a writer will choose to bury a topic sentence in the middle of a paragraph. Rarely is a buried topic sentence effective unless it is used to tone down a negative situation.

The following paragraphs illustrate topic sentences (shown in italics) positioned at the beginning, at the end, and in the middle of a paragraph.

TOPIC SENTENCE AT THE BEGINNING OF A PARAGRAPH

Small businesses provide excellent career opportunities for individuals who prefer to be generalists rather than specialists. The typical small business cannot afford to hire many people; thus, the individuals they hire must be able to handle a variety of duties. By handling a wide range of duties, small business employees gain more experience in a year than employees in large businesses gain in several years.

TOPIC SENTENCE AT THE END OF A PARAGRAPH

Although visuals are not required for effective presentations, they do tend to improve presentations. Listeners can grasp complex concepts much quicker and easier when visual support is provided. <u>Consequently</u>, the time spent preparing visuals is usually invested wisely. *Effective visuals make a good presentation even better.*

TOPIC SENTENCE IN THE MIDDLE OF A PARAGRAPH

We have reviewed your request to increase your credit limit to $5,000. When we extended $3,000 in credit to you six months ago, the maximum limit was granted based on the level of income earned. Your request indicates that your income has not increased; <u>moreover</u>, our records show that you have been late with payments for three of the six months. <u>*Therefore*</u>, *we are unable to extend your credit limit at this time.* We will be happy to consider an increase in your credit limit after you have maintained your account properly for one year.

An effective way to determine if a paragraph has unity is to identify the topic sentence and then examine the other sentences in the paragraph to see if they relate to the topic sentence.

Link sentences using logical structure and by using appropriate transitional words.

Coherence. A paragraph contains ideas that are linked logically to each other. The transition from one idea to the next should be smooth and free flowing. The most important way to ensure coherence is by limiting the ideas in a paragraph to those that logically relate to each other. Coherence is also enhanced by using carefully selected transitional words to link ideas. Examples of transitional words include *thus, consequently, however, subsequently, for example, in addition, therefore, moreover, likewise,* and *also.* Repetition can also be used to link ideas.

Review the three paragraphs on pages 39 and 40 that illustrate topic sentences. Coherence is achieved in two ways. First, all sentences in a paragraph are logically linked to the topic sentence. Second, note the underlined transitional words that help to link ideas in the paragraph.

A good rule of thumb is to emphasize positive ideas that will be received well by the reader and de-emphasize negative or sensitive ideas that are not likely to be received well.

Emphasis. Using emphasis appropriately means stressing important ideas and subordinating less important ideas. A variety of techniques can be used to emphasize ideas.

- **Mechanical techniques**—use capital letters, bold print, large font size, underlining, color, and clip art.
- **Space**—the amount of space devoted to developing an idea indicates the amount of emphasis given that idea. An idea that takes several paragraphs to develop receives more emphasis than an idea developed in a single paragraph.
- **Isolation**—the white space around an idea can be used for emphasis. A one-sentence paragraph can be very emphatic because the space around the paragraph makes it stand out. One-sentence paragraphs should be used sparingly and should be reserved for ideas meriting special attention. A

postscript (P.S.) at the bottom of a letter or memo is an example of a one-sentence paragraph. A postscript should be reserved for ideas meriting special emphasis; it should never be used for something left out of a message.

- **Sentence structure**—simple sentences are direct and emphatic. Complex and compound sentences are less emphatic than simple sentences. In complex sentences, the idea in the main clause (by position) receives more emphasis than the idea in the dependent clause. In compound sentences, the ideas are given equal emphasis.
- **Language**—specific language is more emphatic than general language. Ideas that you wish to stress should be stated very specifically. General language is more appropriate for ideas that need to be de-emphasized, such as sensitive situations.
- **Position**—the first and last sentences are the key emphasis positions in a paragraph. To emphasize important ideas, position them as the first or the last sentence of a paragraph. On the other hand, to de-emphasize negative information, bury it in the middle of the paragraph.

Deciding which ideas to emphasize is a matter of judgment. Always consider the reader and the situation before determining which ideas to emphasize.

(Your instructor may direct you to complete the Guide 8 Application on page 65 at this time.)

GUIDE 9—FORMAT DOCUMENTS EFFECTIVELY

Effective document format accomplishes a number of objectives, including

- creating a good first impression
- supporting document content
- adding organizational structure
- providing a consistent image
- denoting formality
- enhancing readability
- emphasizing important points

Effective document format facilitates communication—it does not simply make a document look aesthetically pleasing.

Many organizations research document design carefully and standardize the format and design elements used for all their company documents. Standardized formats present a consistent image and make document production more efficient. Most companies focus major attention on the logo and trademarks of the organization. Visual design is a key element in corporate identity and image.

Most organizations generate a variety of internal and external documents ranging from letters and memos to forms and reports. This text emphasizes preparing letters and memos, so these are the formats illustrated here. Read the content of these examples for additional formatting information.

Each chapter of this text contains an application in which you are employed as a management trainee by Heritage Productions. Heritage standardized all its documents a year ago; it prepares letters in block format with open punctuation and memos in the format illustrated on pages 42 and 43. Your instructor will indicate which style you should use for other applications.

(Your instructor may direct you to complete the Guide 9 Application on page 67 at this time.)

Position the date a double space below the letterhead or move it up or down depending on letter length. Leave at least three blank lines between the date and inside address.

Double space before and after the salutation.

Leave three or four blank lines for the signature.

Double space before and after additional elements, such as reference initials, enclosures, or copy notations. If necessary, single space the elements to fit the document on one page.

Punctuation is not placed after the salutation or complimentary close when open punctuation style is used.

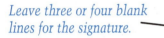

Document Design, Inc.
4385 Madison Road
Cincinnati, OH 45227-5837
(513) 555-0165 ◾ FAX (513) 555-0145

May 15, 19—

Ms. Sadako Chang
10539 Lev Avenue
San Francisco, CA 94134-3958

Dear Ms. Chang

This letter provides the format information you requested. Most companies use either block or modified-block format with open or mixed punctuation.

We recommend the block format with open punctuation that is illustrated in this letter because it is efficient, attractive, and contemporary. Note that all the lines are positioned flush left with the left margin and that punctuation is not used after the salutation or complimentary closing.

The enclosed format guide illustrates other document formats. We hope you find it to be of interest.

Sincerely

Juan Mendosa
Office Manager

rt
Enclosure

Block Style, Open Punctuation

Document Design, Inc.
4385 Madison Road
Cincinnati, OH 45227-5837
(513) 555-0165 ■ FAX (513) 555-0145

May 15, 19—

Ms. Sadako Chang:
10539 Lev Avenue
San Francisco, CA 94134-3958

Dear Ms. Chang:

This letter provides the format information you requested. Most companies use either block or modified-block format with open or mixed punctuation.

Some companies prefer modified-block format with mixed punctuation that is illustrated in this letter because it is efficient, attractive, and traditional. Note that the date and closing lines are positioned at the center and that a colon is placed after the salutation and a comma after the complimentary close.

The enclosed format guide illustrates other document formats. We hope you find it to be of interest.

Sincerely,

Juan Mendosa
Office Manager

rt
Enclosure
c J. A. Stankiewicz

Modified–Block Style, Mixed Punctuation

The same vertical spacing is used for block and modified-block style.

A colon is placed after the salutation, and a comma is placed after the complimentary close when mixed punctuation style is used.

The date and closing line are centered in a modified block style.

Document Design, Inc.
4385 Madison Road
Cincinnati, OH 45227-5837
(513) 555-0165 ■ FAX (513) 555-0145

TO: J. A. Stankiewicz
FROM: Juan Mendosa
DATE: May 15, 19—
SUBJECT: Design Proposal for Ms. Chang

Please prepare the consulting proposal for Ms. Chang that we discussed last week. She indicated that she would be very interested in having us do a complete image assessment of her organization.

rt

Memorandum

Many different memo formats are used; the format illustrated here is a very popular one.

GUIDE 10—EDIT AND PROOFREAD CAREFULLY

The responsibility for effective editing and proofreading always belongs to the writer of a message. In many cases, documents are composed and keyed by the same individual. In other cases, one individual may compose a document, and another may key the document and produce it in final form. Both individuals should share responsibility for the quality of the document.

DISTINCTION BETWEEN EDITING AND PROOFREADING

Often the difference between high-quality and mediocre messages is in how carefully the communication is edited and proofread.

Each document produced should be edited and proofread carefully. Editing and proofreading, however, are separate activities and require a different set of skills. Editing usually precedes proofreading.

Editing focuses on both content and mechanical correctness. From a content perspective, editing checks to ensure that the objective of the message was achieved and that the guides for effective writing were applied appropriately. Editing generally occurs prior to producing a document in final format.

Proofreading focuses on the accuracy of the final document. It includes such activities as ensuring that proper stationery was used, that appropriate mailing notations were used, and that the document is error free. Proofreading generally occurs after a document has been produced in final format; it is the final check to ensure that the document is error free.

Office support staff should and usually do proofread documents carefully. However, editing responsibility belongs primarily, if not exclusively, to the writer.

ELECTRONIC REFERENCE TOOLS

Almost all documents are produced using word processing software. On-line reference tools included in the software aid writers in the editing and proofreading process; they do not replace careful editing and proofreading by the writer of a document. Word processing software contains several reference tools that should be used extensively by writers.

Spelling. All word processing software contains a dictionary. A document can be scanned to determine if all words in the document appear in the dictionary. Words that are misspelled are identified and alternative spellings are suggested. Some words that are identified are not necessarily incorrect words; they simply are not contained in the dictionary. Technical words and proper nouns are common examples of words that may not be contained in the dictionary.

On the other hand, just because words in a document match words in the dictionary does not mean that the words were used properly. For example, if the word *form* is substituted for *from* and *principal* is substituted for *principle,* these words would not be identified as errors because the dictionary contains the words. Other types of errors that are not identified include numbers, spelling of proper nouns, punctuation, and capitalization. The more sophisticated word processing programs offer a helpful option to correct spelling while you key.

Grammar. Virtually all modern word processing software contains tools to determine if basic rules of grammar have been applied correctly. Different sets of grammar rules are available. The Business Writing option usually is the most appropriate one to use. Style analyzers, included in the grammar checking software, identify elements such as passive sentences. The same type of limitations that apply to checking spelling apply to checking grammar and style. Some writing problems identified are not errors; and some problems are not identified. After the grammar check is complete, the program displays readability statistics that indicate the difficulty of the writing. Grammar and style analyzers do not replace careful editing by the writer.

Thesaurus. An electronic thesaurus provides on-line access to a dictionary of synonyms. Many times a writer cannot think of a word that accurately fits the situation being described. The thesaurus provides a list of words meaning approximately the same thing so that the writer can select the best word to convey the meaning intended. An electronic thesaurus can be very helpful in determining appropriate substitutes when particular words are overused.

Annotation and revision tools. In some cases an individual who writes a document may ask someone else to review the document and make suggestions for improvement. In other situations, many documents are written and reviewed by a team of writers. To facilitate the review process, most of the current word processing software contains tools to annotate or revise a document. Annotations are comments about a document that are made in a separate window. The document itself is not changed. The writer can review the annotations for suggested changes and then determine whether to accept those suggestions. Revisions are marked, and the changes are actually made in the document. The revision marks inform the writer as to what changes were made.

The use of these tools facilitate editing and proofreading. However, the writer should always edit and proofread carefully.

EDITING

Editing is a mental process. It involves checking to see that the document meets certain standards. If it does not meet standards, then revisions should be made as part of the editing process. Editing usually is more successful if it is done one step at a time.

- Edit for content accuracy. Determine what needs to be included in the message and ensure that the message contains the information and that all information is accurate.
- Edit for organization. Ensure that ideas are presented logically and that appropriate sentence and paragraph structure is used. Check to see that the material flows smoothly.
- Edit for writing style. Ensure that the message is crisp, concise, and written at the appropriate level for the reader. Clarify vague statements.
- Edit for mechanical correctness. Check for errors in grammar, spelling, punctuation, capitalization, number usage, and word usage.

The proofreader's marks shown on this page are generally accepted symbols that are used to communicate changes or revisions in a paper-based copy of a document; review them carefully.

SYMBOL	MEANING	USE THE SYMBOL	RESULTS
∿	Bold	Illustrate the bold symbol	Illustrate the **bold** symbol
≡	Capitalize	capitalize a letter or word	Capitalize a letter or WORD
/	Lowercase	LØwercase a letter or WORD	Lowercase a letter or word
◡	Close up space	Close up space	Close up space
⌐	Delete	Delete this this word	Delete this word
∧	Insert	Insert word	Insert a word
⋏	Insert a comma	Insert a comma then	Insert a comma, then
#	Insert a space	Insert aspace	Insert a space
⋎	Insert an apostrophe	Insert an apostrophe in Pats title	Insert an apostrophe in Pat's title
M	Insert an em dash	Insert an em dash then	Insert an em dash—then
N	Insert an en dash	Insert an en dash in page range 6 10 N	Insert an en dash in page range 6–10
↗	Move	To move text to another position in a document use this symbol	Use this symbol to move text to another position in a document
⌐⌐	Move down	Move this text down	Move this text down
⊏	Move left	Move this text left to block the paragraph	Move this text left to block the paragraph
⊐	Move right	Move this text right to align the copy properly	Move this text right to align the copy properly
⌐⌐	Move up	Move this text up	Move this text up
∿	Transpose	To properly align text	To align text properly
___ und	Underline	Use underline und	Use underline
___ ital	Use italics	Use italics ital	Use *italics*

PROOFREADING

Most people proofread hard copy better than they proofread copy on a computer screen.

(Your instructor may direct you to complete the review of Guide 10 on page 68, and Application 2B, on page 69, at this time.)

Edit and proofread documents before printing them. Use the computer's print preview to see how the document will look once it has been printed. Then after printing, give the document one final check to ensure that it is error free.

- Check the overall appearance of the document. Check for appropriate stationery, attractive placement, and consistent format.
- Check for content accuracy. Check for accuracy and completeness.
- Check for mechanical correctness. Check for correctness of grammar, spelling, punctuation, capitalization, word usage, and number usage.

GLOBAL CONNECTIONS

The issues of diversity and global competitiveness receive a significant amount of press in business publications. Most people think of these issues as being separate and quite different. They tend to think of diversity as dealing with fair and balanced treatment based on gender, ethnicity, and religion as well as other factors; and global competitiveness as focusing on being able to compete with businesses from virtually any part of the world.

In reality, these issues are very similar and are interrelated. From a business perspective, both diversity and global competitiveness are bottom-line business issues—not social issues. Attracting the best talent from all segments of society is the key to being able to compete domestically and globally. Being able to communicate effectively is critical for doing business regardless of the location.

Understanding cultural differences is important in building relationships, in being able to communicate effectively, and in being able to do business in other countries. The more you know about your international customers and about the international competitors that you face, the better you will be able to do business with them. Taking time to learn about the culture and language of another country shows your interest in that country and helps you to make a good impression.

Most local libraries maintain country-specific references that provide cultural information that is very helpful to know before you visit a country. At the same time, care must be taken not to stereotype or label all people from a country. They are as unique and as different as we are. The rewards of learning about other cultures far exceed the effort required.

If you visit or work in a foreign country, understanding the culture and customs of that country will help you communicate more effectively with your hosts.

THE SUPERHIGHWAY OF COMMUNICATIONS

INTERNET

Of all the reasons for using the Internet, E-mail ranks first. Its popularity probably can be attributed to the fact that it is a quick and easy way to send a short message to one person or to broadcast a message (send it to many people).

An E-mail message differs significantly from a letter or memo sent through the postal service. E-mail tends to be more informal and conversational than traditional letters or memos, and its image leaves much to be desired. Many organizations standardize style for traditional documents to ensure a consistent, high-quality corporate image. Yet, E-mail documents from those same organizations often violate the style standards—partly because screen layout differs from paper layout and partly because the recipient's system may impose limitations. E-mail usually requires a memo style, whereas most organizations limit memo style to internal communications. Important limitations often include screen layout size, small or poor-quality font capabilities, lack of word wrap to adjust line length, and the inability to handle special characters or attachments.

Advantages of E-mail: speed and broadcast capabilities

Limitations of E-mail: informality and image

GUIDES FOR PREPARING E-MAIL MESSAGES:

- Use a short line length—75 to 80 characters maximum
- Keep paragraphs short—4 to 5 lines maximum
- Limit documents to one page
- Avoid using special characters such as em or en dashes and copyright or registered trademark symbols
- Use concise writing style
- Avoid cryptic messages and sarcasm

MISCOMMUNICATIONS

Sign at a local construction site:

> CONSTRUCTION PARKING
> ONLY
> All others will be *toad!*

Hand scribbled response to the error:
Hire a spider to right your signs; you mite get it write.

APPLICATION 2A *Apply Guides for Effective Writing*

Read each sentence or paragraph. Use the space provided to answer the question or to rewrite the sentence, applying the guides for effective writing. Write complete, grammatically correct sentences.

GUIDE 1 PLAN MESSAGES CAREFULLY

Plan messages for the four scenarios by answering the questions after each scenario.

1. As manager of group services for the Turtle Isle Beach Resort, you received a request from Ms. Mary Glenn for information about accommodations for 12 double rooms for one week beginning June 1 for a family vacation she is giving her children and their families. She asked for brochures and indicated a preference for beach houses with a minimum of three bedrooms and two baths per beach house. She also inquired about planned activities, baby-sitting services, and other information about the area.

   a. What do you expect to accomplish by writing the letter?

   b. What do you think Ms. Glenn's objectives are?

   c. How do you visualize Ms. Glenn?

   d. What types of information should you send her?

e. What information must you have before you write the letter?

f. Outline the letter you would send to Ms. Glenn.

2. As an intern working with Joe Marks, a landscape architect, you are responsible for answering all inquiries. Mr. Marks received an inquiry from the owners of Pommery Springs Farms, who want a price quotation for developing a private drive entrance and a site plan for four home sites around a large pond in the center of 150 acres of wooded land.

a. What objectives will you try to achieve with your letter?

b. What objectives do you think the owners of Pommery Springs Farms have?

c. How do you visualize the owners?

d. What types of information should you send them?

e. What information must you have before you write the letter?

f. Outline the letter you would send to the owners.

3. You are the team leader in the manufacturing plant in which you work. Your team of 15 employees have requested that you write to the manager of human resources requesting that the company implement a no smoking policy in the plant. Plan the memo you will write.

a. What objectives will you try to achieve with your memo?

b. How do you think the manager of human resources will respond?

c. What information should you obtain before you write the memo?

d. Outline the memo you would send to the manager of human resources.

4. You have been asked by the local Junior Achievement organization to volunteer as a business consultant. As a business consultant, you would spend one hour each Tuesday morning assisting a local teacher in the Applied Economics class. You would need release time for about 1.5 hours per week for 12 weeks to participate in the program. Plan the memo you would write to your supervisor requesting permission to do this. List the questions that you should consider in planning your memo and provide brief answers to the questions.

a.

b.

c.

d.

e. Outline the memo you plan to write.

GUIDE 2 WRITE FOR THE READER

Rewrite these ten sentences or paragraphs from the perspective of the reader.

1. Tell the girls in the office to get the survey sent out in today's mail.

2. If you had sent your check on time, your statement would not have last month's overdue bill included.

3. I like the new product design report you prepared for me, and I will send it to the Design Committee.

4. Pick up our supplies at the warehouse on your way back from lunch.

5. The Design Committee will consider the new product design at our 10 A.M. meeting on Friday. Prior to the meeting, read the report I sent you and be prepared to discuss it. Also show up on time as we have a lot to cover.

6. Notify each manager to tell his salesmen to attend the new product training session on October 3 at 9:15 A.M.

7. Inform each employee that if he/she wants to hear Jane McKee—the lady attorney from the corporate office—speak, he/she can go to the meeting.

8. Thank you in advance for representing me at the meeting.

9. Fill out the form and bring it to the black guy who prints the tags.

10. I told you that you were not smart to spend your money buying the stock.

GUIDE 3 PRESENT IDEAS POSITIVELY

Rewrite these ten sentences, presenting the ideas positively.

1. Don't schedule the meeting if you don't finish the proposal.

2. Tell the customer not to complain about our product he sent back to us; his worker didn't read the directions for adjusting it properly.

3. Don't call me this morning because I won't be in the office.

4. Jim won't be on time for a 9:15 meeting if he doesn't leave here by 8:30.

5. Never fax a bid without sending a confirmation copy.

6. Why don't you join me for lunch today if you are not busy?

7. Don't forget to mail the tax form today.

8. I received your complaint about your scratched mirror, but we can't replace it until the new mirror arrives.

9. Why don't you call the Help Desk if you don't understand how to install the new software?

10. Never transmit confidential documents from a workstation that has not been cleared for security.

GUIDE 4 WRITE IN A CLEAR, READABLE STYLE

Rewrite these ten sentences

- using a conversational tone and contemporary language to make them clear and easy to read
- stripping long, involved, or wordy sentences of unnecessary words
- enumerating lists or using tables to simplify paragraphs with multiple items

1. The new on-line real estate service lists four homes that may be of interest to you. The first one is at 1028 Maple Street, has 4,200 square feet, and is listed at $258,000. The second one is at 4035 King Street, has 4,600 square feet, and is listed at $264,500. The third one is at 9374 Sims Alley, has 4,100 square feet, and is listed at $224,500. The fourth one is at 9105 Oak Street, has 4,800 square feet, and is listed at $295,725.

2. The supplies you need for the Interior Design I class are a design ruler, a furniture template, an appliance template, graph paper, an architectural symbol guide, several sharpened pencils, an art eraser, and tracing paper.

3. Please make sure that all employees in your department are notified that they must participate in one of the Excellence in Customer Service—The Competitive Edge seminars that are scheduled every Friday morning in October and November and that they must let Leslie Martin, our training coordinator, know which session they will attend so that a seat can be reserved and appropriate supplies made available for them.

4. Pursuant to your request about the above-referenced Excellence in Customer Service seminar, I have scheduled you to participate on Friday, September 15.

Use a dictionary or thesaurus if necessary to simplify the following sentences.

5. Mr. Marcus admonished his youngest offspring about her excessive extravagances, which he speculated would be construed by his neighbors as conspicuous consumption.

6. Isabelle recapitulated the prevalent opinions of both the opponents and proponents of the controversial proposal at the conclusion of the discussion and promised to provide a synopsis in a reasonably expeditious manner.

7. I relinquished my position as treasurer because of a philosophical discrepancy with other administrators in leadership positions in the organization.

8. Will the major ramification of automation of the plant be a permanent displacement of employees or will the major ramification be a redeployment of employees to other positions here or in other localities?

9. In response to your gracious telephone request last week, I contacted our district sales manager and asked her to schedule a demonstration of our new line of printers at our showroom on March 6; she agreed to have two of our representatives make the presentation at two o'clock in the afternoon for eight guests from your office.

10. The selection process is a complicated one involving screening interviews by recruiters on campus; then the second step is have in-company interviews with a manager from the Human Resources Department; and then the manager of the department having an opening to fill interviews the candidates who pass the first two screening hurdles.

GUIDE 5 CHECK FOR COMPLETENESS

For each of the following situations, indicate the information that you should provide and the questions you should anticipate to ensure that the message is complete.

1. You are writing all your employees a memo notifying them of required attendance at a full-day planning retreat at an off-site location.

   Information you must provide:

   Questions you should anticipate:

2. You are writing sales representatives to inform them that the company will provide an automobile allowance for them to use their own cars and will no longer provide automobiles for them to use.

   Information you must provide:

   Questions you should anticipate:

3. You are writing a memo asking your supervisor for permission to purchase a new computer.

   Information you must provide:

   Questions you should anticipate:

4. You are writing a memo to employees to encourage them to participate in a volunteer work project upgrading homes for the elderly who are unable to do so.

   Information you should provide:

   Questions you should anticipate:

Indicate the additional information that is necessary in each of the following situations.

5. The Leadership Seminar is scheduled for November 6 at 10:30 A.M. All department managers are expected to participate in the seminar.

   Additional information that should have been provided:

6. Please reserve a room for me at your hotel for June 16 and 17.

   Additional information that should have been provided:

7. Will you meet me for lunch at the Market Restaurant on Friday, May 6?

   Additional information that should have been provided:

8. You are invited to a reception at my home on Tuesday, March 20 at 6 P.M. honoring Julie McMath for receiving the Innovation Award.

   Additional information that should have been provided:

9. The Planning Retreat scheduled for Friday has been canceled.

   Additional information that should have been provided:

10. Vice President Jennifer Goldberg from our corporate headquarters will be visiting our plant on October 10.

    Additional information that should have been provided:

GUIDE 6 USE AN EFFICIENT, ACTION-ORIENTED STYLE

Rewrite these ten sentences

- using an efficient, action-oriented style
- using active voice unless it is awkward or inappropriate to do so

1. Matt is of the opinion that the settlement of the case may occur this week.

2. Ellen was given an invitation to the reception by the Governor because of her position as a member of the Board of Directors.

3. Please make the announcement that Shelter 2 is available for our use in the event of rain during the picnic.

4. Natalie shipped a box 12 pounds in weight to the city of Columbus in the state of Mississippi.

5. The agreement was read and approved by the owners of the property.

6. The furniture was badly scratched during the move.

7. Joseph made the statement to the two teams that if they did not cooperate together he would seriously take into consideration not giving them the maximum bonus possible next quarter.

8. The gift looks nicer in a box of a larger size and that is rectangular in shape.

9. Did Mary say that John had reverted back to unacceptable behavior?

10. Peggy not only extended kindness and hospitality to us, she also gave us a lot of help and assistance when we moved to our new home.

GUIDE 7 USE CONCRETE LANGUAGE

Read the following sentences and interpret the general language from your perspective. Rewrite the sentences, substituting what you believe to be appropriate specific language. After you complete all ten sentences, compare your revisions with those of your classmates to see if their interpretations were similar to yours.

1. A large percentage of our students work many hours each week in part-time jobs.

2. The flight was very long, and it was also very expensive.

3. Bill wants to know if a good supply of program brochures is available for the mailing that will be sent out before too long.

4. Please return the questionnaire to me as soon as possible.

5. Arnie makes a much better salary as a surgeon than Dan does as a dentist.

6. Susie works quite late on a number of nights each week.

7. Pat insists on taking a long walk quite often.

8. They were very late paying that extremely large bill.

9. Please place your book orders at your earliest convenience.

10. Does your bank pay a high rate of interest on a very large certificate of deposit?

GUIDE 8 USE EFFECTIVE SENTENCE AND PARAGRAPH STRUCTURE

Revise the following sentences and paragraphs

- improving sentence structure
- combining choppy sentences to make them more coherent
- making sentences clear and grammatically correct

1. There is a meeting the president scheduled at two o'clock this afternoon in the auditorium. Do you plan to go? No agenda was sent out. I think the new product line will be discussed.

2. On our trips, we prefer to shop for good bargains, swimming in the ocean, and not dressing up.

3. If your payment on your boat is late again, it will be repossessed.

4. Please place the magazines in the reception office near the guest chairs.

5. When preparing the estimate, the price of the monitor was left out.

For Question 6, place parentheses around the topic sentence and underline transitional words.

6. A number of organizations have eliminated layers of management positions in the process of downsizing. In addition, the number of individuals seeking management positions is increasing. Managers with excellent communication skills are in the best position to move up the career ladder in management. Therefore, managers interested in increasing their chances for promotion should work hard to develop good communication skills.

7. Write a three- or four-sentence paragraph explaining why you would prefer to work in a small business rather than a large business. Put parentheses around the topic sentence and underline transitional words.

8. List the techniques you used for emphasis in the paragraph you just wrote for Question 7.

9. Write a paragraph of at least five sentences describing why good computer skills are necessary for most jobs. Place parentheses around the topic sentence and underline transitional words.

10. List the techniques you used for emphasis in the paragraph you just wrote for Question 9.

GUIDE 9 FORMAT DOCUMENTS EFFECTIVELY

Complete the following exercises.

1. Describe the differences between a block format letter and a modified-block letter.

2. Describe the differences between mixed and open punctuation.

3. You are writing a memo to employees informing them that the division has purchased a new voice mail system that will be installed one week from today. Write an appropriate heading for your memo that includes a subject line.

4. Give several reasons why using effective format is important.

5. The following letter should be formatted using block style with open punctuation. Mark the changes on the copy that must be made in the format, then key the letter using correct format.

Turkey Creek Farms
294 Crown Lake Drive
Hopkins, SC 29061-2756
(803) 555-0135

Ms. Cheryl Mayeaux
3948 Devine Street
Columbia, SC 29209-1847

Dear Ms. Mayeaux:

We have approved the style manual you provided. As you can see from this letter, block format with open punctuation is now our official letter format. We have also implemented the records management system you proposed.

Your check is enclosed. Thank you for all the work you have done for us.

Sincerely

John A. Lafitte

pr

Enclosure

GUIDE 10 EDIT AND PROOFREAD CAREFULLY

Guide 10 is reviewed in Application 2B of this chapter and in application B of all the remaining chapters in this textbook. Write the proofreader's marks you would use to accomplish the following edits.

a. Delete   f. Insert space

b. Transpose   g. Insert an em dash

c. Capitalize   h. Close space

d. Move right   i. Bold

e. Use italics   j. Underline

APPLICATION 2B *Editing and Language Arts Checkpoint*

The Editing and Language Arts Checkpoint is designed to improve your editing and proofreading skills as well as to provide a quick, basic language arts review. Each of the remaining chapters in this text contains an Editing and Language Arts Checkpoint. Carefully read the document that follows; it is packed with errors. Use proofreader's marks to mark all errors in grammar, spelling, word usage, number usage, capitalization, and punctuation. Do not revise sentence or paragraph structure in this activity unless an error exists. After you have marked all corrections directly on this document, access File 2B on your template disk and make the corrections you marked. If you do not have access to the template disk, key the letter, making the corrections as you key. After you have made all corrections, refer to pages 230–231 in Appendix C for the solution, which shows errors that should have been corrected. Note that the solution directs you to review a specific Editing and Language Arts Checkpoint Guide (located on page 226 in Appendix B) that applies to any error that you did not locate in the editing process. This approach targets your review so that you only review guides for errors that you did not detect. You may use on-line reference tools just as you would if you were doing this as part of your job.

Add a memo heading to the document, which will be sent to department managers from you. Use May 20 as the date and supply an appropriate subject line.

The executive committee plans to met on tuesday, June 6 1997, at 2 o'clock to develop a strategic plan for implementing technology changes. At it's meeting last March 15th, the Members of the committee discussed our current status with Ashley Price a leading Consultant with Central Technology services, and asked for her advise. Her agreed to apprise our situation, and to report back to us.

Ashley called Rick our personal manager, this passed week and said "may I interview 5 Managers and about 20 experienced knowledgeable computer users. If it is possible, Rick, please schedule the interviews during the 1st part of next week. Rick are scheduling 3/4 hour slots for managers interviews and an half hour slot for each computer user's interview. All managers should do his best to accommodate these request form Rick for staff and managerial time. If you are unable to schedule an interview early next week please call me immediate so that I can chose someone else whom can participate.

Please report at conference room a in our knew facility on Highway Ten on the South side of town for your interview. This cite is most convenient for staff than the building at 1 Main Street and it is very quite. Reminder. Allow 15 minutes to get their in plenty of time for your interview. Also please read the 12-page report that is attached. The information on Page five about our mainframe computer be of particular interest.

As our Consultant points out in the report, personal computers not mainframe computers are the wave of the future. About seventy-five percent of our computing is handled by our mainframe. 200 personal computers handle the other twenty-five percent of our computing. Of the 200, 50 are 386 processors. Our consultant councils us that the computers, with 386 processors, need to be replaced at one time rather then in a peacemeal fashion. We also need to install a network upgrade software and add more storage capability. If we except our consultants advise, our Long Range Budget committee will, of coarse, have to determine the affect replacing this computers will have on our capitol budget before we precede with this action.

The predicted cost is two million dollars that is significantly-higher than our current budget for computer hardware and software consequently we will have to act very cautious. I estimate it will cost $2,400.00 to replace each 386 computer the software will be an additional five hundred dollars. We only owe $5,000 (five thousand dollars) on the principle of the loan on the mainframe computer therefore, we will probably keep it.

Its eminent that our technology will be upgraded we must compliment our investment in hardware with an investment in our personal. We have explored both self paced training and the new course, arntson computer-based training for windows. We will report on all of these developments at the june meeting.

APPLICATION 2C *Self-Assessment*

I. Have you mastered the concepts learned in Chapter 2? Rewrite the following sentences, applying the guides for effective writing. Check to see that each sentence is complete and grammatically correct.

1. Pursuant to their discussion about the new carpeting for the stadium end zone lounge, Henry sent Ginger a sample of the aforementioned carpet.

2. Never sign the squad list unless you have checked the academic progress of student athletes and have determined that they are not ineligible.

3. Sandy doesn't allow you to make firm appointments, but she doesn't mind if you make tentative appointments if you don't forget to get telephone numbers to confirm or cancel the appointment.

4. If you had read your E-mail, you would know that the meeting was rescheduled and will be held on October 10.

5. Why did Jeff place the computer in the boardroom on the end of the table at the back of the room?

6. We will need a lot of shrimp for the reception because we are having a big crowd.

7. If the payment for your season pass does not arrive before June 15, it will be made available in the general ticket sale.

8. The incentive bonus awards were announced by Steve Austin, manager of Human Resources, and they were presented by President Csiszar.

9. The new suite of software includes word processing, spreadsheet, database, graphics, clip art, project management, scheduling, Internet access, file management, and accounting software.

10. Bring the report to the receptionist by no later than noon on Friday.

II. You have scheduled the quarterly meeting of project managers for October 10. You want each manager to bring a written report summarizing the status of all projects and to be prepared to give a ten minute update on projections for completion of all projects. List the questions you should ask in planning the memo announcing the meeting, and provide short answers for each question.

1.

2.

3.

4.

5.

III. Outline the memo you planned in II.

APPLICATION 2D *Heritage Productions*

Heritage Productions

Last week you attended the brainstorming session devoted to two potential new product lines—EFL videos and cross-cultural training videos. Ms. Anna Eisch, the department manager to whom you are currently assigned, asked you to summarize the discussion on EFL videos because she has been asked to lead the team working on that project. You jotted down the rough notes shown below during the meeting. You are now rewriting the notes—putting the fragments into complete sentences and applying the guides for effective writing before you give them to Ms. Eisch. Pay particular attention to improving sentence and paragraph structure.

Managers' Brainstorming Session

EFL Videos Segment

Managers agreed significant potential for EFL videos. Considered three primary regions—Europe, Asia, and South America. Decided to select best alternative and do a pilot study in one region. If it works, then expand.

Discussed the advantages and disadvantages of each region. Selected Europe as best place to start. Reasons—current line of videos in classes in Europe. Heritage name recognition in Europe. Marketing network already in place. More than 50 countries and about the same number of languages spoken in Europe. Three distinct regions in Europe—Northern and Western Europe, Southern Europe, Central and Eastern Europe. Regions in Europe are quite different and probably need to be looked at separately. English is clearly the official language of business; most business people prefer American version to British or Australian. Central and Eastern Europe have few English teachers available so home study video—good alternative.

Some disadvantages. Extensive competition already exists in Northern and Western Europe. British publishers have bulk of market for general English training and for school-based programs. No one doing much with English training for business use. Market potential not as great as Asia, but easier to enter. Southern Europe market not as large or as competitive as Northern and Western Europe. Turkey is an exception in Southern Europe—large population centers and desire to join European Union increases demand for EFL training. Central and Eastern Europe have very limited development, but rapidly growing economy. The laws protecting intellectual property rights are not as strong nor enforced as well in Central and Eastern Europe as in the other two sections of Europe.

The group reached the conclusion that all three sections of the European market have potential for Heritage to market EFL videos successfully. Some entry barriers exist but the obstacles can be overcome. The most viable and underserved market appears to be Central and Eastern Europe.

Group recommendation—target niche market in Central and Eastern Europe first because market size and ability to speak English prerequisite for high paying jobs in region.

Another recommendation—consider partnering with local distributors. Would need to investigate carefully.

You have decided to use the following headings to organize and structure the information you collected at the meeting:

MANAGERS' BRAINSTORMING SESSION
English as a Foreign Language Videos
Date (use Wednesday of last week)

Potential Markets for EFL Videos
Regions of Europe
Europe Selected as First Market Site
    Advantages
    Disadvantages
Conclusions and Recommendations

3

POSITIVE LETTERS AND MEMOS

Performance Goals

After you complete Chapter 3, you should be able to

❑ *Use a direct strategy for writing positive and neutral messages*
❑ *Edit communications more effectively*

OVERVIEW

Good writers recognize that both strategy and style determine the success of their writing. Effective writing strategy requires that messages be adapted to meet the needs of the reader and the specific situation necessitating the message. The writer's style also influences the manner in which a message is written. The purpose of any message is to communicate to the reader. Therefore, when the reader's needs and the writer's style conflict, primary consideration should be given to the reader's needs so that the objective can be attained.

Anticipating the reader's reaction to a message provides clues to the type of strategy that might work best. Typically, readers react in one of *four* ways to messages received.

1. A reader may be pleased with the message and to respond to it favorably. This type of message is known as a *positive* or *good-news message*.
2. A reader may react to information with little emotion—being neither pleased nor displeased with the message. This type of message is known as a *neutral* or *routine message*.
3. A reader may be displeased with the message and respond to it unfavorably. This type of message is known as a *negative* or *bad-news message*. In some cases, a reader may react favorably to some parts of a message and unfavorably to other parts. A message that elicits both favorable and unfavorable reactions is sometimes called a *mixed-news message*.
4. A reader may question a message and respond with thoughts such as "Why should I do what the writer asks? Of what value is this to me?"

A message that must convince a reader to respond to the writer's request is known as a *persuasive message*.

The reader's predicted response generally is a product of the situation. If a reader is likely to respond unfavorably, the situation is a sensitive one that needs to be treated very carefully. If the reader is likely to respond favorably, the situation is not likely to be very sensitive.

Strategy and style are the key determinants of successful writing.

A different strategy is appropriate for each type of message.

Good strategy depends on the situation and the anticipated reaction of the reader.

75

Chapter 3 focuses on writing good-news and neutral messages. Chapter 4 presents strategies for writing bad-news and mixed-news messages. Chapter 5 covers strategies for persuasive messages.

PLANNING GOOD-NEWS MESSAGES

The first guide for effective writing presented in Chapter 2 emphasized the need for careful planning. The planning stage provides the opportunity to determine how the reader is likely to react, to understand the situation involved, to compare the reader's likely reaction to your point of view, and to develop an appropriate strategy for writing that takes all these factors into consideration.

As you review the following steps in the planning process, that you learned in Chapter 2, think specifically about applying the steps to situations in which the reader is likely to respond favorably.

Use cues from previous communications rather than a crystal ball to visualize the reader and the situation effectively.

- **Determine objectives.** What are your objectives when you write the message, and what do you think the objectives of the reader will be? In a positive situation, the objectives of both the reader and the writer are likely to be similar. In a negative situation, the objectives of the reader and the writer are more likely to conflict. Communication is much easier when both the writer and the reader want to accomplish the same thing.
- **Analyze the reader.** As you visualize the reader, build on the fact that in this good-news situation, the reader should be receptive to the information. Your challenge then is to present the information in a way that enhances the reader's ability to understand and use the information appropriately. Use information—such as age, gender, education, occupation, or technical knowledge—that you either know about the reader or that you can judge by reviewing previous communications from the reader to determine the vocabulary level, the amount of detail that should be provided, and ways to personalize the message.
- **Make decisions.** All the decisions that must be communicated to the reader should be made prior to writing the message. Favorable decisions should be communicated quickly and with only necessary details provided. As soon as a reader determines that the writer is providing favorable information, the reader wants that good news immediately without having to read long justifications explaining why the writer did what was requested.
- **Collect information.** Two types of information are needed in planning and writing a message. The first type is background information about the reader that can be used by the writer in planning and preparing the message. Background information includes copies of letters or memos, notes from telephone calls, and various other types of information normally found in business files.

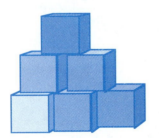

A good plan ensures that all the building blocks are present and organized effectively.

The second type of information is that which must be supplied to the reader. For example, a reader may ask about specific features of a product or service. You may have to obtain this information from other employees in your company before you can answer a reader's specific question. Having all information prior to writing enables you to organize the material so that it can be communicated effectively.

- **Develop a writing plan.** A written outline for each message helps an inexperienced writer prepare effective messages in an efficient manner. A more experienced writer may write effective messages using a few marginal notes or may work from a mental outline.
- **Implement the plan.** Most writers like to write positive letters because they tend to be short and easy to write. Once good news is presented, the reader rarely questions it; therefore, detailed information is usually not necessary.

STRATEGY FOR WRITING GOOD-NEWS MESSAGES

A direct, straightforward approach typically produces the best results in writing positive messages.

GOOD-NEWS STRATEGY

- State the good news as early as possible in the message, preferably in the first sentence or paragraph.
- Provide supporting details and any needed explanation.
- Use a positive, friendly closing paragraph designed to build goodwill.

People like to hear good news; therefore, telling them good news immediately is logical. More important from a psychological perspective, presenting good news immediately creates a good first impression and sets the tone for the entire message. First impressions tend to be lasting impressions. The reader—pleased with good news—becomes comfortable with the message and is free to focus on the details provided.

Another psychological benefit of using a direct approach is that it applies techniques of emphasis effectively. In Guide 8 of Chapter 2, you learned that the beginning and ending of paragraphs or messages are the key emphasis positions. The direct strategy uses emphasis techniques masterfully because it

- provides the information the reader wants to hear immediately
- minimizes and subordinates the detail supplied
- closes on a positive note

The letter on page 78 illustrates the use of direct strategy for presenting positive information. As you analyze the letter, pay careful attention to the opening paragraph, which sets the tone by presenting good news right at the beginning. Note that the details are positioned in the least emphatic position— the middle of the letter—and that the closing paragraph builds goodwill and leaves the reader with positive thoughts.

STRATEGY FOR WRITING NEUTRAL MESSAGES

Neutral messages by definition evoke little emotion or reaction from readers; they convey routine information that readers expect to receive. Many business messages, such as inquiries, responses to inquiries, and transmittal messages, fall into the routine category. In fact, some messages are so routine that the same letter or memo could be sent to different individuals needing the information. Messages sent to multiple individuals with little customized information are called *form messages*. In Chapter 7, you will learn how to develop effective form letters and memos using the writing strategies contained in this chapter.

A direct approach for good news provides important psychological advantages.

To use emphasis by position, begin and end with the best or most positive points; sandwich the filler or negatives in the middle.

A chocolate lover's version of emphasis by position.

The same planning and writing approach that you used for good-news messages applies to neutral messages. The most important step in the planning process is determining specifically what you want to accomplish and what the reader needs to know. Then analyze the reader, collect the information, develop a writing plan, and implement it using the same direct, straightforward strategy you used for good-news messages.

- Present the most important information first, preferably in the first sentence or paragraph.
- Provide supporting details and any needed explanation.
- Close with a positive, friendly paragraph designed to build goodwill.

Example of Good-News Letter

American Junior Soccer League
8452 Stewart Street ■ Seattle, Washington
98101-4837 ■ (206) 555-0139

October 18, 19—

Mr. Marcus Zuerlein
Athletics Director
Central Midlands University
4834 South Marion Street
Columbia, SC 29205-2746

Dear Mr. Zuerlein

Presents good news early and sets tone for entire letter

Congratulations! Central Midlands University has been selected from more than sixty bids to host next year's American Junior Soccer Classic. The reputation of your outstanding soccer program, the popular youth training camps your coaches offer, your excellent facilities, and your tremendous fan support made Central Midlands University the obvious choice for the Classic.

Provides supporting information

The contract will be finalized during the Classic Planning Team visit scheduled on November 14–15. The enclosed planning manual provides detailed procedures the Team uses in working with site coordinators. Please note that Appendix A of the planning manual contains a checklist of items to be accoomplished during the visit.

Closes on a friendly, goodwill building note

We look forward to working with you to make the American Junior Soccer Classic tournament at Central Midlands University one of the greatest events ever for our young soccer players and their fans.

Sincerely

Angela Mendez
Commissioner

ms

Enclosure Planning Manual

c American Junior Soccer Classic Planning Team

Using the direct approach for neutral messages has the same logical and psychological advantages as using the direct approach for positive messages. When you tell a reader the important information up front, the initial reaction to your message is favorable. The tone is set for the entire message. Successful routine messages depend on the effective presentation of information. Presenting the information in order of importance and in a concise manner works best. Building goodwill is a priority for all messages; therefore, the closing paragraph should be friendly and helpful. The memo on page 80 illustrates the use of direct strategy for presenting routine information. As you analyze the memo, pay careful attention to the opening paragraph, which sets the tone by presenting the most important information right at the beginning. Note that less important details are presented in the middle position, which is less emphatic, and that the closing paragraph builds goodwill and leaves the reader with positive thoughts.

Most people feel overwhelmed with paperwork; conciseness is appreciated.

USING STRATEGIES WISELY

Using the strategy approach to writing helps inexperienced writers get started quickly and produce good results in the early stages of writing. Usually the most difficult part of writing is starting the message. Using a writing strategy makes it easy to determine what information should be placed in the first paragraph. Once the initial sentence or two has been written, the remainder of the message tends to flow smoothly. A caution is in order, however, about using strategies. Using a particular strategy as a model or formula that can be applied to all messages can lead to stereotyped messages. Stereotyped messages sound alike. Good writers avoid stereotyped messages by planning carefully. The objective of each message is different, and each reader is different. A custom-designed message that is targeted to meet specific objectives and that is adapted to meet the needs of a particular reader will be different from a message targeted to meet the needs of a different situation and a different reader.

A subtle but important difference exists between following a model and using a strategy designed to meet the reader's needs.

A model is a general planning tool; a strategy designed to meet the needs of a reader is more specific.

Example of Routine Memo

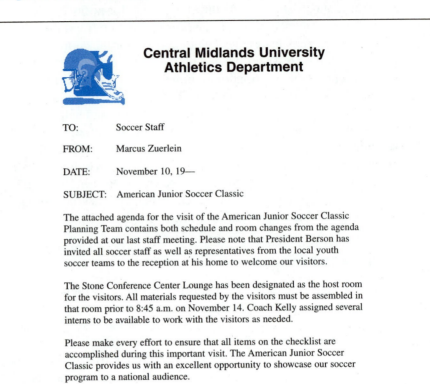

Central Midlands University
Athletics Department

TO: Soccer Staff

FROM: Marcus Zuerlein

DATE: November 10, 19—

SUBJECT: American Junior Soccer Classic

Presents the most important information first

The attached agenda for the visit of the American Junior Soccer Classic Planning Team contains both schedule and room changes from the agenda provided at our last staff meeting. Please note that President Berson has invited all soccer staff as well as representatives from the local youth soccer teams to the reception at his home to welcome our visitors.

Follows with less important details

The Stone Conference Center Lounge has been designated as the host room for the visitors. All materials requested by the visitors must be assembled in that room prior to 8:45 a.m. on November 14. Coach Kelly assigned several interns to be available to work with the visitors as needed.

Closes on a friendly, optimistic note

Please make every effort to ensure that all items on the checklist are accomplished during this important visit. The American Junior Soccer Classic provides us with an excellent opportunity to showcase our soccer program to a national audience.

og

Attachment

GLOBAL CONNECTIONS

Communicating effectively with employees and customers is a challenge for most organizations. That challenge increases dramatically when communications with employees and customers involve translating into other languages. In this section, the emphasis on global communications is at the strategic or executive level. In the next chapter, the emphasis is on global communications issues that affect all employees. The keys to managing communication globally are

- developing and implementing a strategic communication plan
- distributing strategic information
- assessing communication effectiveness

A strategic communication plan must ensure consistent, accurate, coordinated messages for very diverse groups. Organizations place major priority on communicating a consistent image and protecting trademarks. The pitfalls of language translation create major concerns about accurate communications. Companies have found that statements such as the product "adds life" might be translated as the product "brings back the dead," that "diet foods" imply illness rather than low fat and calorie content, and that "fried chicken fingers" make your fingers fall off.

Distributing communications to other countries also presents challenges. The best medium in one country may be ineffective in another country. Most companies work hard to ensure that employees read information about the company before that information appears in the press. Electronic communication has made the job easier, but numerous technical and nontechnical pitfalls exist, such as country holidays that were not anticipated.

The greatest challenge of all is ensuring the effectiveness of communications. In addition to language translation problems, cultural and style differences make it almost impossible to use the same message in different regions of the world. Continuous assessment is needed to ensure that the needs of diverse groups are being met.

THE SUPERHIGHWAY OF COMMUNICATIONS

INTERNET

Messages sent via company-owned networks are private, but they belong to the organization that owns the network, not to the employees who write the messages. Employees need to be aware that employers have the legal right to read those messages and that deleting messages and using passwords does not prevent employers from reading the messages. Deleting messages removes them from the user's desktop. However, the messages remain in the system until the network administrator clears them out.

Using the Internet provides less privacy than using proprietary intranets, which explains why many companies prefer to use their own networks rather than the public Internet. Most companies do not allow sensitive data to be transmitted over the Internet. Hackers can easily break most security codes. Clever marketers often develop profiles of Internet users by tracking the web sites they contact and by accessing the information that users provide in various transactions.

MISCOMMUNICATIONS

The following question, which appeared on the ballot in a local referendum in 43 counties in the last election, confused many voters. What is your interpretation of the question?

Shall the prohibition on Sunday work continue in this county subject to an employee's right to elect not to work on Sunday if the prohibition is not continued after certification of the result of this referendum to the Secretary of State? ❑ Yes ❑ No

Interpretation:

A voter who wants businesses to be able to open any hours desired on Sunday should vote "No."

A voter who wants to continue restricting the hours in which businesses may be open on Sunday should vote "Yes."

APPLICATION 3A *Review Guide 1: Plan Messages Carefully*

1. Ms. Poh-Lin Wong requested that you (as credit manager of South Side Furniture Gallery) raise her credit limit from $1,000 to $5,000 so that she can purchase additional dining room and bedroom furniture. She originally bought an expensive dining table and a king-size bed more than a year ago. Ms. Wong opened an account at that time and paid all bills in a timely manner. Therefore, your company desires to sell her more furniture, and you will grant her request. The new limit is available immediately under the same terms and conditions as the current account. Plan the letter to Ms. Wong.

   a. What objectives do you wish to accomplish?

   b. What objectives do you think Ms. Wong wants to accomplish?

   c. What do you know about Ms. Wong that will help you write this letter?

   d. What information should you present first? Why?

   e. Outline the letter you plan to write.

2. The offices in your department are going to be painted next weekend. Employees must be notified that the work will be going on and that they will not have access to their offices from noon on Friday until Monday morning. On Friday afternoon, employees may work from home, from the departmental conference room, the employee lounge, or the customer demonstration room. They also must clear their desks and furniture tops before noon. Employees should take appropriate measures to ensure the security of their files and documents. Plan the memo.

   a. What objectives do you wish to accomplish?

b. What objectives do you think employees want to accomplish?

c. In view of the situation and likely reaction of employees, what strategy is best for this memo? Why?

d. Outline the memo you plan to write.

3. Roberto Mendoza has conducted several seminars on financial planning for groups of employees. You have two additional groups that need to be trained within the next month or two. You would like Mr. Mendoza to conduct the same basic seminar using the same materials and time frame that he used in the previous seminars conducted for your employees. You paid Mr. Mendoza $1,500 per day for the previous seminars and intend to pay the same amount for these two seminars. Plan the letter.

a. What objectives do you wish to accomplish?

b. What objectives do you think Mr. Mendoza wants to accomplish?

c. What do you know about Mr. Mendoza that will help you write this letter?

d. What information should you present first? Why?

e. Outline the letter you plan to write.

APPLICATION 3B *Editing and Language Arts Checkpoint*

Carefully read the document that follows; it is packed with errors. Use proofreader's marks to mark all errors in grammar, spelling, word usage, number usage, capitalization, and punctuation. Do not revise sentence or paragraph structure in this activity unless an error exists. After you have marked all corrections directly on this document, access File 3B on your template disk and make the corrections you marked. If you do not have access to the template disk, key the letter, making the corrections as you key. After you have made all corrections, refer to page 232 in Appendix C for the solution and check to see that you corrected all errors. You may use on-line reference tools just as you would if you were doing this letter as part of your job.

Add a memo heading to the document, which will be sent to Jan Marks, Training Manager, from you. Use June 8 as the date and supply an appropriate subject line. Reformat the memo using single spacing and block format. Save the file as 3B-sol.

Thank you for giving me a opportunity to review the *Effective Team Building training* materials. I examine the training package form both the prospective of the trainer and our personal who would take the coarse. I also tried to apprise the value relative to it's cost.

From the trainers perspective, the materials is comprehensive. The package include an outline a trainee manual, audio and video tapes slides, and an assessment. The content is relevant and is write in a clear concise way. Very little reinforcement is provided however. From the learners perspective, the material has only one major flaws. The learner is not required to participate active. Overall though the program is quiet good.

The complete program with materials for seventy-five trainees is price at $6,000.00 or about eighty dollars per trainee. Additional training packets are sixty dollars each which will make the per employee cost slight lower if we train all them employees whom work in a team environment. This program is the more expensive of the 3 programs that we have evaluated. These costs do not of course include the time of our employees.

Since one additional training program is scheduled to arrive for review on June 15th, I recommend that the decision be postpone to see if that program is more cost affective then this one. I plan to be at the Highway Twelve Training Center on the 16 of June and I will be happy to review the materials while I am their if you would like me to do so.

APPLICATION 3C *Writing Positive and Neutral Messages*

Check the address file in Appendix A beginning on page 223 for addresses.

1. Write the letter to Ms. Wong that you planned in Application 3A-1 on page 83. Save as 3C1.

2. Write the memo to employees that you planned in Application 3A-2 on pages 83–84. Save as 3C2.

3. Write the letter to Mr. Mendoza that you planned in Application 3A-3 on page 84. Save as 3C3.

4. Brad Cubbage, shipping manager, asked you to find a new supplier for shipping containers for the gas grills that your company manufactures. The shipping damage rate is at an unacceptable level. You have located a container made by the Kerry Container Company that meets all specifications of the shipping department. Cost of the container is approximately the same as the container currently being used; however, it weighs six pounds more—which will have a slight impact on shipping cost. Savings from the lower damage rate will more than offset the additional shipping costs. Plan and write the memo recommending the Kerry Container Company as the new supplier. Attach the cost analysis you have prepared and the technical specifications to your memo. Save as 3C4.

5. Mr. Cubbage approved your recommendation. Plan and write the letter to Mr. William Kerry telling him that Kerry Container Company has been selected as the new supplier for the shipping containers for all grills that your company manufactures. Invite Mr. Kerry or his representatives to meet with your shipping team next Tuesday at 2:30 p.m. to establish the procedures to be used for inventory management, quality control, and billing. Save as 3C5.

6. Ms. Ursula Pharr requested that Holiday Air sponsor the Central University MBA Case Competition team by providing six round-trip airline tickets to the three host cities. You are delighted to do so. Plan and write the letter to Ms. Pharr indicating that you will supply the tickets requested. Ask her to provide you with the names, addresses, and telephone numbers of the participants as well as the preferred flight dates and schedules. Then inform her that a reservation agent will call her to finalize the trip arrangements. Sign the letter with your name and the title marketing manager. Save as 3C6.

7. Plan and write one memo to all six student members of the MBA Case Competition team informing them that Holiday Air is sponsoring their trips to the three competitions. Indicate that you are providing Holiday Air with their names, addresses, and telephone numbers as well as with flight information for the three trips. Suggest that each student write Bruce Rosenfield, marketing manager of Holiday Air, and thank him for sponsoring the team. Save as 3C7.

8. Because the MBA team is preparing for the first competition in Montreal in March, you have been asked to search the Internet for travel information about Montreal, a city in Quebec, Canada. Try to obtain information on attractions to visit, restaurants, weather, and so on. Plan and write a memo to the team sharing the information you found. You may attach copies of material printed from the Internet. Save as 3C8.

9. Fred C. Stands, MD, has asked you to prepare a letter to Mr. J. T. Teng to give him the good news that the results of all his laboratory work were negative. Dr. Stands wants you to remind Mr. Teng that it is important for him to follow the prescribed diet and exercise program carefully. He should schedule a follow-up appointment in six weeks—sooner if he experiences any problems. Save as 3C9. Prepare the letter for Dr. Stands' signature.

Chapter 3

APPLICATION 3D *Self-Assessment*

1. Use complete, grammatically correct sentences to answer each of the following items.

 a. Describe the most appropriate strategy for a message that conveys routine information. Justify your choice of strategy.

 b. Describe the most appropriate strategy for a message that conveys good news. Justify your choice of strategy.

 c. What should be done to avoid creating stereotyped messages?

 d. How does the good-news strategy use emphasis techniques effectively?

 e. Describe the steps involved in planning a good-news message.

2. Plan the following letter.

   You reviewed a proposal submitted by Dr. Evelyn Jervey to evaluate your entire customer service operation. She has experience in designing and evaluating communication and computer software to facilitate handling customer calls and records. You are interested in her proposal and expect to hire her to do the job, but you would like to have her meet with your key supervisors to discuss the processes she uses before you make a final decision on the proposal. Plan a letter inviting her to meet with your group next Tuesday or Thursday morning at 9:30 for about an hour.

   a. What objectives do you wish to accomplish?

   b. What objectives do you think Dr. Jervey wants to accomplish?

   c. What do you know about Dr. Jervey that will help you write this letter?

   d. What information should you present first? Why?

   e. Outline the letter you plan to write.

3. Write the letter to Dr. Jervey. Her address is Jervey and Associates, P.O. Box 2847, Hopkins, SC 29061-2847. Use today's date and sign your name and your title, manager of customer service. Format the letter appropriately. Use the on-line reference tools available to assist in editing the letter. Save the file as 3D3.

Heritage Productions

APPLICATION 3E *Heritage Productions*

You have now rotated to the research and development department of Heritage Productions. As assistant manager, you report to Mr. Gary Kiely, the manager of the department. (If necessary, review information on pages 17 and 73 that describe your previous position in Heritage Productions.) Mr. Kiely was impressed with the contributions you made in the last meeting on EFL and cross-cultural videos to be used in training programs. He has asked that you spend some time "surfing" the Internet to see if information is readily available about training videos for EFL classes, programs, and self-learning opportunities. Mr. Kiely suggested that you search the World Wide Web using a software browser such as Netscape® and search engines such as Yahoo® or Excite®. Mr. Kiely also suggested that you try the following key words for your search. (If you do not have access to the Internet, use library resources to find sources of information on the following topics.)

English as Foreign Language, or EFL
English as Second Language, or ESL
video training for EFL
video training for ESL

Plan a memo to Mr. Kiely reporting your findings by answering the following questions:

1. Is information about EFL or ESL readily available on the Internet (or library references if you do not have access to the Internet)? If so, what types of information?

2. Who is providing information about EFL or ESL—universities, language training institutes, publishers, and so on?

3. Did you find specific references to training videos for EFL/ESL? If so, give examples.

4. Can you suggest references (home pages on the web, addresses, or other on-line or hard-copy sources of information) that Mr. Kiely can access so that he can view the types of material available?

5. Did you locate any information about EFL/ESL in Central or Eastern European countries?

6. Write the memo to Mr. Kiely. Save as 3E6.

NEGATIVE LETTERS AND MEMOS

4

Performance Goals

After you complete Chapter 4, you should be able to
- ❏ *Use an indirect strategy for writing negative messages*
- ❏ *Modify a direct strategy for mixed news messages*
- ❏ *Determine when a direct strategy is appropriate for negative news*
- ❏ *Edit communications more effectively*

OVERVIEW

The good-news messages you wrote in Chapter 3 used a direct strategy because the reader was likely to respond positively. In this chapter, your challenge is to use strategy effectively when the situation is such that the reader is likely to be displeased with the message and to respond to it unfavorably. This type of message is known as a *negative* or *bad-news message*.

In some cases, the message may not be all positive or all negative. A reader may react favorably to some parts of a message and unfavorably to other parts. A message that elicits both favorable and unfavorable reactions is sometimes called a *mixed-news message.*

In a few situations, negative news should be treated as though it were positive news. These situations usually relate to legitimate claims from customers or clients relative to product or service problems.

Remember, good strategy depends on both the situation and the anticipated reaction of the reader—the situation may be bad but the reader may like the way it is being handled.

PLANNING BAD-NEWS MESSAGES

Planning a bad-news message differs significantly from planning a good-news message. People generally are eager to give and receive good news; therefore, little time is spent trying to ensure that the message is justified and determining whether it should be put in writing. Rarely is anyone eager to give or receive bad news. Before bad news is communicated, efforts should be made to ensure that it is justified and to determine the best way of communicating it.

Verify and justify the decision. Decisions should be made carefully and the facts on which decisions are made should be verified for accuracy. Conveying bad news is difficult. Conveying bad news only to find out later that an error was made and the bad news should not have been conveyed can create a far more disastrous situation.

Key questions—
- *Is the bad news justified?*
- *Is a written message the best way to convey the bad news?*
- *Who should convey it?*
- *What strategy is likely to be most effective?*

Newspapers frequently print horror stories of bad news conveyed in error. A recent story featured a picture of a lady who had returned to her home and was horrified to find that it had been bulldozed as part of an urban renewal project. The letter from the city notifying her of the pending action had been delayed in the mail. Thus, she had no opportunity to notify the city that the letter was sent in error—the house slated to be destroyed was located in the next block. The bulldozer arrived and demolished the wrong house.

Determine the severity and the sensitivity of the situation. The severity and sensitivity of bad-news situations vary widely. Some situations may be drastic whereas others may result in only mild disappointment. The reaction to the house that was bulldozed was not just one of being upset; it had major legal and financial ramifications. The degree of sensitivity influences how a bad-news message should be written. Consider the following examples:

1. How do you think a reader who believes a claim filed was legitimate and expects to be paid would react upon receiving a letter indicating the claim was turned down because of a technicality?
2. How do you think a reader who ordered a product and received a message that it was temporarily out of stock would react?
3. How do you think a reader who receives a very detailed complaint letter providing numerous examples of a problem in the software purchased from the reader will react?

The range of reactions in these three situations would probably be from one extreme to another.

1. In the first situation, the reader is likely to be very angry. Expectations play a major role in reactions. Because the reader actually expected a positive response, the reaction to the negative response is likely to be extremely intense.
2. In the second situation, the reader might be disappointed but is not likely to be very angry about the news conveyed unless the reader needed the product for a special event.
3. In the third situation, the reader may even receive the bad news positively. Although no one is pleased to receive a complaint, the reader may believe that the information will help solve the problem.

Decide on the best media to convey bad news. The degree of sensitivity influences the decision about the best way to convey bad news. In some cases, conveying bad news using written media may not be appropriate. Consider the best way to communicate information in the following examples:

1. A doctor receives results of lab tests that indicate a patient has severe medical problems. How should the doctor tell the patient?
2. A manager is going to fire an employee. How should the manager tell the employee?
3. A plant is going to shut down for two weeks because of excessive inventory, with the obvious result that hourly employees will be without pay for those two weeks. How does the supervisor tell the hourly employee?
4. A subcontractor who placed a large order for several types of commercial carpet for a large building project just learned that the project is in financial trouble; therefore, the subcontractor wants to cancel the order before carpet is cut. How does the subcontractor notify the carpet store?

5. A customer is one month late paying for purchases charged at the hardware store. How does the store manager notify the customer?
6. The company needs to notify employees that it has decided to discontinue the annual picnic because of reduced participation in recent years and cost cutting efforts. How does the company president notify the employees?

Options for conveying information.

The best medium for these situations varies considerably. In some cases, the choice is clear-cut—one option is clearly better than all other options. In other cases, the choice is not clear-cut.

1. Generally the results of medical tests arrive several days after a physician meets with a patient; thus, the results are usually conveyed in writing. A physician who has determined from a test that a patient has a major medical problem would be more effective talking to the patient in a face-to-face conversation.

2. Under most conditions, an employee who is being fired should be told in person rather than notified in writing. In this situation, a brief written statement may be needed for documentation. The statement would be handed to the employee after the situation has been discussed.
3. One fact that must be considered is that plants typically have two or three work shifts. If one shift is told, the grapevine will probably convey the news to the workers on the other shifts before management has an opportunity to meet with them. With multiple shifts to ensure that everybody receives the message at the same time, mail may be the preferred option. Employee expectations should also be considered. Employees may expect periodic shutdowns and may feel that a temporary shutdown of the entire plant is preferable to layoffs. The more knowledge you have of the circumstances and the anticipated reaction of the people, the easier it is to decide how to convey the news.

4. Two factors must be considered in canceling this large order before carpet is cut. The first is the urgency of the situation, and the second is making sure that the right order and the entire order is canceled. Fax offers obvious advantages. The message can be transmitted immediately, and a copy of the order to be canceled can be faxed with the message.

5. A tactful, impersonal letter to remind the customer that the payment is late is preferable to other media at this stage. A fax would convey too urgent a message, and a phone call may embarrass a customer having temporary problems.
6. The reasons for canceling the picnic are valid, and this situation is not likely to be very sensitive; therefore, an E-mail message would be a very reasonable way to notify everyone of the change.

Determine who should convey the bad news. Many employees have conveyed bad news to key customers only to have those customers appeal successfully to someone with greater authority in the organization to overturn the decision. In situations that are extremely sensitive or that have a very negative impact on major customers, the best approach is to discuss the situations with individuals in positions of higher authority before making final decisions. You may even be asked to prepare the letter for the signature of someone in a position of higher authority.

Tone often refers to strength or impact of the message.

Be tactful and sincere. No one likes to receive bad news; therefore, the writer should make a special effort to present the bad news as tactfully and sincerely as possible. The way something is said may be more important than what is said. Tone is especially important. A strong or undesirable tone often produces a strong emotional reaction on the part of the reader. Bad news presented in a milder manner is less likely to create a strong emotional reaction on the part of the reader.

Prepare the reader. Most people can accept bad news more easily when they have been prepared appropriately for it. Surprises, particularly negative ones, generally are not received very well. Usually, when bad news is presented, obstacles must be overcome before the negative news can be communicated effectively.

Use empathy. Perhaps the best way to think about the difference in writing a positive or a negative message is to put yourself in the position of the reader. Try to visualize what your reactions would be if you were in each of the following situations:

Honesty and integrity are critical.

- Suppose you have just been told by your employer that you would receive a 15 percent increase in salary. What would your reaction be? Most people would be very pleased. Would you inquire why you got such a generous raise? Would you question the judgment of the person making the decision? Most people would express pleasure in the result and would not question the process at all.

Getting bad news from an honest and sincere writer is difficult; getting bad news from a dishonest or insincere writer is intolerable.

- Suppose the situation were reversed—you have just been told by your employer that you would receive no raise or, even worse, your salary would be cut by 15 percent. What would your reaction be? Most people would be very displeased and angry. What would your first question be? Most people would want to know why. Because most people immediately react to bad news by wanting to know the reasons why, a good strategy usually is to explain the reasons before you present the bad news.

Readers of good-news messages rarely question the logic of the situation; therefore, lengthy explanations serve no useful purpose. Because readers of bad-news messages usually question the logic of the situation, adequate explanations are necessary. Thus, bad-news messages tend to be longer than good-news messages.

Analyze the situation carefully. If the situation is sensitive and the reader is likely to react negatively, an indirect style usually works best. If the situation is routine or if the reader is likely to receive the information without being upset, a more direct style would be appropriate. If the reader is likely to accept the news positively even though it is bad news, use a direct style.

A few readers prefer a direct style because of their personality type. They tend to be open, frank, and even blunt in their communication to others, and they expect the same type of communication in return. Providing such people information in a roundabout way may upset them more than providing negative information without preparing them adequately for it. They want the information immediately regardless of whether it is good or bad. A caution is in order, however. Just because you prefer a direct approach does not mean that it is the best approach to use with others.

STRATEGY FOR WRITING BAD-NEWS MESSAGES

Clients, customers, and even friends may make requests that are not in your best interest or the best interest of your company. Although you must reply negatively to a particular request or situation, you value the patronage and friendship of these individuals. Therefore, when you disagree with them, you do not want to be perceived as being disagreeable.

Good writers master the art of disagreeing without being disagreeable.

BAD-NEWS STRATEGY

The most appropriate strategy for writing negative messages usually is an indirect approach. Here are the steps to using an indirect approach for negative messages:

- Begin with a buffer to soften the bad news.
- Explain the reasons for your decisions in a logical manner using a positive tone.
- Present your refusal clearly as an outgrowth of the logical decisions, and communicate in a positive, tactful manner.
- Offer helpful suggestions or alternatives when they are appropriate.
- Close on a positive—or at least neutral—note.

Use a balanced approach—a fine line exists between presenting negative information too quickly and delaying it too long.

A *buffer* is a neutral statement that enables you to explain the situation logically before you present the negative news. An effective buffer is a reasonably short statement that enables you to begin on an agreeable note, but does not mislead the reader into thinking that the message contains good news. The best use of a buffer is to establish that you have been logical, fair, and reasonable in making the decisions you are conveying. Consider the following example:

You are a logical, fair person who receives a request to replace merchandise that the customer states is defective.

- What would you do first to begin resolving the problem?
  Most logical people would begin by examining the merchandise to determine the actual problem. The reported problem may be the same as the actual problem or the actual problem may be something different than was reported.
- What would you do next?
  You would try to determine the best course of action to solve the problem. If the merchandise was defective, you would have it repaired or replaced. If the merchandise was damaged by the customer, you would probably decline to repair or replace it without charge. You may offer other alternatives if they are available.

Assume in this scenario that you sent the merchandise to quality control, and the inspector found that the merchandise had been damaged by the customer. Therefore, company policy will not allow you to replace it without charge. What type of buffer could you use in this situation that would enable you to explain the logical process you used to make a decision and that would also prepare the reader for a negative decision? An appropriate buffer might be: *Our quality control inspector carefully checked the merchandise you returned to us.*

A good buffer deals directly with the problem and does not mislead the reader.

The opening statement establishes that you used a reasonable approach to determine the problem. At this point, however, the customer does not know what decision the quality control inspector has made. Note that the buffer relates to the situation—the problem with the merchandise. It does not mislead the reader into thinking that a positive response will follow.

The next logical step would be to present the inspector's findings. Review the facts and give the reasons for the decision before actually disclosing the decision. If you present good, logical reasons, the reader is likely to have an open mind and view the facts objectively.

Reasons differ from policy statements. Giving reasons is very different from stating that your organization's policy does not permit you to do what the customer requested. Customers are not interested in an organization's policy as such. They want to know why you made the unfavorable decision. Therefore, present the reason behind the policy rather than stating a policy.

Carefully stated reasons should lead logically to a gentle statement of refusal. It should be clear that the request cannot be granted, but rarely is it necessary to refuse in a negative or high-impact tone. A good technique is to focus on what you can do rather than on what you cannot do.

On some occasions, you will have no reasonable alternative to offer the reader. In those situations, try to close the letter on a positive—or at least neutral—note. On other occasions, you may have an alternative to suggest or a way to assist the reader. Provide alternatives only if they are reasonable and helpful. Providing an alternative enables you to close the letter on a positive note.

An example of a reasonable alternative in this scenario would be to offer to repair the merchandise and charge only for the parts or to offer a replacement at a substantial discount. Although you were not responsible for the problem, you would probably build goodwill by trying to accommodate the customer. Companies value customer goodwill, and most companies try to accommodate customers when it is possible to do so.

DE-EMPHASIZE NEGATIVE INFORMATION

Use a low-impact style to minimize attention placed on negative aspects of a situation.

In Chapter 2, you learned six techniques to emphasize ideas. When you present negative information, you should strive to give it as little emphasis as possible. In effect, you reverse those six techniques to de-emphasize ideas.

- **Mechanical techniques**—use regular font; avoid attributes such as bold, all capitals, and underline.
- **Space**—limit the amount of space devoted to the negative information.
- **Isolation**—ensure that negative statements are placed in multiple-line or multiple-sentence paragraphs to avoid the emphasis by isolation created by white space surrounding a one-line paragraph.
- **Sentence structure**—use compound and complex sentences to present negative information because they are less emphatic than simple, direct sentences. In complex sentences, placing the idea in the dependent clause receives less emphasis than placing the idea in the independent clause.
- **Language**—use general language and passive voice because they are less emphatic than specific language and active voice.
- **Position**—the middle paragraphs of a message receive less emphasis than the first and last paragraphs. Likewise, the middle sentences of a paragraph receive less emphasis than the first and last sentences of a paragraph.

Review the guides for effective writing in Chapter 2 for illustrations of effective use of these techniques.

HANDLE MISTAKES EFFECTIVELY

Negative messages often deal with mistakes made by either the writer's company or the reader's company. The way that a mistake is handled may be more important than the fact that a mistake was made. Negative messages that deal with mistakes made by the reader or the reader's company usually result from the reader's unwillingness to accept responsibility for the mistake. In some cases, the reader accepts responsibility for the mistake but expects the writer's company to correct the mistake even though it was not responsible for it. In other cases, both the reader and the writer contributed to the mistake. The writer gains no advantage by accusing the reader or by sermonizing the reader, regardless of which of the three situations occurred.

The examples in the box illustrate the scenarios just discussed.

SCENARIO	ANALYSIS
The 41-inch stair treads we ordered are too short. Although your order form specifies that custom stair treads are cut to order and may not be returned, we know that you want to have satisified customers and will exchange these treads for 42-inch treads.	The customer admits making the mistake but still expects the company to correct it.
Our order specified Color 39, light yellow, but the carpet you shipped us was Color 39, ivory. We wanted light yellow carpet. Please exchange it for light yellow carpet.	The company shipped the carpet by color number—Color 39 is actually ivory. The light yellow carpet the customer wanted is Color 37. The customer ordered the wrong color. The company should have known that the number and color specified did not match.
If you had verified the number in the color brochure we sent you last week, you would have known that the light yellow carpet is color 37.	Sermonizing the customer serves no purpose and is likely to make the customer angry.

The most effective way to handle a mistake made by the writer or the writer's company is to admit the mistake, apologize for it, and emphasize what is going to be done to correct the mistake. The apology for a mistake should be simple and straightforward. It should be given quickly and only once. The apology should not be repeated or positioned in the closing paragraph. The reader should remember the corrective action that has been taken, not the mistake that was made.

USE AN EFFECTIVE CLOSING

Close a negative message with care. Stereotyped closings that writers use in most of their letters often lead to inappropriate closings. Make sure that the closing does not include ironic statements, statements that imply the problem will happen again, or statements that invite prolonged correspondence. Review the closing statements in the box.

The closing provides the last impression—use it to build goodwill.

Please let me know when you have problems with our service in the future.	This statement implies that the reader is likely to have problems with your service in the future.
We are sorry we were unable to grant your request this time, but please let us know if we can help you again in the future.	This statement is ironic. It implies you have helped the reader when you have not done so.
If you have further questions about our decision not to replace your carpet, please let us know.	Encouraging the reader to try again means you have to say no again.

The letter below illustrates the use of indirect style to give negative information—the rejection of a proposal. Review it and the margin comments carefully.

Indirect Approach to Bad News

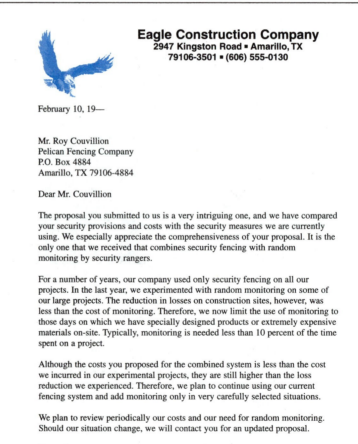

Eagle Construction Company
2947 Kingston Road ▪ Amarillo, TX
79106-3501 ▪ (606) 555-0130

February 10, 19—

Mr. Roy Couvillion
Pelican Fencing Company
P.O. Box 4884
Amarillo, TX 79106-4884

Dear Mr. Couvillion

Opens with a buffer to set the tone of logical decision making

The proposal you submitted to us is a very intriguing one, and we have compared your security provisions and costs with the security measures we are currently using. We especially appreciate the comprehensiveness of your proposal. It is the only one that we received that combines security fencing with random monitoring by security rangers.

Presents the basis for making decisions

For a number of years, our company used only security fencing on all our projects. In the last year, we experimented with random monitoring on some of our large projects. The reduction in losses on construction sites, however, was less than the cost of monitoring. Therefore, we now limit the use of monitoring to those days on which we have specially designed products or extremely expensive materials on-site. Typically, monitoring is needed less than 10 percent of the time spent on a project.

Presents the facts that justify the decision

Although the costs you proposed for the combined system is less than the cost we incurred in our experimental projects, they are still higher than the loss reduction we experienced. Therefore, we plan to continue using our current fencing system and add monitoring only in very carefully selected situations.

Closes on a friendly, goodwill-building note

We plan to review periodically our costs and our need for random monitoring. Should our situation change, we will contact you for an updated proposal.

Sincerely

Sharon Kramer
General Manager

ms

STRATEGY FOR WRITING MIXED-NEWS MESSAGES

A mixed-news message contains both good and bad news. The reader is likely to be pleased with part of the information and displeased with the rest of the information. The best psychological approach is to use a direct writing style for the good news and modify it slightly to accommodate the bad news.

- Present the good news first.
- Explain the reasons for the negative portion of your message.
- Let the reasons lead logically to the negative information.
- Present the negative information in as positive a tone as possible.
- Close with a goodwill-building statement.

This strategy follows the same principles that you learned in Chapter 3 and in this chapter. The opening and closing paragraphs are reserved for positive information. The reasons are presented prior to presenting the negative news, and the negative news is buried in the middle.

When you present good news in a mixed-news message, keep in mind that bad news follows; therefore, use a conservative approach.

   The letter on page 100 illustrates the strategy that is generally most appropriate for a mixed-news message. Pay particular attention to the way that the bad news is introduced after the good news has been presented.

ALTERNATIVE STRATEGIES FOR NEGATIVE MESSAGES

The emphasis in this chapter on using an indirect style for writing most bad-news messages does not imply that all situations require an indirect style. In some situations, a direct style may be the most effective style to use. Letters that report problems with products or services to the supplier or manufacturer present bad news, but the response to this bad news is usually very positive. These letters are generally called claim letters. Most organizations are very eager to correct problems for several reasons:

Some negative situations can be handled very effectively using a direct strategy.

- Their reputations depend on good products and good service.
- Customer feedback helps to improve products.
- They want to maintain good relationships or even partnerships with their customers.
- They want to keep the customer.

Therefore, a high-impact style is not needed to get action. If a claim is justified, presenting the information factually is all that is necessary. A good tone is important in maintaining good relations with suppliers and manufacturers.

   The following strategy is generally used for reporting problems with products and services:

- Present the problem factually, giving enough information to allow the reader to identify the situation.
- Present additional details necessary to explain the situation and justify your request for action.
- Request the action that you desire.
- Close on a friendly note.

The letter on page 101 illustrates effective use of presenting negative information using a direct strategy. Review the letter carefully. Pay particular attention to the tone used.

Modified Direct Approach for Mixed News

VanHuss Industries, Inc.
292 Crown Lake Drive ▪ Hopkins, SC 29061-4736
(803) 555-0181

TO: Marty Mostafa

FROM: Jan Boudreaux

DATE: March 24, 19—

SUBJECT: Facilities Request

Presents the positive information first

The six offices vacated by the marketing group have been reassigned to your department as you requested. The additional space should help to accommodate the additional staff in your group. The offices are being painted and will be ready for occupancy next week.

Explains the reasons for the negative information

We have also reviewed your request for new furniture for these offices. Our facilities staff has checked the furniture carefully. They have elected to touch up and clean the furniture rather than use the limited funds in the facilities budget to replace the furniture. You may, of course, use your own departmental funds to replace the furniture.

Presents a realistic alternative

The facilities staff plans to complete the work on the furniture before your employees move into the offices. If you plan to replace the furniture, please notify facilities before they begin the work on the furniture.

Closes on a friendly, optimistic note

We hope that the additional office space will improve the working conditions in your department.

og

Attachment

Direct Strategy for Claims Letter

VanHuss Industries, Inc.
292 Crown Lake Drive ▪ Hopkins, SC 29061-4736
(803) 555-0181

July 26, 19—

Mr. Leonard Robinson
Office SuperStore
6849 Garners Ferry Road
Columbia, SC 29209-4801

Dear Mr. Robinson

The printer that we purchased from your store one month ago continues to malfunction. Frequently, when the printer is turned on, the message on the screen indicates a 013 error. According to your manual, this is a memory-related error. The printer has 12 megabytes of memory installed.

Your service representative has checked and "adjusted" the printer on three different occasions. Each time, the printer works for three or four days, and then the error appears again. Turning the printer on and off several times will finally clear the error. However, it appears again the next time the printer is turned on.

Please have one of your service managers or a factory representative fix this printer. If the problem is not corrected this time, then we want the printer replaced with a new printer or our money refunded so that we can purchase a printer that functions properly.

We look forward to a quick resolution to this problem. We are pleased with the quality of the printing and would like to continue using your product.

Sincerely

Kimberly C. Mayfield
Administrative Manager

ms

Presents the problem factually, giving enough information to allow the reader to understand the situation

Presents additional details to explain the situation and justify your request for action

Requests the action desired

Closes on a friendly note

Communicating effectively with fellow employees and with customers is a challenge for employees whose companies do business globally. Most companies use electronic mail, fax, and the telephone to communicate with international customers because of the delivery time required for regular mail. Time differences must also be taken into consideration. Employees must recognize that communication styles are very different in the various regions of the world. Therefore, learn more about the cultures of the countries in which you must deal with customers. The more you know about the culture of the country, the better able you are to tailor your messages to meet the needs of your reader. Your reader will appreciate the efforts that you make.

Americans tend to be more casual than their customers in other countries. Observe the level of formality in the communications you receive from international customers. Use that information as a guide in determining how formal you should be in corresponding with the customer. Be especially careful about addressing individuals without the use of a proper title. In many cases, using a first name is considered inappropriate and rude.

The length of communications varies significantly in different countries. In some countries, it is rude to write concise, to-the-point messages. In other countries, extensive information and particularly statistical details are expected. Be aware of these differences and try to accommodate the expectations of your reader.

Although English is the international language of business, remember that your reader may have limited English skills. Use words that are very familiar and that can be translated easily. Avoid slang and expressions that are common only to the region in which you live. These expressions often have no equivalent in foreign languages and are likely to be misinterpreted.

Patience is required. Always be willing to explain things in detail and to clarify questions that might arise.

INTERNET

THE SUPERHIGHWAY OF COMMUNICATIONS

Netiquette is a word coined from *network etiquette.* Netiquette refers to appropriate behavior when using the various resources of the network. It is important to sort out information that is appropriate for business use from the myriad information available. This text focuses exclusively on network business applications. In this section, E-mail etiquette is covered. In later chapters, other aspects of netiquette are covered.

Consider the following ideas before sending E-mail messages:

- You represent your company when you send business messages using E-mail. Always try to convey a positive image.
- Avoid the gimmicks used in casual E-mail, such as *smileys* (symbols to represent a smiling face) or all CAPS within a message to get attention (considered shouting on the Internet).

- Check to ensure that the E-mail address is correct. E-mail addresses cannot have spaces embedded in the address, and the system, site, and domain elements are separated by periods. The address elements include the reader's log-on name, the @ symbol (sometimes followed by the name of the system-specific computer account), the site (name of the company, on-line service, or school network), and the domain (the type of network, such as *com* for commercial or *edu* for education).
- Limit each E-mail to one subject and use a concise, descriptive subject line.
- Apply guides for effective writing to E-mail messages.
- Use the Reply feature (rather than creating a new message) for responding to an E-mail so that the two messages will be linked.
- Limit copies to those who need to know the information.

MISCOMMUNICATIONS

Summary of responses to an exit poll on election day:

Women prefer Democrats to men.

Sign in the window of a loan company:

Ask about our plans for owning your home.

APPLICATION 4A *Review Guide 2: Write for the Reader*

Revise the following sentences to make them more reader-oriented.

1. I expect you to meet with your employees and make them read the new procedures and also make them come to the meeting explaining how the procedures are to be implemented.

2. If you had read your instructions carefully, you would not have messed this project up. Correct it immediately.

3. I want each department head to ensure that his expenditures are within his budget.

4. I reviewed the project, and I thank you for the excellent work you did to ensure that it was successful.

5. Ask the girls in the office to find an appropriate room for the meeting and to set it up properly.

APPLICATION 4B *Editing and Language Arts Checkpoint*

Read carefully the document that follows; it is packed with errors. Use proof-reader's marks to mark all errors in grammar, spelling, word usage, number usage, capitalization, and punctuation. Do not revise sentence or paragraph structure in this activity unless an error exists.

After you have marked all corrections directly on this document, access File 4B on your template disk and make the corrections you marked. If you do not have access to the template disk, key the letter, making the corrections as you key.

After you have made all corrections, refer to page 233 in Appendix C for the solution and check to see that you corrected all errors. You may use on-line reference tools just as you would if you were doing this document as part of your job.

Add a memo heading to the document, which will be sent to members of the Economic Alliance from you. Use March 10 as the date and supply an appropriate subject line. Reformat the memo using single spacing and block format. Save the file as 4B-sol.

---

the Board of Directors of the Economic Alliance have scheduled a meeting with Robert West, Mayor of Horrell Hill Judy Ledbetter, President of County Counsel and Wayne Roxbury Secretary of Commerce at 1;45 on Tuesday March 26. The primary purpose of the meeting is to identify two peaces of land North of Highway Ten that have one hundred acres per cite and take initially steps to obtain options to purchase this land. These step is critical so that we will not loose out on economic development prospects again because of our inability to locate suitable sights for manufacturing plants immediately.

The Economic Alliance will also review Bob Smith's and Tom Graham's proposal to upgrade the conference room and shift form portable projection equipment to a stationery multimedia platform for presentations to visiting prospects. The funds are available for the project permission is need to build a base platform that is twelve feet long, six feet deep, and ten inches high. The multimedia podium will be mounted on this base platform.

The last item propose is a plan to beautify Rosewood Boulevard between 1st and 9th Street. This area is the gateway to our city and need to be enhanced with landscaping, benches,and appropriate lighting to create a positive first impression for visitors to the city. The landscape architect with who we have consulted has provided a cost estimate for the project. a architectural drawing of the area will be on display at the meeting.

The Board welcome your comments or suggestions on these topics prior to the meeting. Please send them to me as early as possible.

APPLICATION 4C *Writing Negative and Mixed-News Messages*

Plan and write the following messages. Check Appendix A for addresses.

1. Ms. Ursula Pharr requested that Holiday Air sponsor the Central University MBA Case Competition team by providing six round-trip airline tickets to Montreal leaving on December 27 and returning on January 3. You would like to do so, but the holiday season is your peak time and you even block out tickets for all frequent flier coupons during this period. Therefore, you are unable to provide six tickets during the holiday period. You would be happy to provide six tickets for the team to any destination you fly if the team has other competitions scheduled during a nonholiday period.

   Plan the letter to Ms. Pharr by answering the following questions:

   a. How is the reader likely to feel about your decision?

   b. What objectives would you like to accomplish?

   c. What buffer would be appropriate to open the letter?

   d. What reasons support your decision?

   e. What alternatives, if any, can you offer?

   f. What would be an appropriate closing to build goodwill?

2. Write the bad-news letter to Ms. Pharr using an indirect approach. Sign your name; use the title marketing manager. Save as 4C2.

3. You ordered (Order No. 395867) two swimsuits with matching jackets from the Resort Wear Boutique to take on a cruise. Today, you received the jacket of one set and the swimsuit of the second set along with a notice that the other items were out of stock and were back ordered. The notice from Ms. Renee Marks indicated you could expect them in approximately three weeks. Because your cruise departs in two weeks, you want to cancel the order for the items that were out of stock and return the jacket. You plan to keep the swimsuit because you really like it even though you did not get the jacket to match it. You will request a refund of $94.

    Plan the letter by answering the following questions:

    a. How is the reader likely to respond to your keeping the swimsuit? How is the reader likely to respond to your canceling your order for out of stock items and returning the jacket?

    b. Would it be better to start with the good news or the bad news? Why?

    c. What reasons can you offer that lead to your decision to cancel the order and return the jacket?

    d. What closing would be appropriate?

4. Write the mixed-news message to Resort Wear Boutique. Sign your name. Save as 4C4.

5. You purchased ConstructionEstimator, a software package designed to estimate the amount of supplies needed for construction jobs. You have used the software for six different projects. On the three large projects, the quantity of supplies was grossly underestimated. On the three small projects, the quantity of supplies was grossly overestimated. At your request, a technician reviewed the procedures you used and verified that you were using the software properly. The overestimates required you to pay restocking fees, and the underestimates caused you to lose time ordering additional supplies and waiting for them to be delivered. You have purchased several other software packages from Custom Construction Software and have been very pleased with them; but these errors are extremely costly to your construction business, and you are dissatisfied with the software. You would like a full refund of the $995 you paid for ConstructionEstimator.

   Plan the letter by answering the following questions:

   a. Would it be appropriate to use a direct approach for this situation? Why?

   b. How do you expect the reader to feel about your request?

   c. Outline the letter you plan to write.

6. Write the letter to David Scheatzle at Custom Construction Software. Save as 4C6.

7. Mr. Arthur Rosenblaum, an owner of several small apartment complexes, requested that Appliance Superstore increase his current $2,500 line of credit to $10,000 so that he can purchase appliances as needed for apartment units. Mr. Rosenblaum was granted the $2,500 line of credit approximately nine months ago. You base credit decisions on income and credit record. Mr. Rosenblaum's income justified only $2,500 when you extended the credit, and his payment record has not been satisfactory. During the past nine months, he has

been late with his payments three times and did not pay the minimum required on two occasions. You would reconsider his request after he has maintained his account properly for one year. Plan and write the letter declining his request to extend his credit limit. Sign your name and use the title credit manager. Save as 4C7.

8. A number of employees have sent you E-mail notes requesting that VanHuss Industries provide an employee cafeteria to serve breakfast and lunch at its Kilgore facility. You do provide cafeterias at some of the large industrial facilities, but providing a cafeteria to serve breakfast and lunch at a small facility with less than thirty employees would not be cost effective. You will, however, expand the current employee lounge, provide a microwave oven, and add several vending machines with a variety of sandwiches, cereal packs, snacks, and beverages appropriate for breakfast and lunch. Plan and write a draft of the memo that you will send by E-mail to all employees. Use your name and an appropriate subject line in the heading. Save as 4C8.

9. When you returned from a business trip on Holiday Air flight 485 from Atlanta to Charlotte last week, your luggage was not on the flight. A delivery service dropped off your luggage at the main desk of your company. When you picked up the suitcase, you noticed that it had been badly damaged. The baggage had tire marks and appeared to have been run over by the baggage trailer. You called the airline, and the customer service representative instructed you to take it to Reggie's Repair Shop, have them repair it and bill Holiday Air direct. The repair job left deep scars on the bag and is not acceptable. Reggie's Repair Shop indicated you should contact Ms. Carolyn Brandt, manager of customer service at Holiday Air. You paid $275 for the luggage less than six months ago, and you want it replaced. Plan and write the claims letter. Sign your name. Save as 4C9.

10. Jan Evans, an employee of VanHuss Industries, requested and was granted permission to attend a two-day telecommunications training seminar offered by Southside Community College. The $350 fee was paid by the training department. A week later, Southside Community College refunded $250 to the training department because the employee did not attend the seminar. A nonrefundable $100 fee was retained for failure to cancel the registration. You had no notification from the employee; therefore, you verified with the college that Jan Evans did not attend the seminar either day nor call to cancel the registration. Company policy requires that an employee who does not attend a scheduled training program notify the training department and reimburse the company for any fees incurred. Exceptions are made only in circumstances beyond the control of the employee. The training manager notifies the employee of the amount that must be refunded and the reasons why. A copy is sent to the employee's supervisor (Lynn Adamson). Any disciplinary action is taken by the supervisor. Write the bad-news memo. Use your name, the title training manager, the current date, and an appropriate subject line in the heading. Save as 4C10.

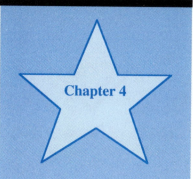

APPLICATION 4D *Self-Assessment*

1. Use complete, grammatically correct sentences to answer each of the following items.

   a. Describe the most appropriate strategy for a message that conveys negative information. Explain your choice of strategy.

   b. Describe a good buffer and how it should be used in a bad-news message.

   c. What type of situation is most appropriate for conveying negative news using a direct approach?

   d. What factors should be considered in deciding which medium is best to convey negative information?

   e. Describe several techniques that can be used to de-emphasize negative information.

2. Approximately 30 percent of employees at VanHuss Industries have preschool children, and a group of them got together and requested that the company provide a day-care center on company facilities for their children. The employees indicated that they are willing to pay a major portion of the costs. You have investigated the situation and decided not to provide the center this year. Several factors influenced your decision. Space, adapting space for a center, and locating competent employees to work in the center are major problems. The current budget does not have funds available for creating and operating such a facility. You also have concerns about the liability that might result from such a facility. You will appoint a committee to study the issue and to make recommendations when next year's budget is being prepared. Write the memo to all employees from you as human resources manager. Use an appropriate subject line. Save as 4D2.

Heritage Productions

APPLICATION 4E *Heritage Productions*

You are still working in the research and development department of Heritage Productions. As assistant manager, you report to Mr. Gary Kiely, the manager of the department. (If necessary, review pages 17, 73, and 90 for information describing Heritage products as well as your present and previous positions in Heritage Productions.)

Mr. Kiely received an invitation to visit Stonehedge Publishing Company, Ltd., a British publishing house that produces EFL books designed for elementary students. He has asked you to find out as much as you can about Stonehedge and then to talk with the task force responsible for marketing Heritage's EFL products for business to find out if a trip to London would be justified. He wants to maintain good relations with the company, but does not want to make a special trip to London unless compelling business reasons (such as gaining immediate knowledge about the business market or contacts with distributors in the countries you are targeting) make it urgent to go now. He asked that you draft a letter for his signature that can be faxed to Stonehedge either accepting or declining the invitation. If you decline the invitation, be sure to leave the door open for a future visit.

Your research produced the following information:

- Business people in the targeted countries definitely prefer American English to British English.
- Stonehedge has no experience in publishing for the business community—only in publishing for elementary classes.
- Stonehedge has distributors in the countries targeted, but they are strictly in the education market—not the business market.
- Stonehedge currently is not a direct competitor because they publish EFL materials for elementary schools and Heritage publishes EFL materials for secondary and postsecondary schools.
- Stonehedge primarily produces textbooks; their videos for elementary classes are tapes of entertainment programs in English rather than specially designed training programs. At some point in the future, Heritage would like to explore joint video projects for EFL classes in elementary schools.

Do the following:

1. Analyze the information carefully and decide what you will recommend to Mr. Kiely.

2. Plan and write a mixed-news memo to Mr. Kiely presenting your recommendation and the information your research produced.

3. Plan and draft the letter to Elizabeth Addison, Director of Product Development at Stonehedge Publishing Company, Ltd. The address is in Appendix A. If the letter is negative, use an indirect approach; if it is positive, use a direct approach. Also prepare a fax cover sheet. Save as 4E3 and 4E3B.

PERSUASIVE LETTERS AND MEMOS

Performance Goals

After you complete Chapter 5, you should be able to

- ❏ *Use logical appeals for writing persuasive messages*
- ❏ *Use emotional appeals for writing persuasive messages*
- ❏ *Determine when to use logical appeals and when to use emotional appeals*
- ❏ *Edit communications more effectively*

OVERVIEW

To persuade means to induce or to convince someone to do something. The need for persuasion implies that the reader may not take the requested action unless convinced to do so. If the reader is likely to do something, very little, if any, persuasion is needed. A routine request is all that is necessary. Individuals and organizations often make requests of other individuals or organizations. Many requests involve the commitment of resources, such as money, time, or effort. Most individuals and organizations rightfully tend to guard their limited resources very carefully.

Persuasion often involves ethical issues. Persuasion does not include force. A writer in a position of power who uses force to cause a reader to take certain action may be using intimidation rather than persuasion. Persuasion that manipulates, misrepresents, misleads, or takes advantage of someone else is inappropriate. Communications must be honest. Deliberately withholding information from a reader may be just as deceitful as presenting incorrect information. Intent or motive is a key issue in ethical situations. The intent to deceive a reader by providing incorrect information or by withholding needed information obviously represents an unethical situation. At the same time, writers should take care that persuasive efforts do not unintentionally mislead the reader.

In Chapters 3 and 4, you focused on writing positive and negative messages. The primary emphasis was on conveying information, and the primary concern was on doing so in an effective manner. In this chapter, you will focus on writing effective persuasive messages. Because persuasive messages can have either positive or negative overtones, you will have the opportunity to build on what you learned in previous chapters. The emphasis is different,

Honest efforts to convince a reader to take the action requested is ethical persuasion.

Efforts that include deceiving a reader in order to convince the reader to take the action requested is unethical persuasion.

however. An approach that works well for conveying positive or negative information may not be effective in convincing someone to take action.

Persuasive messages ask readers to do things they might not be likely to do; therefore, the writer should expect and prepare for some resistance. The primary focus should be trying to convince the reader to take the action requested. In some cases, the reader may like the request or think that it is a reasonable one, but the reader may feel hesitant to commit the time or resources involved. In other cases, the reader may be negative toward the request, but could be convinced that it is in their—or their organiztion's—best interest to grant the request.

Planning Persuasive Messages

Many different types of messages fit into the broad category of persuasive messages. The approach that works best for one type of persuasive message may differ from the approach that works best for another type of persuasive message. For example, the approach to persuade someone to buy a product differs from the approach to persuade someone to pay a delinquent bill or from the approach to convince someone to devote time to work on a community service or charitable project.

These situations all have similarities and differences. They are similar in that you have to get the reader's attention before you can present the request. They are also similar in that in each case the primary objective is to convince the reader to take action. They are different in the knowledge needed to be effective in each situation. In the sales situation, planning involves careful analysis of the customer's needs, how your product fits those needs, the competitive products that are available, and the entire market situation. Convincing the customer of the need for the product may even be required. The collection letter may require an understanding of the problem and potential ways to solve it before focusing on persuading the individual to take the necessary steps to pay the delinquent bill. In the last situation, appealing to the emotions of the individual may persuade the individual to take the desired action.

In many organizations, writing specialized messages, such as sales letters and collection letters, is handled by specialists within the organization or by external consultants who concentrate only on those types of messages. The emphasis in this chapter focuses on general persuasive messages. The degree of persuasion can vary from a minor element of persuasion to a very persuasive message.

Planning a persuasive message first requires focusing on getting the reader's attention. Then emphasis is placed on developing interest in the request and creating the desire to do what is asked. The final consideration is making it easy for the reader to do what is requested.

Factors That Influence Persuasion

Earlier in this chapter, persuasive messages were defined as messages that ask readers to do something that they might not be likely to do. Persuasion requires influencing or changing the behavior of individuals. Therefore, factors that can be used to influence a person's behavior must be analyzed carefully. The two key factors that influence persuasion are the credibility of the writer of the message and the appeal used in the message.

CREDIBILITY

Both the writer and the message must have credibility. To have credibility, the reader must perceive the writer as

- being knowledgeable or having expertise on the topic
- being sincere, honest, and forthright
- being in control of the situation

To be credible is to be believable or trustworthy.

If any of those elements are missing, the reader is not likely to believe the writer. If the writer is not credible, the reader is not likely to believe the message. Even if a writer is credible, the message may not be credible. For a message to be credible, it must be judged by the reader to be

- accurate
- clear and easy to understand
- supported with adequate information to make a decision

Credibility of the writer and the message is always judged by the reader—not the writer.

APPEAL

A message can have a logical or a psychological appeal. In some cases, the logical and psychological appeals can be combined. A message has a logical appeal when the reader believes good reasons exist for taking the action requested. To be logical, the message must make sense; the request must come across to the reader as being reasonable. A message with a logical appeal is developed by presenting facts and supporting evidence, analyzing that evidence, and drawing logical conclusions from it. Believability is conditioned upon the reader perceiving the facts to be accurate, the analysis to be proper, and the conclusions justified by appropriate analysis of the facts.

An appeal is an enticement to do something.

Logical appeals focus on rationality.

A message has a psychological appeal when it stimulates the reader's emotions or when it relates to a reader's goals, values, or perceived needs. A psychological appeal is created when a reader feels a request has inherent value or when it satisfies the reader's motives or needs. A psychological appeal makes the reader feel good or righteous about taking the action that was requested. Psychological appeals often focus on fair play, appreciating one's good fortune and helping the less fortunate, and doing things just because they are good things to do.

Psychological appeals focus on emotionality.

STRATEGY FOR WRITING PERSUASIVE MESSAGES

The best strategy for writing a persuasive message depends on what you are trying to accomplish and how difficult the task is. Many different types of messages require an element of persuasion. Some messages require more persuasion than others. The degree of persuasion needed is the key element to use in determining the strategy that is likely to produce the best results.

The best strategy for a simple request that requires very little persuasion is the direct strategy that you learned in Chapter 3 for positive and routine messages. The key is to present the reasons for the request effectively so that the reader will believe that the reasons are good and the request is justified.

The best strategy for messages that require more persuasion is an indirect strategy that is similar to the strategy you used in writing negative messages. The indirect strategy works better in persuasive situations because the reasons or justification are presented before the request is made.

- Attract the reader's attention and interest.
- Explain the request carefully, making sure that it is fully justified.
- Minimize the obstacles and make it as easy as possible for the reader to act.
- Request the desired action confidently.

Getting the reader's attention is not always easy. In some cases, the reader may have an interest in your message, and getting attention is relatively easy. In other cases, creativity and imagination are crucial in getting the reader's attention.

Getting attention is only the first step. The opening paragraph must also prepare the reader for the justification that follows. Using the right appeal for the situation is important. Most people respond to things that appeal either to their emotions or to their reasoning power.

As a rule of thumb, use a logical appeal when the situation has some direct benefit to the reader and a psychological appeal when the benefit is indirect or when the request has no benefit at all to the reader. Analyze the situation carefully before deciding which type of appeal to use. Be creative in developing appeals.

BRAINSTORMING

Use brainstorming techniques to stimulate creative thinking. A free wheeling, questioning tactic is helpful. Ask yourself questions such as:

- What benefit, if any, does this request have for the reader?
- How important is the benefit—is it a direct benefit or an indirect benefit?
- If I were the reader, would I be likely to do what was asked?
- Why would anyone who does not have to do what I am asking be willing to do it?
- Would the reader grant the request because it makes good business sense to do so or does it make the reader feel that it is a good thing to do?
- What reasons would convince me to do what is being asked of the reader?
- What would motivate me to take action on the request?
- What would convince the reader of my credibility?
- What would be the most effective way to appeal to the reader?

The purpose of brainstorming is to generate as many ideas as possible. Accept all the ideas without being judgmental about them. Resist the temptation to criticize the ideas; rather, try to build on the ideas that you generate. One idea may have no value on its own, but it may lead you to think of other ideas that could prove to be valuable. After you have generated as many ideas as possible, begin to evaluate them to determine their strengths and weaknesses. As you evaluate the ideas, do a quick credibility check. Ask questions such as:

- Would I believe this idea?
- Would I think this is a good reason to do what I am asking?
- Why wouldn't I believe this idea?
- How could I change this idea so that it would be believable?

The ideas that you select as the basis for your appeal should be given a final check for credibility. Some writers try to use a gimmick to open the letter and get the reader's attention. The idea may be clever or cute, but if the reader does not believe it, the opening will not be effective.

Sincerity is especially important in persuasive messages. Warm and friendly messages that contain factual information tend to build trust. Some writers tend to exaggerate to make a point in persuasive messages. Effective writers avoid this temptation because they do not want to risk jeopardizing their credibility with the reader. Empathy is a great technique for evaluating sincerity. Read the message carefully. If you received the message, would you believe it? If it does not seem sincere to you, it probably will not seem sincere to the reader.

Review the two illustrations on pages 118 and 119. Note that the first illustration is a relatively simple request that could provide benefit for the reader. Therefore, using a logical appeal or combining a logical and psychological appeal is appropriate. The second illustration has no direct benefit to the reader and would require a significant amount of persuasion to convince the reader to take the action requested. Therefore, an indirect style with a psychological appeal is appropriate in this case.

GLOBAL CONNECTIONS

The following specific writing techniques will help to ensure that messages written to individuals in other countries are easier to interpret.

- Use a simple, straightforward writing style. Complex and compound sentences are more difficult to interpret than simple sentences.
- Use concrete language. Specific writing results in less ambiguity than general or abstract language does.
- Avoid idioms, slang, and nonstandard English, which often have no equivalent in the language of other countries. An expression such as *slick as a whistle* may totally confuse the recipient.
- Use bulleted items, graphs, charts, and illustrations to clarify and simplify data.
- Use familiar words, short sentences, and short paragraphs to make the document more readable.

Attracts the reader's attention and stimulates interest

Explains the request and combines a logical and a psychological appeal to persuade the reader to take the desired action

Requests action confidently; makes it easy for reader to act

Star Publishing Co.
3847 Elmwood Drive ▪ Muncie, IN 47303-6857
(219) 555-0190

April 6, 19—

Ms. Marcia Metcalf
Metcalf and Associates
2847 Carriage Lane
Muncie, IN 47302-1082

Dear Ms. Metcalf

During the past several years, you and your staff have conducted a number of excellent training programs for Star Publishing Co. Our employees have reacted very favorably to the training, and our company has benefitted immensely from the investment in these training sessions. Today, when the Community Services of Muncie Board of Directors agreed that training our volunteers must be our first priority, I immediately thought of Metcalf and Associates and the excellent work you do.

Would you please consider contributing one day of training in early May for all volunteers working with Community Services of Muncie? As you know, Community Services and its volunteers have improved the quality of life for many of the less fortunate members of our community. In addition to knowing that you have made a major contribution to our community by helping our volunteers to do an even better job, you will have an opportunity to showcase your training to the leading companies in the Muncie area. Many of these leading companies provide the volunteers who work with Community Services of Muncie.

Please check your calendar, and I will call you next week to see if we can work out an appropriate time for you to conduct the training session.

Sincerely

Student's Name
Chair, Board of Directors

ms

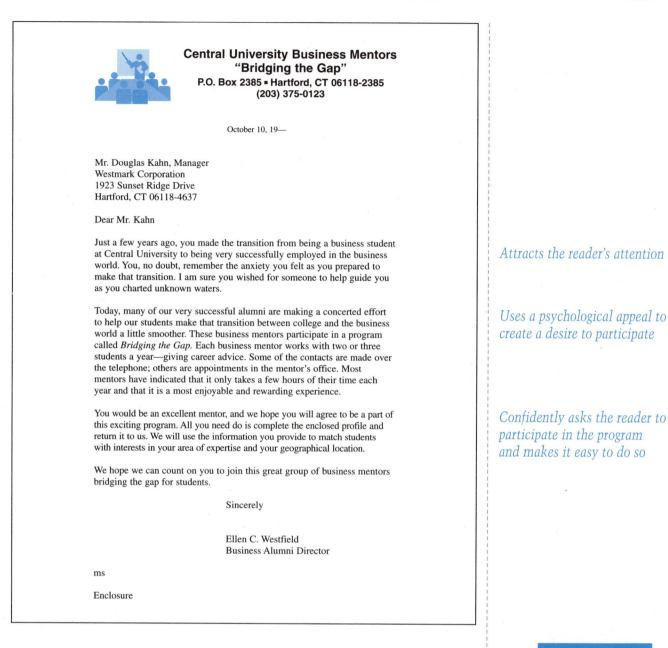

Central University Business Mentors
"Bridging the Gap"
P.O. Box 2385 ▪ Hartford, CT 06118-2385
(203) 375-0123

October 10, 19—

Mr. Douglas Kahn, Manager
Westmark Corporation
1923 Sunset Ridge Drive
Hartford, CT 06118-4637

Dear Mr. Kahn

Just a few years ago, you made the transition from being a business student at Central University to being very successfully employed in the business world. You, no doubt, remember the anxiety you felt as you prepared to make that transition. I am sure you wished for someone to help guide you as you charted unknown waters.

Attracts the reader's attention

Today, many of our very successful alumni are making a concerted effort to help our students make that transition between college and the business world a little smoother. These business mentors participate in a program called *Bridging the Gap*. Each business mentor works with two or three students a year—giving career advice. Some of the contacts are made over the telephone; others are appointments in the mentor's office. Most mentors have indicated that it only takes a few hours of their time each year and that it is a most enjoyable and rewarding experience.

Uses a psychological appeal to create a desire to participate

You would be an excellent mentor, and we hope you will agree to be a part of this exciting program. All you need do is complete the enclosed profile and return it to us. We will use the information you provide to match students with interests in your area of expertise and your geographical location.

Confidently asks the reader to participate in the program and makes it easy to do so

We hope we can count on you to join this great group of business mentors bridging the gap for students.

Sincerely

Ellen C. Westfield
Business Alumni Director

ms

Enclosure

THE SUPERHIGHWAY OF COMMUNICATIONS

INTERNET

The Internet contains a wealth of information that can be used effectively by business. Many individuals and organizations are eager to share their information resources with others. Three key problems occur with using information from the Internet. The first is locating the information needed in an efficient manner. Surfing the Internet can be time consuming. Learning to use keyword searches effectively is important. The second problem is that not all information shared is good information. Good netiquette requires that information shared on the network be accurate. Material placed on the Internet should be dated. Good netiquette also requires that copyright laws be followed and that materials be cited when used. The third problem is the wasted time that often results from the excessive use of graphics. Good netiquette requires concise materials and graphics limited to those that make a contribution to the content.

Some information on the Internet is available at no charge. Other information is available on a subscription basis. The accessibility and volume of information make subscriptions a bargain in many cases. Quality of information is always an issue and should be monitored carefully to determine if the subscription is worthwhile.

MISCOMMUNICATIONS

Accurate reporting of statistical information

The star guard went on a scoring tare in the final 2 minutes and 16 seconds of the basketball game—scoring 7 points on 2 three-point goals and 2 of 3 free throws.

Maybe a scoring tear would have produced 8 points.

APPLICATION 5A *Review Guide 3: Present Ideas Positively*

Revise the following negative sentences to make them more positive.

1. Don't complete the application if you have not read all of the instructions.

2. Call Judy and see if she doesn't need extra help in getting ready for the meeting.

3. We regret that we were negligent and failed to include the specifications with the proposal and you could not evaluate it effectively.

4. We don't put post office boxes on our mailing labels because overnight delivery service cannot deliver to post office boxes.

5. Jan did not do as well on the verbal portion of the exam as she did on the math portion of it.

APPLICATION 5B *Editing and Language Arts Checkpoint*

Carefully read the document that follows; it is packed with errors. Use proofreader's marks to mark all errors in grammar, spelling, word usage, number usage, capitalization, and punctuation. Do not revise sentence or paragraph structure in this activity unless an error exists.

After you have marked all corrections directly on this document, access File 5B on your template disk and make the corrections you marked. If you do not have access to the template disk, key the letter, making the corrections as you key.

After you have made all corrections, refer to page 234 in Appendix C for the solution and check to see that you corrected all errors. You may use online reference tools just as you would if you were doing this as part of your job.

Add a memo heading to the document, which will be sent to Janice T. Babcock from you. Use August 15 as the date and supply an appropriate subject line. Reformat the memo using single spacing and block format. Save the file as 5B-sol.

Thank you for giving me the opportunity to review the Productivity Improvement and Cost Reduction proposal christopher McBride submit to you and to give my assessment of it. I analyzed the proposal careful and I have a number of reservation about it even though Christopher McBride is an imminent consultant.

My principle concern is that the approach Christopher proposed is an standard industrial engineering approach. It's major emphasis is on efficiency rather than on affectiveness. The industrial engineering approach works reasonably good for some factory and routine clerical operations however it generally does not produce good results in a work setting involving professionals. My second concern are the cost quoted. The first phase cost of $25,000.00 is about twenty percent to high.

As we discussed earlier, most of your personal are professional employees—many of who are doing routine work that could be delegate to support staff. Delegating affectively would reduce cost's and enhance the positions of your support staff substantial. Christophers proposal do not address this issue at all.

My advise to you is to try to obtain a proposal that focus on effectiveness and that is designed for professional employees. I have a meeting in your building on monday March 14 form 2;15 to 3;15 in conference room c and could meet with you about the proposal at 3:30. Just leave me know if you want to meet at that time.

APPLICATION 5C *Writing Persuasive Messages*

Plan and write the following messages. Use the appeal that would be most effective. Use your name as the signature on each document. Check the address file in Appendix A for addresses.

1. As a business communications instructor, you would like to secure examples of the types of letters and memos that are written in local businesses. You would use these documents as illustrations in your classes. You would protect the confidentiality of the company by removing the company name and any other identifying information. To determine the type of response you might get, you selected Henderson & Henderson, an advertising, public relations, and marketing consulting firm. This firm has a great image and excellent reputation for being a good corporate citizen.

   a. What benefit, if any, would Henderson & Henderson gain by granting your request?

   b. What obstacles would you anticipate in trying to persuade the firm to send you samples?

   c. How could you overcome those obstacles and make it easy for the firm to grant your request?

   d. What appeal do you think will produce the best results?

2. Write the persuasive letter to Ms. Martha Henderson, one of the owners.

3. VanHuss Industries currently uses proprietary project management software. The program needs to be updated because of changes in computer technology. As a senior project manager, you are convinced that VanHuss should abandon the proprietary software and purchase a project management software package off the shelf. You have analyzed several packages—all of which work well. The package you recommend is IPM (Integrated Project Management). You recommend the program because it does everything your current software does and more. The key advantage of the program is that it is part of the integrated suite of products that includes the word processing, database, spreadsheet, and graphics software that VanHuss uses. Another factor is the time involved in updating proprietary software. It takes three to six months to make programming changes in your current software. The IPM program is available now and upgrades are offered periodically. Costs are comparable. Plan a memo to the Technology Task Force trying to persuade them to make this change. The Technology Task Force was responsible several years ago for having the current software developed, and they have been hesitant to abandon it.

a. What benefits, if any, would VanHuss Industries gain by changing the software?

b. What obstacles should you anticipate when you write the memo to the Technology Task Force?

c. How could you overcome those obstacles?

d. What appeal do you think will work best in the situation?

4. Write the memo to the Technology Task Force.

5. Currently Hess Industries has a compensation plan for sales representatives in their first three years that consists of 25 percent salary and 75 percent commission. After three years, the compensation changes to 50 percent salary and 50 percent commission. Your sales managers have reported to you, as marketing manager, that they have lost several candidates for sales positions to competitors. You have also noted that turnover in the sales force is much greater in the first years of tenure than at any other time. The company has always felt that commission provided a greater incentive than salary for new hires. You have given a lot of thought to the issue and believe that concern about economic security is now a factor that is offsetting the commission incentive. You propose changing the ratio of salary and commission. The total dollar amount paid to new sales representatives is not expected to change significantly. Plan the memo to the Compensation Committee.

a. What benefits, if any, would Hess Industries gain from changing the commission plan?

b. What obstacles would you anticipate in trying to persuade the Compensation Committee to change the compensation to 50 percent salary and 50 percent commission for all sales representatives?

c. How can you overcome these obstacles?

d. What appeal do you think will produce the best results?

6. Write the memo to the Compensation Committee.

7. You are manager of community relations for Hess Industries. You want to strongly encourage all employees to contribute to the Community Chest Fund. The Community Chest supports about fifty local charitable causes. The bulk of all funds are collected through the workplace. Employees can donate through payroll deductions, check, or credit card. Hess Industries wants to be viewed as a good corporate citizen

and matches each gift an employee makes. At the same time, Hess does not want to pressure employees to give to the Community Chest Fund. Hess prefers to appeal to the need to help take care of the homeless, the hungry, abused or neglected children, and many other groups needing community support. Plan and write the memo to employees encouraging them to contribute generously to the Community Chest Fund. Refer employees to an enclosed brochure that describes the various agencies that receive support from the Community Chest Fund.

8. As president of Computer Testing Associates (CTA), you have prepared a proposal to send to Dr. Karen Roskowski, vice president of Office Systems and Services (OSS). You now must prepare a transmittal letter to Dr. Roskowski persuading her to accept your proposal. You want to hire Dr. Roskowski and her associates to work as consultants to establish business partnerships with carefully selected educational institutions in more than fifty cities. These institutions would serve as CTA training and assessment centers. You spoke with Dr. Roskowski briefly on the telephone about the project and told her you would send the proposal to her this week. You selected OSS because all the associates in OSS are educators who are well respected in their fields. You believe that educators would be more effective at convincing the educational institutions to become CTA centers than your sales representatives would.

    The contract proposed is a very lucrative one. It includes major financial incentives for meeting tight deadlines as well as the standard consulting fees that OSS normally charges. Encourage Dr. Roskowski to give careful consideration to the proposal. You must have her answer no later than one week from today.

9. Hess Industries has contracted with the Topping Management Center of the College of Business Administration at Central University to develop a certificate program entitled *The Hess Leadership Institute* for its managers. The program consists of eight three-day segments taken over a two-year period (one per quarter) and is available to all employees whose positions are Grade 10 or higher. Four of the segments are required for all participants, and four are elected from a list of ten alternatives that are designed to meet the needs of employees in a variety of different positions in the company. The programs are conducted on work time, and Hess Industries pays for all costs including books and training materials. The program requires some work assignments between the segments offered. Write a memo that will be sent to all eligible employees persuading them to participate in the program and to obtain the certificate offered. You do not want employees to feel that they are being pressured or forced to participate.

10. As a professor of Human Resource Management, you are writing a textbook. Someone in a company you work for as a consultant showed you a compensation survey sent to human resource directors of large companies within the state. The survey instrument included short job descriptions for benchmark jobs. You felt the survey design and job descriptions were excellent and would like to include them as examples in your textbook. You will give full credit to Ms. Yolanda DeShane, human resources director of Hess Industries, who designed the survey instrument. Write Ms. DeShane requesting permission to use the survey instrument with the job descriptions.

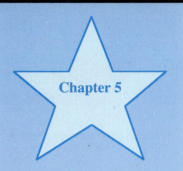

APPLICATION 5D *Self-Assessment*

1. Use complete, grammatically correct sentences to answer each of the following items.

   a. Describe the most appropriate strategy for a persuasive message. Justify your choice.

   b. Describe two types of appeals normally used in persuasive messages.

   c. Describe the situation in which each type of appeal is most effective.

   d. Why is credibility of major importance in persuasive messages?

   e. Give examples of ethical persuasion and unethical persuasion.

2. You own The Woodworking Shop. Almost a year ago, you built a custom-designed entertainment center for a customer who abandoned the project when it was in the final stages of construction. The unit was designed to fit an extremely large recreation room and was designed specifically for a five-foot television screen and specialized stereo equipment. You have had the $3,500 entertainment center in your shop for months, and it is obvious that the opportunities to sell it to someone else are very limited. Fred Baker, a good customer of yours, recently visited the shop and showed the unit to his neighbor Roger Whetstone, who was getting ready to contract with a competitor for a similar unit. Roger indicated to Fred that the unit was similar in size and design, but not exactly like the one he planned to have built. You have decided to sell the unit for $1,000, less than a third of the contract price, to recover your expenses. Fred suggested you write Roger and try to persuade him to take the unit at the bargain price rather than build a much more expensive unit. Save the document as 5D2.

Heritage Productions

APPLICATION 5E *Heritage Productions*

You have completed your rotation in the Research and Development Department of Heritage Productions where you have worked on EFL projects. Your new assignment in the Custom Products Department is designed to give you an orientation to the second product line that Heritage is developing—cross-cultural videos. (Refer to Application 1C, page 17 to review Heritage product lines if necessary.) You will serve as assistant manager to Ms. Mary Turnquist, the department manager. The Custom Products Department develops cross-cultural training videos under contract for specific companies. These products later are expanded for a general product line offered to the public.

MetroMark Manufacturing Company is building a large plant in Malaysia and has contracted with Heritage to develop cross-cultural training videos to be used with American employees who will be sent to work in Malaysia. Some of the employees will be there for a few weeks; others may be sent for as long as three years. Employees assigned for three months or longer may take their families with them. Therefore, the videos should provide information for families as well as for those conducting business. Ms. Turnquist has been in contact with several other noncompetitive companies that have facilities in Malaysia who have a need for cross-cultural training videos for Malaysia.

You are looking for all types of accurate information that would be helpful for a family moving to Malaysia for the first time. Your first task is to brainstorm and come up with a list of the types of information that would be important to include in the video. Surf the Internet (or use library resources if you do not have access to the Internet) to discover the types of information available. Remember to use only credible sources of information. Chat rooms may have biased information. Using *Malaysia* as a keyword for the search, you should be able to access information from the U.S. Department of State and other governmental agencies. Then compose a letter to the American–Malaysian Chamber of Commerce and to the Embassy of Malaysia requesting the types of information you decided you need. Remember that you are writing to representatives of Malaysia; be very sensitive in the way you request information.

Save all information you accumulate on Malaysia. You will use this information in later assignments.

Ethics question: Is it ethical to use materials developed under contract for MetroMark in programs provided to other companies? If so, under what conditions?

LETTER AND MEMO REPORTS

Performance Goals

After you complete Chapter 6, you should be able to

- *Write effective messages that can be used to make decisions*
- *Use both personal and objective styles for writing reports*
- *Use effective organizational approaches for decision-making messages*
- *Edit communications more effectively*

OVERVIEW

Reports can best be described as documents used to convey information for decision making or as documentation to individuals within or outside of an organization. The format of a report varies depending on the length, complexity, formality, and destination of the report. General formats include letter report format, memo report format, and standard report format. Letter format is typically used for short, relatively simple, informal reports written to individuals **outside** the organization. Memo format is typically used for short, relatively simple, informal reports written to individuals **within** the organization. Standard report format may be used either internally or externally for both formal and informal documents. Long, formal, or highly complex documents usually are formatted using standard report format.

An **external** report may be a **letter** reporting to a customer that a project is about two weeks behind schedule because the shipment of materials needed for the project has been delayed. The customer may then use the information to decide what other action must be taken, such as rescheduling other phases of the project, to accommodate this two-week delay. An **internal** report may be a **memo** to the crew leader working on the project reporting that the materials needed for the project will be delayed for two weeks and that the project schedule must be adjusted accordingly. The type of report just described is often called a progress or status report.

The most common type of report is one that a superior assigns to a subordinate requesting that the subordinate collect and analyze information about a particular problem and report back with recommendations for solving that problem. The report could be in memo format or standard report format.

Most companies consider reports to be key documents for conducting business.

Internal reports move up the chain of command; therefore, they can impact an employee's career by providing an opportunity to showcase quality work to managers.

129

Effective reports are a critical TQM tool.

The total quality management (TQM) movement of the past decade resulted in many organizations focusing on continuous quality improvement. This focus requires extensive communication among groups within an organization as well as with customers, suppliers, and others outside the organization. Written communications provide better documentation for future use than oral communications; therefore, reports are used extensively in business.

Classifying a report as a document for decision making or as documentation clearly emphasizes the need for accuracy and objectivity in report writing. Good decisions result from careful analysis of accurate information. Inaccurate or biased information negatively affects decision making. Obviously, reports for documentation purposes must contain accurate, unbiased information.

Formality and Writing Style

The degree of formality of a report often determines the best writing style—objective or personal—for that report. Formal reports tend to be written in objective style, and informal reports tend to be written in personal style.

Appearances count—and objective style appears to be less biased than personal style.

A report written in objective style is written in third person and uses formal language. Third-person style means that first and second person pronouns (I, we, our, us, and you) are not used. Third-person pronouns (they, he, she, them, it) are used. Formal language would preclude using contractions, colorful, or very conversational style. A report written in personal style could include the use of first and second person pronouns and could be less formal than an objective-style report.

Just because a report is written in objective style does not necessarily mean that the report is actually objective or unbiased. Conversely, just because a report is written in personal style does not necessarily mean that the report is biased. Care must be taken to ensure that all information is accurate and presented in an objective manner.

Style is a matter of organizational or personal preference. Some organizations tend to be more formal than others. A factor to consider in determining style is that objective style is not only more formal than personal style, but it also tends to be more persuasive. Limiting pronouns to third person pronouns gives the appearance of objectivity, whereas using first person pronouns gives the appearance of presenting the writer's opinion. Information presented with words such as *I believe, I think,* or *I feel* often are interpreted by readers as being the opinions of the writer rather than conclusions drawn from an objective analysis of factual information.

Compare the following pairs of sentences. The first sentence of each pair is written in personal style, and the second sentence is written in objective style.

A reader who objects to Alternative 1 may respond with: I believe Alternative 2 is better because . . . The issue then becomes personalized.

P   I evaluated the three alternatives, and I believe that Alternative 1 is the best for us because it generates more revenue over a three-year period than do the other two alternatives.

O   A careful evaluation of the three alternatives shows that Alternative 1 produces greater revenue over a three-year period; therefore, Alternative 1 is recommended.

P   I studied the data carefully and concluded that the training program improved productivity.

O   The data clearly show that the training program improved productivity.

P   I feel that it is time for us to change the name of the organization so that we can broaden our appeal to a wider constituency.

O   The timing is ideal to change the name of the organization so that it will appeal to a wider constituency.

Some writers trying to use objective style substitute terms such as *the writer* or *the researcher* in place of first person pronouns. Good writers avoid this practice. Writing in objective style is a little more difficult than writing in personal style, but the results make the extra effort worthwhile.

Objective style places the emphasis on the issue studied rather than on the person who studied the issue.

REPORT CONTENT AND FORMAT

Earlier in this chapter, you learned that short reports may be formatted in letter, memo, or standard report format. This section focuses on the content of the report and on the internal format of the letter, memo, or report.

Most reports contain headings, visuals, and summaries. If the report is very short, the summary may be omitted. Title pages and transmittal letters or memos should be prepared when reports are formatted in standard report format. Obviously, they are not needed when letter or memo format is used.

Report content varies depending on the length, complexity, and type of report. The following components are types or categories of information frequently included in reports.

Identifying information. Most readers want to know who prepared a report, the title of the report, the date it was prepared, and, in some cases, who authorized or requested the report. When standard report format is used, the title page usually contains this information. When memo format is used, the memo heading normally contains the identifying information.

Writers often use different headings for the various components of reports. The headings may be functional or may relate to the content.

A letter report may or may not contain all the information. Standard letter format requires the date and the signature of the person who prepared the report. The person who requested or authorized the information is generally the person to whom the letter is addressed. The title of the report may be included in a subject line. In some cases, the first paragraph of the letter is used to present the identifying information.

Problem statement. This section explains the purpose of the report. The problem statement should clearly present what you are trying to accomplish in the report. In some cases a brief summary of the background information that led to the problem is presented. Background information is particularly useful when the reader is not familiar with the reasons for studying the problem. Care must be taken not to repeat information the reader already knows.

Supporting data. Information collected to solve the problem is presented in this section. A brief statement indicating the sources of the data and how the information was collected should precede the actual presentation of the data.

Data analysis. The data analysis consists of a discussion of the facts and an interpretation of how those facts can be used to solve the problem that is being studied. Both qualitative (judgment) techniques and quantitative (statistical) techniques may be used to analyze data.

The data analysis section may also be called findings *or* results.

Conclusions. The results obtained by analyzing and interpreting the facts are the conclusions. Each conclusion presented should be supported by data presented in the data analysis section. Some reports, such as progress or status reports, may not contain conclusions; these reports simply convey information to the reader.

Recommendations. Suggested actions based on conclusions are called recommendations. Generally the writer of a report is in the best position to recommend specific action to take. However, not all reports contain conclusions. Reports that contain conclusions and recommendations are called analytical reports.

Summary. The summary consists of a brief synopsis of the report. The summary should contain a brief statement of what you studied, how you studied it, and the results you obtained. In short reports, the summary is often combined with the conclusions and recommendations section. In long reports, the summary is usually a separate section. An executive summary frequently is included with long (ten or more pages) reports. An executive summary presents a brief statement of the problem studied, a statement of how it was studied, and a summary of the results, conclusions, and recommendations. Executive summaries are prepared as stand-alone documents; that is, they do not relate to specific pages of the report. The summary can be read and understood as a separate document by people who do not have access to the complete report.

An executive summary is usually placed at the beginning of a report. A regular summary is usually placed at the end of a report.

REPORT ORGANIZATION

Information contained in a report can be organized in a number of different ways. The way that information is organized can influence the results obtained. Organizational patterns can be applied to any type of document ranging from very simple documents to highly complex documents. Each organizational style has both advantages and disadvantages. Four frequently used organizational styles are described and compared in the following material. Then one very simple scenario is used to illustrate each of the four report styles to show how easily they can be applied to almost any situation.

Narrative. A narrative report simply gives an account of events in the sequence they occurred. The advantages of a narrative style are that a narrative report is easy to write and it provides a record of events that took place. The disadvantages of the style are that it does not facilitate comparing information, and it makes poor use of position as an emphasis technique. The first and last positions of a document are the key emphasis positions. The activities that occur first and last, however, may not be the activities that deserve emphasis.

Direct, or deductive, style. A report that uses the direct approach presents the key information or the conclusion first and then provides the data necessary to support that conclusion. Many people in industry like this approach and often refer to it as the bottom-line approach because you get to the heart of the matter immediately. The advantages of this organizational style are that it is straightforward and it places emphasis on the most important information. The primary disadvantage is that the style is not persuasive. The style is best used when the reader is likely to agree with the conclusion of the report. If the reader disagrees with the conclusion that is presented first, the reader is likely to question the facts as they are presented rather than read them with an open mind.

Indirect, or inductive, style. A report written using an indirect approach presents the facts and supporting information first; then lets those facts lead to logical conclusions. The primary advantage of the indirect style is that it is a persuasive style—it presents facts in an objective manner before telling the reader the conclusion. The reader is more likely to consider facts objectively and less likely to raise objections if the conclusion is not known. The primary disadvantage of the indirect style is that it is a roundabout, slow-moving style.

Weighted style. A report that uses the weighted approach presents the information in the order of importance. The most important information is presented first; then the second most important information is presented. This procedure continues until all information is presented. A closing statement summarizing the two or three most important points is essential to avoid ending the report with the least important information. The primary advantages of the weighted style are that it effectively uses position as an emphasis technique and it makes comparing data easy. The primary disadvantage is that it is not a very persuasive style.

Read the following scenario carefully. Then examine the short reports on pages 135–142 that were used to illustrate each of the approaches that could be used to organize the report.

SCENARIO:

Jay Johnson, a very talented high school football player, is being recruited by Hillview, Stonehedge, and Meadowbrook Universities, and he made an official visit to each on a weekend in November. Jay kept the following **rough** notes of his trips so that he could compare the three visits objectively. He will use the information to decide which university's scholarship offer to accept.

HILLVIEW UNIVERSITY (HU) (11/5–11/7)

Friday evening—met by student-athlete host and taken to dinner; joined by assistant coach. Friendly, enjoyable evening, but weather cold, snowy. Saturday, had breakfast with all recruits and coaching staff. Then toured campus and athletic facilities—campus was beautiful; athletic facilities were reasonably good. Met with counselor in Athletics Department who talked about the academic programs. Said they have a good business program. Gave me material about the program. Had lunch; then met with head coach and position coaches separately. Coach felt I could play as a freshman; said I have all-star potential. Team was first or second in conference last three years—conference is reasonably good. Most of time spent talking about goals of football program and how I fit in them. Had dinner at stadium; athletic director spoke to group. Then we attended a football game. Sunday morning—taken to airport by student host.

Jay Johnson

Hillview Bears

Stonehedge Eagles

Meadowbrook Lions

Read the rough notes carefully; then analyze the additional information and decide what you would recommend. Think about how you would organize the information if you had to write the report.
Then review the illustrations on pages 135–142.

STONEHEDGE UNIVERSITY (SU) (11/12–11/14)

Friday—Accompanied by parents on trip at the urging of the head coach. Met by position coach and student-athlete host; then was taken to dinner. Great evening—friendly, relaxed evening; warm weather. Saturday—breakfast with recruits, parents, coaching staff, and faculty members representing the majors of interest to recruits. Then went to faculty member's office; talked about program of study and was given materials about program; then toured academic facilities. Great business program. Student host gave a campus and athletic facilities tour. Met with position coaches; had lunch followed by visit to the Athletics Academic Enrichment Center; counselors explained the academic support provided and the emphasis placed on academic success. Met with head coach; may "redshirt" me first year to learn system and get established in school; said I have great potential. Football team ranked in top half of conference past three years; getting better each year. This is new coach's third year. Strong conference. Had dinner at stadium with recruits, parents, and some coaches—head coach and athletics director talked about importance of getting a degree. Then attended football game. Taken to airport Sunday after breakfast.

MEADOWBROOK UNIVERSITY (MU) (11/19–11/21)

Friday—Met by position coach and student-athlete host; taken to dinner. Nice evening—friendly, enjoyable group; nice weather. Saturday—breakfast with recruits, coaching staff, and several faculty members. At breakfast, faculty members talked about academics and gave materials about program. Good business program. Student host then gave a campus and athletic facilities tour. Met with position coaches; had lunch. Met with head coach; may play or may "redshirt" depending on other recruits signed. Said I have great potential. Team ranked in top third of conference past three years; reasonably strong conference. Spent afternoon with student hosts. Had dinner at stadium with recruits and coaches—head coach and athletics director talked mostly about future of football program; talked some about importance of education. Attended football game. Taken to airport Sunday after breakfast.

SCENARIO, CONTINUED

Jay had a hard time making a decision and asked Mrs. Ruth Cogwell—his business communication teacher, a former basketball star, and a trusted advisor—to help him analyze the situation and make a decision. Jay and Mrs. Cogwell agreed to use the information to write a report illustrating the formats and organizational approaches that could be used. Mrs. Cogwell read Jay's notes and asked him to rank the three universities (from best to worse) on the following criteria.

Best overall for education if he did not play football: SU, MU, HU

Best business program: SU, MU, HU

Best opportunity to play football: HU, SU, MU

Best football program now: HU, MU, SU

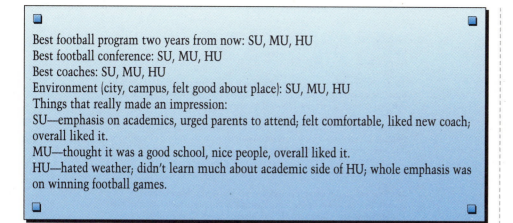

Best football program two years from now: SU, MU, HU
Best football conference: SU, MU, HU
Best coaches: SU, MU, HU
Environment (city, campus, felt good about place): SU, MU, HU
Things that really made an impression:
SU—emphasis on academics, urged parents to attend; felt comfortable, liked new coach; overall liked it.
MU—thought it was a good school, nice people, overall liked it.
HU—hated weather; didn't learn much about academic side of HU; whole emphasis was on winning football games.

Mountain View Academy
121 Coyote Creek Road
Eugene, OR 97402-4298
(541) 555-0128

TO: Jay Johnson

FROM: Ruth Cogwell

DATE: Current date

SUBJECT: Scholarship Offers

Jay, as you requested, I have reviewed your notes and the additional information you provided me about your official recruiting trips to Hillview, Stonehedge, and Meadowbrook Universities. All three universities offered you a full scholarship to play football. The information collected on each of the three trips was summarized, analyzed, and evaluated to determine the one that matches your needs best. Information was analyzed from the perspective of the academic program, the athletic program, and your overall reaction to the university.

Hillview University

The first official visit was to Hillview University. Hillview placed little emphasis on academics. A counselor in the Athletics Department provided information about the business program, but the opportunity to meet with representatives of the Business Department was not offered. According to the counselor and the materials provided, Hillview has a good business program.

Hillview places major emphasis on athletics and thought you would be able to play as a freshman and would excel in football. Hillview has a very strong football program in a reasonably good conference. The coach felt you would fit in with the goals of having a winning football program.

Overall, the football program is a strong one in an acceptable conference. Academics appears to be secondary to athletics, and little was learned about the business program. The weather is a major disadvantage of attending Hillview University.

Stonehedge University

The second official visit was to Stonehedge University. Stonehedge placed major emphasis on academics. A business faculty member was actively involved in the recruiting process and provided extensive information about the excellent business program. Athletic personnel also placed major emphasis on academic achievement and emphasized the importance of graduating. Parents were included in activities.

Standard memo heading.

First- and second-person pronouns are acceptable when personal writing style is used.

Narrative organizational style presents events in the order in which they occurred.

A heading is used on second and succeeding pages of letter and memo reports.

Data are difficult to compare when information is presented in sequential order.

Jay Johnson
Page 2
Current date

The football program has a new coach who is building a program that is getting better each year. The conference is a very strong one, and Stonehedge has the potential of being a very good football program in this strong conference.

Overall, Stonehedge is a very good place to attend college and to play football. Faculty and parents interact effectively with the Athletic Department. The atmosphere is very comfortable.

Meadowbrook University

The final official visit was to Meadowbrook University. Meadowbrook devoted time to both academics and football. A business faculty member was involved in the recruiting process, and Meadowbrook has a good business program. Athletics personnel placed some attention on academics but major emphasis was on football.

The football program is a reasonably good one, and the conference is reasonably strong. The opportunity to play as a freshman depends on the quality of other recruits.

Overall, you were pleased with the football program, the business program, the people, and the atmosphere.

Conclusions and Recommendation

All three offers of a scholarship provide good opportunities for a football career and college education. From an academic perspective, Stonehedge is the best offer. At the present time, Hillview has the best football record, but Stonehedge plays in a stronger conference and has excellent potential. Meadowbrook is not quite as strong in academics as Stonehedge or in football as Hillview. Overall, Stonehedge and Meadowbrook are more desirable places to attend college than Hillview.

Stonehedge presents the best scholarship offer when all three perspectives—academic, athletic, and your overall reaction—are considered. Therefore, I recommend that you accept the scholarship and become a student-athlete at Stonehedge University.

ms

Narrative Organizational Style   Memo Format   Personal Writing Style

Mountain View Academy
121 Coyote Creek Road
Eugene, OR 97402-4298
(541) 555-0128

Current date

Mr. Jay Johnson, Student
3981 Cedar Ridge Road
Eugene, OR 97401-2562

Dear Jay

Of the three alternatives, Stonehedge presents the best scholarship offer when all three perspectives—academic, athletic, and overall reaction—are considered. Thus, the recommendation made is to accept the scholarship and become a student-athlete at Stonehedge University.

This recommendation is based on an analysis of the information gathered during the three official visits to Hillview, Stonehedge, and Meadowbrook Universities. The data were analyzed based on the academic strengths of the business program, the quality of the football program, and the overall environment.

Stonehedge clearly placed more emphasis on academics than the other two universities. Faculty members were involved in the process, and the cooperation between the academic and athletic programs was obvious. Athletics personnel also stressed academic achievement.

Hillview clearly placed more emphasis on football than the other two universities. Currently, Hillview has a very good football team in an acceptable conference. The entire recruiting visit revolved around football with only indirect exposure to the academic program. Playing as a freshman had the best prospects at Hillview. Meadowbrook also has a good football program in a reasonably strong conference. Playing as a freshman was conditioned on the quality of the other athletes recruited. Meadowbrook stressed football more than academics, but faculty were involved in the visit. Stonehedge has a steadily improving football team with a new coach in a strong football conference.

Block letter format is used in this example.

Direct organizational style presents the conclusions first, then presents the supporting data.

First- and second-person pronouns are not used when a report is written in objective style.

Note that headings were not used in this example; headings may be used with letter, memo, or standard report format.

A heading is used on second and succeeding pages.

Mr. Jay Johnson
Page 2
Current date

Stonehedge provided the best overall environment for an education and a football career. The fit with Stonehedge was good, and the involvement of parents in the program was impressive. Meadowbrook was also a good environment. Hillview has the least desirable overall environment for getting an education. The cold, snowy climate was also considered a disadvantage for Hillview.

All these factors support the recommendation to accept the Stonehedge scholarship offer.

Sincerely

Ruth Cogwell
Business Communications Instructor

ms

Direct Organizational Style   Letter Format   Objective Writing Style

EVALUATION OF SCHOLARSHIP OFFERS FROM HILLVIEW, STONEHEDGE, AND MEADOWBROOK UNIVERSITIES

Jay Johnson was invited to make official recruiting trips to Hillview, Stonehedge, and Meadowbrook Universities to consider scholarship offers to play football. All three schools used the same general format for the weekend recruiting trips. Data from these three trips were analyzed to determine the offer that should be recommended.

Methodology

Three criteria were used as the basis of analysis—academic strength of the business program, quality of the football program, and reaction to the overall environment. Data consisted of detailed notes made after each visit and additional evaluative information provided after all three visits were made.

Academic Perspective

Stonehedge placed the most emphasis on academic achievement. Meadowbrook has a good academic program but was not quite as good as Stonehedge. Hillview placed the least emphasis on academic success, and the opportunity to learn more about the business program was not offered. At Stonehedge, a faculty member from the business program was involved in the recruiting process, and the athletics personnel emphasized the importance of academic achievement.

Football Perspective

Hillview has a very strong football program in an acceptable conference. The coaching staff at Hillview placed more emphasis on football and on the possibility of playing as a freshman than the other two schools. Meadowbrook has a strong team in a reasonably strong conference. Stonehedge's football program is not quite as strong but the conference is the strongest. With the new coach, Stonehedge's football program has been improving and the potential for the future appears to be excellent.

Overall Reaction

The reaction to Stonehedge and Meadowbrook was better than the reaction to Hillview. Stonehedge and Meadowbrook seemed to be more comfortable and a better fit than Hillview. Stonehedge was the only school that involved parents in the recruiting process. Hillview had the additional disadvantage of the cold, snowy climate conditions.

A title page generally is prepared when standard report format is used.

Indirect organizational style presents the supporting data first, then presents the conclusions.

Headings help to add to the organizational structure of a report.

Conclusion and Recommendation

When all three perspectives are considered, Stonehedge appears to provide the best situation. Therefore, the Stonehedge offer should be accepted.

**Indirect Organizational Style   Short Report Format
Objective Writing Style**

EVALUATION OF SCHOLARSHIP OFFERS FROM HILLVIEW, STONEHEDGE, AND MEADOWBROOK UNIVERSITIES

Jay Johnson was invited to make official recruiting trips to Hillview, Stonehedge, and Meadowbrook Universities to consider scholarship offers to play football. All three schools used the same general format for the weekend recruiting trips. Data from these three trips were analyzed to determine the offer that should be recommended.

Methodology

Three criteria were used as the basis of analysis—academic strength of the business program, quality of the football program, and reaction to the overall environment. Data consisted of detailed notes made after each visit and additional evaluative information provided after all three visits were made.

Academic Perspective

The most important factor in selecting a school is the quality of the academic program. Stonehedge placed the most emphasis on academic achievement. Meadowbrook has a good academic program but was not quite as good as Stonehedge. Hillview placed the least emphasis on academic success, and the opportunity to learn more about the business program was not offered. At Stonehedge, a faculty member from the business program was involved in the recruiting process, and the athletics personnel emphasized the importance of academic achievement.

Football Perspective

The second most important factor in selecting a school is the quality of the football program. Hillview has a very strong football program in an acceptable conference. The coaching staff at Hillview placed more emphasis on football and on the possibility of playing as a freshman than the other two schools. Meadowbrook has a strong team in a reasonably strong conference. Stonehedge's football program is not quite as strong but the conference is the strongest. With the new coach, Stonehedge's football program has been improving and the potential for the future appears to be excellent.

Overall Reaction

Other factors considered in selecting a school are categorized as overall reaction. The reaction to Stonehedge and Meadowbrook was better than the reaction to Hillview. Stonehedge and Meadowbrook seemed to be more comfortable and a better fit than Hillview. Stonehedge was the only school that involved parents in the recruiting process. Hillview had the additional disadvantage of the cold, snowy climate conditions.

A title page generally is prepared when standard report format is used.

The weighted organizational style presents the data in order of importance. Key factors are summarized; then the conclusion and recommendations follow.

Headings help to add to the organizational structure of a report.

Conclusion and Recommendation

The quality of the academic program is most important, and the quality of
the football program is also a very important factor. Stonehedge has the
strongest business program and has a very good football program. When
all three perspectives are considered, Stonehedge appears to provide the
best situation. Therefore, the Stonehedge offer should be accepted.

**Weighted Organizational Style   Short Report Format
Objective Writing Style**

GLOBAL CONNECTIONS

The organizational approaches for reports taught in this chapter may not be as effective in other cultures. Whereas most Americans prefer a direct or bottom-line style of writing, other cultures view organizational approaches from a different perspective. In many cultures, trust must be built before the reader is ready to accept conclusions or recommendations. Presenting conclusions before documenting those conclusions extensively and carefully would likely result in a loss of credibility.

Color makes charts and graphs easy to interpret. Color often communicates different meanings in different cultures. The use of some colors might be offensive or totally inappropriate; therefore, color selections for charts and graphs that will be sent to other cultures should be researched carefully. For example, in many Asian countries, black and white are considered unlucky or tragic colors.

The personal style used in many short reports in industry might create a bad impression in other cultures. Many cultures prefer the formality that is associated with objective style.

Many reports include time lines. The attitudes toward time vary significantly among cultures. Some cultures interpret time lines in a report as flexible guides. In other cases, time lines are totally unrealistic because of lack of knowledge of the culture. For example, in one country, most companies may take the entire month of August off for holidays. Companies in another country involved in the business may take the entire month of July off for holidays.

Values differ among cultures. What may be considered persuasive in one culture may be considered to be very materialistic and offensive in another culture.

Doing business with individuals or organizations in different cultures can be very pleasant, satisfying, and lucrative. To be effective, however, knowledge about the culture of the individuals with whom you are dealing is essential. The more you know about the culture, the more likely you will be able to meet the needs of your reader.

THE SUPERHIGHWAY OF COMMUNICATIONS

INTERNET

E-mail has been discussed in several chapters as an efficient way to transmit short, informal documents globally. Most reports do not fit the definition of being short, informal documents. However, that does not mean that reports cannot be transmitted through electronic mail.

Most electronic mail software provides an option by which a file can be attached. The E-mail message simply becomes the letter or memo of transmittal for the document. The file containing the document can be downloaded and printed. Not all electronic mail systems are compatible; therefore, it is important to ascertain that the attached document was received in usable format. Copies of the file are distributed to everyone who receives the E-mail message.

The issue of security when E-mail is used was discussed in earlier chapters. Obviously, the same concerns apply to documents contained in files attached to E-mail messages. Those documents have the same vulnerability as the E-mail message.

Faxing is another alternative for distributing reports internationally. Some documents that include color or that are bound are not suitable for fax distribution. Faxing also has security problems in many situations.

Express mail typically is used when electronic distribution is not suitable and time is of the essence. The express mail alternative is more expensive than electronic distribution, but it is considered to be a more secure and reliable alternative.

MISCOMMUNICATIONS

Signs posted:

On a neighborhood pharmacy:

> We dispense with
> accuracy!

In a cemetery:

> Persons are prohibited
> from picking flowers from
> any but their own graves.

APPLICATION 6A *Review Guide 4: Write in a Clear, Readable Style*

Revise the following sentences

■ Using a conversational tone and contemporary language to make them clear and easy to read

■ Stripping long, involved, or wordy sentences of unnecessary words

■ Enumerating lists or using tables to simplify paragraphs with multiple items

1. An investigation of the circumstances precipitating the incident revealed no apparent way to anticipate or prevent the occurrence of the assault.

2. Please send us your complete name including middle initial; complete address including street address, city, state, and postal code; the name of the county in which you reside; your social security number; your telephone number including the area code; and two credit card references.

3. The Executive Committee will meet in the morning in the Vista Conference Room to discuss the location of the new facilities then we will have lunch in the Vista Dining Room and then we will return to the Vista Conference Room to finalize our decision on the location of the new facilities.

4. Pursuant to our discussion this morning, I herewith enclose a copy of the proposal you requested; and I trust that you will kindly advise me when you are ready to discuss it.

5. The manager gave notification to employees that compliance with the provisions of the policy of adhering to smoking exclusively in designated areas was now mandatory rather than voluntary.

APPLICATION 6B *Editing and Language Arts Checkpoint*

Carefully read the document that follows. It is packed with errors. Use proofreader's marks to mark all errors in grammar, spelling, word usage, number usage, capitalization, and punctuation. Do not revise sentence or paragraph structure in this activity unless an error exists.

After you have marked all corrections directly on this document, access File 6B on your template disk and make the corrections you marked. If you do not have access to the template disk, key the letter, making the corrections as you key.

After you have made all corrections, refer to pages 235–236 in Appendix C for the solution and check to see that you corrected all errors. You may use on-line reference tools just as you would if you were doing this as part of your job.

Add a memo heading to the report, which will be sent to the Executive Committee from you. Use the current date, and the subject line should be Addendum to Outsourcing Printing Report. Reformat the report using single spacing and block format. Save the file as 6B-sol.

Data from the Outsourcing Printing Report clearly showed that the cost of printing could be reduced substantial by discontinuing the outsourcing of many of VanHuss Industries printing jobs. Therefore, a 2nd phase of the report were authorize to determine the feasibility of setting up an in-house electronic publishing system.

Problem

The primary purpose of these phase of the project were to determine the percentage and type of work which could be handle internally. This information can then be use to determine the best and most cost affective system too meet the needs of VanHuss Industries.

Supporting Data

All of the request forms for outside printing for the passed year were collected and analyzed to determine the type and volume of printing. In many cases, job samples have to be obtained and were analyzed by the printing production team whom determined whether or not the job could be handled internally. Four electronic printing system proposals from local vendors were analyzed to determine capabilities and prices.

Data Analysis

The analyze of the request forms for outside printing showed that during the past year about ninety percent of the black and white printing and about forty percent of the color printing could have been done internal on an electronic publishing systems. All four of the systems that demonstrated to the evaluation team could have handled them jobs that were identified as internal jobs.

All four system include high resolution laser printers with the capability of handling color as well as black and white copy. The proposals form all four vendors includes software scanners and 2 workstations with 2-page display monitors. The Hess system use two separate printers—one for color printing and the other for black and white printing. The cost of the Hess system is $41,750.00. This cost is two thousand dollars more then the other systems however the system have advanced features that make it feasible to do additional jobs internally. Specifications for the four systems and a complete cost analysis are attached.

Conclusion

The conclusion of the Outsourcing Printing Report indicated that an in-house system could be justified at a cost of eighty thousand dollars if at least forty percent of the printing volume could be shifted internally. The volume of printing that could be shifted internally for exceeds the minimum requirements and all systems evaluated meet the cost restrictions. The Hess electronic publishing system meets the needs of VanHuss Industries best than the other three systems.

Recommendation

The Hess system should be purchased and installed within the next 6 weeks. This time frame allows time far personal in the Printing Center to be adequately trained before the outsourcing contract non-renewal notice must be given.

APPLICATION 6C *Writing Letter and Memo Reports*

Plan and write the following messages. Use the format and organizational approach that would be most effective unless you are directed to use a specific format or organizational approach. Use your name as the sender on each document. Supply an appropriate address when one is needed.

1. You have been hired as a consultant by the Training and Assessment Division of VanHuss Industries to evaluate potential sites for training centers. Your job is to visit the potential site and to evaluate the facilities, the equipment, the staff, the organization, and the location for its suitability as a VanHuss Authorized Training Center (VATC). Within two or three days after each trip, you usually write a short memo report using personal writing style and a narrative approach. You enclose a completed standard evaluation form that VanHuss uses. VanHuss Industries then contracts with the Center to administer the VanHuss Training Program along with the other training programs the center offers.

    Yesterday, you returned from a visit to the McKie Center in Wilmington, Delaware. You were very impressed with the McKie Center and will recommend that a VATC be established in the McKie Center. The McKie Center has two locations in Wilmington. The facilities are excellent and are located in good areas of town. Equipment is satisfactory. Two-thirds of the equipment is state of the art, and McKie has a replacement plan in place to upgrade equipment on a three-year cycle. Larry McKie has an excellent management staff with two center managers, a technical manager, a training manager, and 15 employees who are well trained. Mr. McKie focuses on strategic planning, business development, and marketing. The manager of each center coordinates and schedules all training and handles registration and all financial record keeping as well as all administrative work of the center. Managers also do the follow-up contacts with companies. The technical manager is responsible for selecting, purchasing, and maintaining all hardware and software for both centers. The training manager designs, creates, or purchases all training materials; selects, hires, and trains trainers; evaluates training sessions, and has total responsibility for the training programs. You were very impressed with the professionalism and the technical expertise of the managers and the training staff. They already have the technical expertise VanHuss would need for its training program. Write the memo report to Ms. Kerry Gallman, Director of the Training and Assessment Division, recommending that VanHuss contract for a VATC at both locations of the McKie Center.

2. Revise the memo report you just completed in 6C1 using objective writing style and a direct or deductive organizational approach. Format the report as a letter report.

3. Local businesses work with Century TEC in a program called Business Mentors that is designed to help students with the transition to the workplace. Four businesses have been working with a team of eight students for the past year. At its last meeting, the business executives talked about doing business with clients and customers over lunch or dinner. They also mentioned that they often take candidates interviewing for a job to lunch or dinner to evaluate the social skills and the way the job candidates would fit in and interact with their clients. The companies offered to take the team to a business dinner instead of the regular meeting on Wednesday, March 20. You were asked to evaluate restaurants that you thought were appropriate for a business meal with a client and to make a recommendation (justifying your selection) to the Business Mentors for approval. You decide that you will use this opportunity to showcase your report writing skills and your good judgment because you would like to be considered for a position at one of the four companies when you graduate in June.

   You narrowed down the options to three restaurants that were available on the date needed, that could accommodate a group of 12 at one table in a private room (or two tables of six in the main dining room), and that were suitable based on the broad general guidelines discussed during the meeting with the mentors. Your notes on the restaurants follow.

   Chez Patrick. Very formal, small French restaurant with fancy, hard-to-pronounce names for all menu items. Great food and atmosphere. Ad indicated coat and tie required. Prices for entrees at the very top of the acceptable price range Business Mentors discussed. All items were a la carte.

   Daniel's Ribs. Relatively informal; ribs and pasta are the primary items featured on the menu. Nice atmosphere but most people dress reasonably casual (not jeans) because ribs can be messy. Prices in the middle to upper middle of the range discussed. Food is very good. Trip to salad bar and garlic bread are provided with all entrees. Known for providing large servings.

   The Riverside. Reasonably formal, very nice restaurant with a nice atmosphere. Menu is varied with a broad range of seafood, veal, chicken, and beef items. Great food. One or two items are served with each entree. Diners generally dress nicely. Entree prices in the middle to upper middle of the range.

   Decide which restaurant you will recommend, justify your choice, and write the memo report.

4. As an employee in the Human Resources Department of Candler Publishing Company, you were asked by Mr. Gary Douglas, vice president of Human Resources, to take on a sensitive assignment. He is somewhat concerned that the attire worn by many employees creates an unprofessional image to many company clients. He has identified ten benchmark companies which he has asked you to visit to inquire about specific services they offer. While at the companies, you were to observe the attire worn by various types of employees. You were also asked to talk with employees in Candler Publishing Company and with clients you know well to get their reactions on appropriate attire for employees.

In the benchmark companies, most of the managers and sales staff dressed very professionally. Men typically wore coats and ties; women typically wore business suits or tailored dresses. Attire worn by office staff also was professional, but was a little less formal. The attire of technical people tended to be more casual than that of other employees. In most cases, men wore slacks with shirts that had collars, and women wore slacks or skirts and blouses. In two of the benchmark companies, employees did not dress as professionally as those in the other eight companies. A few employees in those two companies were in jeans or jogging outfits.

Most of the clients (75 percent) that you talked with indicated that they preferred to deal with companies whose employees had a professional appearance; 15 percent liked the casual atmosphere, and 10 percent did not have a preference. Employee reaction at Candler was varied. Many felt that some employees dressed too casually. Others liked the comfortable, if somewhat sloppy attire worn at Candler. You have also learned that a number of companies have casual days on Fridays only.

Your initial reaction is to propose a very general dress code for Candler Publishing. Employees who have contact with clients should wear professional attire—coats and ties for men and suits or tailored dresses for women. Employees who do not have contact with clients may dress more casually; slacks and shirts with collars for men and slacks or skirts and blouses for women would be appropriate. All employees would have the option of dressing more casually on Fridays, but T-shirts, shorts, and jogging outfits should not be worn to the office. Neat jeans may be worn on Fridays if employees are not meeting with clients.

Your assignment is to finalize your recommendation and write the report. You may follow your initial reaction or modify it somewhat. If you make changes, be sure that you can justify them. Select an appropriate organizational approach, format, and writing style.

5. Your company, Wexford Industries, provides Midtown University with a $10,000 fellowship to be awarded to an incoming MBA student. You were asked by Ms. Lauren Adams, vice president of community relations, to represent the company and participate as a judge in the final selection of the recipient. You were provided with copies of the applications of the ten finalists a week before the event. The on-campus activities consisted of a get-acquainted dinner on Thursday evening for finalists, judges, and administrators of the College of Business Administration. On Friday, the judges interviewed the finalists and ranked candidates on a point system. The judges met and agreed on the recipient. The recipient was announced at a large reception at the Faculty House on Friday evening. Susan J. Walker was selected as the Wexford Industries MBA Fellowship recipient.

Write a trip report to Ms. Adams. Be sure to convey to her that all ten finalists were highly qualified and that Midtown University handled the entire event in an extremely professional manner. Your overall assessment was that Wexford gained excellent public relations benefits from this activity.

Chapter 6

APPLICATION 6D *Self-Assessment*

1. Use complete, grammatically correct sentences to answer each of the following items.

   a. Describe the differences between personal and objective style of writing for reports.

   b. Describe the differences between a direct (deductive) and an indirect (inductive) organizational approach for writing reports.

   c. Describe the situation in which each type of organizational approach (direct and indirect) is most effective.

   d. Describe a narrative organizational approach and indicate the type of situation in which it would be most effective.

   e. Explain the difference between conclusions and recommendations in a report.

2. You manage Pat's Fitness Center. Each Monday, you prepare a memo report summarizing the activities of the previous week and send it to Lynn Watson, operations manager, at the parent company, Custom Fitness Centers. Use the sketchy notes below to write the memo report for last week. Use complete sentences and organize the information carefully.

   This past week was the best you have had in the two years you have managed the center. Memberships sold: 4 lifetime, 10 one-year, and 6 three-year. Participation: high also. Weight room: used by 300 members, handball and racquetball courts used an average of 9 hours per day; 3 aerobics classes each day with average attendance of 22 per class; 6 special fitness programs with average of 18 per program. Problems: inadequate number of handball and racquetball courts to meet demand especially from 4 to 10 p.m. Expansion plans have been taken to three contractors for price estimates for building two more handball and two more racquetball courts. Expect bids within 10 days. Other services: vending and babysitting services continue to be profitable. A standard financial report for the week is attached.

APPLICATION 6E *Heritage Productions*

Heritage Productions

In your last assignment (see page 128), you accumulated material on Malaysia. In the meantime, Ms. Mary Turnquist, Manager of the Custom Products Department, obtained tentative agreements with four companies doing business in Malaysia to share the costs of developing cross-cultural training videos with MetroMark Manufacturing Company. MetroMark and the other four companies agree that a cooperative venture with costs shared equally is in the best interest of all. Heritage Productions retains ownership and can adapt the material for future products if desired.

Heritage produces a concise training guide with each training film that participants can take with them for future reference. Two of the companies requested that a much more comprehensive reference guide be prepared for Malaysia. Ms. Turnquist asked you to investigate the pros and cons of developing the guide and prepare a report recommending either to develop or not to develop the guide. She must make a final decision and notify the companies.

You have met with representatives of the five companies and with the team that produces the regular training guides for Heritage training films and have accumulated the following information.

- Two companies expressed strong desire to have the comprehensive reference; one company felt it would be nice to have but was not necessary; two companies preferred not to have the comprehensive guide if preparing it resulted in additional costs or time delays on the project.

- The current production team has a full schedule and could not produce the comprehensive guide in the time frame that was established for the regular training guide. If this team produces the comprehensive guide, an additional four to six weeks would be needed; and the total project cost would increase about 10 percent.

- If an external production house is used, the comprehensive guide could be produced in the same time frame that the regular training guide is produced, but the additional cost is estimated to be approximately 20 percent of the total project cost.

- The material you received from the American–Malaysian Chamber of Commerce and the Embassy of Malaysia included a number of brochures that contained much of the material that would probably be included in a comprehensive guide. In addition, you have a significant amount of material from various governmental agencies that you located on the Internet. You used this material to prepare a bibliography of books that provide cross-cultural information about Malaysia.

An alternative you are considering recommending to Ms. Turnquist is to provide each company with a packet of materials collected and information about how to obtain multiple copies. That way the companies could assemble their own packets for employees if they so desired.

Analyze objectively the information that you have accumulated and decide what you will recommend to Ms. Turnquist. Many of the reports you have seen from this department use short report format with headings and objective writing style and include the components shown on pages 139-140 of this chapter. You also know that the companies are not in agreement about this issue. Therefore, you want to use a persuasive organizational approach. Your goal is to write a report that Ms. Turnquist could send to the other companies with minor adaptations if she agrees with your findings. Decide how you will organize and format the report. Then prepare the report.

FORM LETTERS AND MEMOS

Performance Goals

After you complete Chapter 7, you should be able to
- ❏ *Write effective and efficient form messages*
- ❏ *Edit communications more effectively*

OVERVIEW

Employees often write messages with similar content to several different individuals. To be more efficient, employees can develop one form message that can be sent to the different individuals. Form messages must be designed carefully to ensure that they meet the needs of all individuals who receive the message. They must also be edited and proofread carefully. An error in a form message will repeat each time the form is used.

Some organizations use carefully designed form messages to compensate for employees with limited skills and training in letter writing.

Form messages should be used only when they are both efficient and effective. Form messages are efficient because the completed message is sent to a number of individuals with little effort. The difference in the time required to send one message, ten form messages, or hundreds of form messages is very little. Form messages are cost effective because they require little time to develop and produce. However, form messages are not always effective. A message is effective only when it accomplishes the objectives intended.

TYPES OF FORM MESSAGES

A good writer first determines if a form message could be used effectively, then determines the best type of form message to use. Unless a form message truly meets the needs of the reader and the situation, an original letter or memo should be written.

An effective form message is difficult to distinguish from an original message.

Four different types of form messages are commonly used. Each type of form has both advantages and disadvantages.

Complete forms. Identical letters or memos sent to multiple readers are called complete forms. The messages are not changed or personalized in any way. One document is prepared, and a copy is reproduced or printed for each individual who receives the form.

Printed forms rarely appeal to readers. Use them very selectively.

Efficiency and cost-effectiveness are the primary advantages of using a complete form. Reproducing a document in bulk costs virtually nothing and can be done in very little time. With equipment that folds the document, inserts it in an envelope, seals it, and affixes postage, the entire process of sending out large numbers of messages can be done in minimal time.

With complete forms, the reader knows immediately that the document is a form. Moreover, no attempt is made to personalize the form. The significance of these disadvantages depends on the expectations of the reader. If the reader expected a personalized message, the disadvantages are significant. If the reader expected a total form, the disadvantages may be minimal. Thus, the situation usually determines whether a complete form is appropriate. For example, a letter often accompanies tickets to athletic events that are mailed to purchasers. The typical ticket buyer knows that thousands of purchasers receive the same letter and does not expect a personalized letter. The same situation may apply to printed informational letters that accompany invoices or bills.

Effective use of form messages requires good judgment.

On the other hand, special ticket buyers may expect the letter that accompanies the tickets to athletic events to be personalized. Athletic boosters who contribute $10,000 to $20,000 a year in order to obtain premium tickets know that a relatively small number of people make that contribution and expect the letter accompanying those tickets to be personalized. In this situation, a complete form would not be as effective as other types of forms or as effective as an original letter.

Variable forms. Often, letters or memos with minor variations in information can be sent to many individuals. The information that varies, called a variable, might consist of the inside address and salutation. Everything else may be identical, but the message is personalized. In some cases, a number of variables may be used.

Variable forms are often called mail merge documents because of the word processing software feature used to create them.

For example, form letters are used extensively in credit and collection situations and in insurance and banking settings. Credit accounts may have variables that include the terms of the account and the credit limit placed on the account. Collection letters may have variables that indicate the number of days the account is past due and the amount that is outstanding.

Today's technology makes it easy to set up the variable information in a data file or to extract the information from the company database and merge it into the body of the letter. Depending on the sophistication of the technology used, the process is normally a fairly simple one that can be accomplished in minimal time and with minimal effort. Careful personalization and customization of letters makes them very effective.

Variable forms offer many advantages, including efficiency, cost-effectiveness, and personalization. The disadvantages are that form messages often do not work in many situations. Usually, variable messages work best when the variables are relatively short. Technology, however, is minimizing that disadvantage. Bookmarks and other word processing software features make it possible to insert extended amounts of text from other documents. In some cases, however, when the variations are significant, an original letter may be easier to prepare than a form message.

Form paragraphs. Documents can be created by combining a series of stored paragraphs with the appropriate opening and closing letter or memo components. Form paragraphs must be designed and structured so that the message flows smoothly when the paragraphs are combined to produce a document. Usually, form paragraphs are designed and labeled or coded specifically as beginning, middle, or ending paragraphs.

Options for creating form paragraphs vary depending on the software used; but the concepts are basically the same.

The primary advantage of using form paragraphs is that they offer tremendous flexibility in meeting specific needs. The primary disadvantage of form paragraphs is the difficulty of designing and developing paragraphs that fit together and flow smoothly. This process can be time consuming; however, once the paragraphs are designed, they are very easy to combine to create documents.

Technology offers a number of alternative ways to store and use blocks of text to create documents. Text blocks can be stored as individual documents, and the documents can be combined to create a new document. The document can then be merged with a data file to create personalized letters. Form paragraphs can be stored as subdocuments, and a master document feature can be used to assemble the document. Text can be inserted using a bookmark feature.

Guide forms. Often companies provide employees with model documents that illustrate the type of document that must be written for various situations. First, the employee selects the guide form that is appropriate for a situation. Then, the employee writes an original document patterned after the guide, or sample, form. Guide forms are used primarily when a number of messages are similar, but the messages must be tailored to meet very specific needs. The advantage of the guide form is that, from the reader's perspective, the message is an original one. The disadvantages are that guide forms are not as efficient or as cost-effective as other types of forms. They also require the writer to have greater communication skills than other forms.

Guide forms serve as templates for content rather than formatting.

Review the illustrations on pages 159–162 showing form paragraphs and letters with variables to create form messages.

𝒯ECHNOLOGICAL 𝒞ONNECTIONS

Form messages have been used for many years. However, until recent years, many businesspeople felt that form messages were an inexpensive but relatively undesirable alternative to an original letter. Today, technology has elevated the use of form messages to a combination of science and art. The technology is available to create form messages that are extremely difficult to distinguish from original letters.

The key is helping employees learn how to create effective form messages that have a custom-designed appearance. Sophisticated suites of application software, including word processing, database, spreadsheet, and graphics, make integrating data from different sources relatively easy.

INTERNET

THE SUPERHIGHWAY OF COMMUNICATIONS

Some organizations use the Internet to send electronic form messages. For example, E-mail sent to a distribution list is very similar to a complete form document. Alternately the same E-mail message can be sent with a personalized address. Mailing lists on the Internet are another way to send form messages electronically. Some web sites automatically generate responses to inquiries such as insurance or stock quotations. As more and more business is conducted on the web, the use of electronic form messages is likely to increase dramatically.

MISCOMMUNICATIONS

Sign posted:

> We strive to give all our customers the lowest possible prices and workmanship.

Form Paragraphs Skilled Temps, Inc. Uses to Respond to Inquiries

- **C7** = Chapter 7
- **Ill** = Illustration
- **-B** = Beginning paragraph (the number following indicates which beginning paragraph)
- **-M** = Middle paragraph (the number following indicates which middle paragraph)
- **-E** = Ending paragraph (the number following indicates which ending paragraph)

The file names used for form paragraphs can easily be translated.

File: C7Ill-B1

Thank you for inquiring about Skilled Temps who can handle word processing applications. We have Skilled Temps available who are trained and who have experience using all of the leading word processing software packages. You do not waste your valuable time orienting our employees to your software. Skilled Temps begin productive work immediately.

File: C7Ill-B2

Thank you for inquiring about Skilled Temps who can handle receptionist duties. We have Skilled Temps available who have extensive training and experience as receptionists. All they need is a brief introduction to your organization, and they can begin productive work immediately.

File: C7Ill-M1

All Skilled Temps complete extensive assessments on each software application package and must be certified on a particular software package before they are placed on a job using that software. They are then classified into three skill levels on each software package. These levels allow you to save money by matching your job requirements with the skill levels of our employees. We keep a profile of your company on record that indicates the application software you use and that describes the work to be performed. Changes in the profile can be made any time you request service.

File: C7Ill-M2

All Skilled Temps complete extensive assessments and are certified as having mastered specific skills before they are placed on a job. This certification program enables us to match your job requirements with the skill levels of our employees. We keep a profile of your company on record that describes the skills you require and the type of work to be performed. Changes in the profile can be made any time you request service.

File: C7Ill-E1

The enclosed brochure provides complete job descriptions and a cost schedule. One of our representatives will telephone you next week to answer any questions that you may have about Skilled Temps.

File: C7Ill-E2

The enclosed brochure provides complete job descriptions and a cost schedule. One of our representatives will visit your organization next week to answer your questions and to talk about establishing a profile of your company needs.

Variable Information:

Mr. Steven Garcia, Manager	Ms. Carla Montoya, President
Metro Research, Inc.	Montoya Associates
824 Motley Drive	3847 Preston Oaks Road
Mesquite, TX 75150-9274	Dallas, TX 75240-1073

This letter was created from the form paragraphs on page 159.

1654 Highland Road
Dallas, TX 75218-2059
(214) 555-0134

Current date

Mr. Steven Garcia, Manager
Metro Research, Inc.
824 Motley Drive
Mesquite, TX 75150-9274

Dear Mr. Garcia

Thank you for inquiring about Skilled Temps who can handle word processing applications. We have Skilled Temps available who are trained and who have experience using all of the leading word processing software packages. You do not waste your valuable time orienting our employees to your software. Skilled Temps begin productive work immediately.

All Skilled Temps complete extensive assessments and are certified as having mastered specific skills before they are placed on a job. This certification program enables us to match your job requirements with the skill levels of our employees. We keep a profile of your company on record that describes the skills you require and the type of work to be performed. Changes in the profile can be made any time you request service.

The enclosed brochure provides complete job descriptions and a cost schedule. One of our representatives will visit your organization next week to answer your questions and to talk about establishing a profile of your company needs.

Sincerely

Lisa C. Martinez
Corporate Placement Director

ms

Enclosure

Variables: March 24, 19—; Ms; Carla; Montoya; President;
Montoya Associates; 3847 Preston Oaks; Dallas; TX; 75240-1073;
word processing; visit

<Date>

<Title> <First Name> <Last Name> <Position>
<Company>
<Street Address>
<City>, <State> <Postal Code>

Dear <Title> <Last Name>

Thank you for inquiring about Skilled Temps who can handle <software>
applications. We have Skilled Temps available who are trained and who
have experience using all of the leading <application> software packages.
You do not waste your valuable time orienting our employees to your
software. Skilled Temps begin productive work immediately.

All Skilled Temps complete extensive assessments and are certified as
having mastered specific skills before they are placed on a job. This
certification program enables us to match your job requirements with the
skill levels of our employees. We keep a profile of your company on record
that describes the skills you require and the type of work to be performed.
Changes in the profile can be made any time you request service.

The enclosed brochure provides complete job descriptions and a cost
schedule. One of our representatives will <visit/ telephone> your
organization next week to answer your questions and to talk about
establishing a profile of your company needs.

Sincerely

Lisa C. Martinez
Corporate Placement Director

ms

Enclosure

Variable Form

This form was used to create the form letter on page 162.

Notice the same letter can be created from either a variable form or form paragraphs depending on the preference of the writer.

**1654 Highland Road
Dallas, TX 75218-2059
(214) 555-0134**

Current date

Ms. Carla Montoya, President
Montoya Associates
3847 Preston Oaks
Dallas, TX 75240-1073

Dear Ms. Montoya

Thank you for inquiring about Skilled Temps who can handle word processing applications. We have Skilled Temps available who are trained and who have experience using all of the leading word processing software packages. You do not waste your valuable time orienting our employees to your software. Skilled Temps begin productive work immediately.

All Skilled Temps complete extensive assessments and are certified as having mastered specific skills before they are placed on a job. This certification program enables us to match your job requirements with the skill levels of our employees. We keep a profile of your company on record that describes the skills you require and the type of work to be performed. Changes in the profile can be made any time you request service.

The enclosed brochure provides complete job descriptions and a cost schedule. One of our representatives will visit your organization next week to answer your questions and to talk about establishing a profile of your company needs.

Sincerely

Lisa C. Martinez
Corporate Placement Director

ms

Enclosure

APPLICATION 7A *Review Guide 5:*
Check for Completeness

For each of the following situations, indicate the information that you should provide and the questions you should anticipate.

1. You currently are using word processing, database, graphics, and presentation software from the Office Pro suite, and spreadsheet software from the Office Master suite. You are planning a memo to request permission to convert from the current Office Master spreadsheet software to the Office Pro spreadsheet software. You already have the software, but you need permission to convert all the departmental documents that are in Office Master to Office Pro.

   Information you must provide:

   Questions you should anticipate:

2. You are planning a memo inviting the members of your department to attend a day of football activity including the tailgate celebration and tickets for all to the game.

   Information you must provide:

   Questions you should anticipate:

3. You are planning a memo requesting the training department to provide a customer service training program for all frontline employees in your area.

   Information you must provide:

   Questions you should anticipate:

4. You are planning a memo to tell three branch managers that you have made all travel and hotel reservations for their four-day trip to the corporate office next month.

   Information you must provide:

   Assumptions you could logically make:

   Questions you should anticipate:

5. You are writing a memo to notify all employees about the new company policy that limits smoking to the lounge adjacent to the cafeteria.

   Information you must provide:

   Assumptions you could logically make:

   Questions you should anticipate:

APPLICATION 7B *Editing and Language Arts Checkpoint*

Carefully read the document that follows; it is packed with errors. Use proof-reader's marks to mark all errors in grammar, spelling, word usage, number usage, capitalization, and punctuation. Do not revise sentence or paragraph structure in this activity unless an error exists.

    After you have marked all corrections directly on this document, access File 7B on your template disk and make the corrections you marked. If you do not have access to the template disk, key the document, making the corrections as you key.

    After you have made all corrections, refer to page 237 in Appendix C for the solution and check to see that you corrected all errors. You may use on-line reference tools just as you would if you were doing this as part of your job. Save the file as 7B-sol.

PRESENTATION TO SELECTED STAFF—NOVEMBER 15, 19—

Would you like to have twelve extra hour a week to devote to the responsibilities you think are the more important of everything you do in your job. Dr. Ashu Sopios an imminent expert completed a communications audit for our company. His conclusion were that staff members in the business services department and the Claims Department could save an average of 12 hours per week if the company develop an extensive file of from documents for situations that lends themselves to form applications.

As a way of preceding with this task, dr. Sopios suggested that we first identify situations in that form letters could be used effective. The 2nd step is to determine the type of form that would be best for each situation. Then form letters can be drafted by a team of employees whom are knowledgeable in the area. A cross functional team will review the letters before approving they.

10 supervisors identified about 50 situations in which form letters would save a significant amount of time. To qualify as a situation requiring a form letter, an average of five letters a week must be written to customers to solve that situation. Variable forms or form paragraphs could be used affectively in most of the situations. Because complete forms are impersonal and guide forms are inefficient, the supervisors recommended that neither complete forms or guide forms be used.

Supervisors plan to name 5 teams this week to develop the first draft of the form letters. Each team will be asked to prepare ten form letters. After all letters have been drafted the cross functional team will review the letters and either approve them or suggest revisions. Employees who drafts correspondence in these two areas will be provided with a list and a brief description of all form letters as well as with a disk containing the form letters

APPLICATION 7C *Writing Form Messages*

Use the following information to prepare form messages.

1. Review the Skilled Temps form paragraphs illustrated on page 159. You have been getting requests for information on Skilled Temps who can handle various spreadsheet and database applications. Develop two additional beginning paragraphs that can be used to handle these requests. Save the files as **C7III-B3** and **C7III-B4** and store them on the template diskette with the other form paragraphs. Note: Effective file names are critical when form paragraphs are used. The file names used in this chapter can easily be translated:

   - **C7** = Chapter 7
   - **III** = Illustration
   - **-B** = Beginning paragraph (the number following indicates which beginning paragraph)
   - **-M** = Middle paragraph (the number following indicates which middle paragraph)
   - **-E** = Ending paragraph (the number following indicates which ending paragraph)

2. Retrieve Files **C7III-B4** (the database paragraph you just wrote), **C7III-M2,** and **C7III-E1.** Send the letter to Ms. Elizabeth Davis, Clearwater Industries, 4938 Maple Walk Street, Humble, TX 77346-5802.

3. One of your responsibilities as a personnel assistant in VanHuss Industries is to contact all references listed by job applicants who are being called back for a second interview. The name and address of each person that you contact is provided on the application that the job applicant signed, thus giving you the authority to contact each person listed as a reference. Set up a letter in the format illustrated on page 161. Use appropriate variables for the date, inside address, and salutation.

   Draft the form message indicating that the <applicant> (use a variable for the applicant's name) has applied for a position as a <type of position> and listed the individual as a reference on his or her application. Request that the individual complete the evaluation form, which you will enclose with the letter. Tell the person that you hope to make a decision within the next three weeks and tactfully ask that they send the reference so that the information can be considered in the decision-making process. Sign your name and use Personnel Assistant as your title.

4. Use the form message you just developed to request a reference on Kenneth W. Willis, who applied for a position as a sales representative. Ken listed Marcus Schwartz, Marketing Manager, Midtown Medical Supplies, 3958 Ridgecrest Street, Las Cruces, NM 88005-1486 as one of his references. Use the current date.

5. Your Credit Department always sends individual letters to accounts that are more than three months past due. You have developed a series of guide forms that get progressively stronger. Earlier reminders are printed notices included with duplicate copies of the unpaid statement. The first individual letter tries to convince the person to pay the bill. The second letter points out the consequences of not paying the bill. The third letter gives the customer ten days to pay the bill before it is turned over to a collection agency.

   Use the following guide form for a first individual letter. You may make changes in the letter if you feel you can improve it.

Guide Form: C7-5GF1

Dear

   Success in any endeavor is dependent on making good decisions. You made an excellent decision when you purchased your new luggage from the *Travel Master Shop.* Travel Master decided more than twenty years ago to provide our customers with the finest travel products available at a reasonable price. And that decision is one of the primary reasons we have been successful for so many years.

   Until now you have always made excellent decisions on the way you maintained your account with us. However, your $1,850 account is now more than three months past due. We hope you will make another excellent decision—the decision to protect your fine credit rating.

   You can do so by sending us your check for $1,850 in the enclosed envelope. Please take action now.

   Sincerely

Adapt the guide form appropriately and send the letter to Ms. Roseanne Desselles, 12 Essex Street, Beverly, MA 01915-3867, whose $2,290 account is now more than three months past due. Use the current date, sign your name, and use the title Credit Manager.

6. As marketing manager of Video Productions you are marketing three video training programs that each contain two modules. The programs are entitled:

   > *The Creativity Connection*
   > *The Art of Negotiating*
   > *Self-Directed Teams Revisited*

You enclosed the following complete form with each copy of *The Creativity Connection* shipped.

Thank You for Ordering
The Creativity Connection

The videocassettes for Modules 1 and 2 of *The Creativity Connection* are enclosed. Thank you for ordering our training program. We are confident you will be pleased with the quality of our training and will find it to be very beneficial to your employees.

The videotapes on which the program is recorded are high-quality tapes designed for extensive use. They are carefully checked prior to shipment. However, should a tape be defective or damaged in shipment, it will be replaced immediately if it is returned within two weeks of receipt of the tapes. Worn-out or damaged tapes will be repaired or replaced within one year from the date of purchase at a cost of 25 percent of the current catalog price. The damaged tape must be returned with your request for reimbursement. The video programs are protected by copyright and may not be videotaped, duplicated, or copied in any form or medium.

Please call us if you need additional copies or if you would like us to develop custom-designed materials for your organization to complement the program. Thank you again for ordering *The Creativity Connection.*

You are considering using a form with variables for all three training programs and personalizing each letter to be more effective. Using the information contained in the complete form, prepare a variable form letter that could be personalized and that would have variables so that it could be used for each of the three video training products available. Determine which document would be more effective—the complete form or the letter created from the form with variables. Be prepared to justify your answer.

7. Complete the variable form for Mr. Jody Swinney, Training Manager, Sports Marketing, Inc., 3748 Devine Street, Columbia, SC 29209-3847. Mr. Swinney ordered *The Art of Negotiating.*

Chapter 7

APPLICATION 7D *Self-Assessment*

Use complete, grammatically correct sentences to answer each of the following items.

1. Describe each of the following types of forms, giving the advantages and disadvantages of each.

   a. Complete forms

   b. Variable forms

   c. Form paragraphs

   d. Guide forms

2. **C7D-MH** Store the memo head shown below either as a macro or as the file name listed at the beginning of this paragraph.

   To:
   From:
   Date: (Insert date code)
   Subject: Your Travel Request

   C7D-B1
   Write a paragraph telling the employee that his or her travel request has been received and reviewed. Indicate that the request has been processed, but that modifications in the request were required because the request did not fully conform to the travel policies established by the Executive Committee of VanHuss Industries.

C7D-B2

Write a paragraph telling the employee that his or her request for international travel has been received and reviewed. Point out that the travel request cannot be processed because VanHuss travel policies require that all international travel requests be signed by a senior vice president.

C7D-M1

Write a paragraph telling the employee that the changes made on the travel request are highlighted on the enclosed copy of the Travel Request form. Indicate that the changes were made to lower the total cost of the trip as mandated by VanHuss travel policies. Ask the employee to call immediately for an exception if the revisions present a hardship or would have a negative effect on the purpose of the trip.

C7D-M2

Write a paragraph telling the employee that you are enclosing an Exception to Travel Policy form. Ask the employee to return the form with the signature of the appropriate senior vice president. Indicate that you will process the travel request as soon as you receive the signed form.

C7D-E1

Write a paragraph telling the employee that tickets and confirmation for any other services required will be delivered to the employee at least two days prior to departure. Indicate that any changes made in the travel arrangements should be made through the Corporate Travel Department. Be sure to remind the employee that restricted tickets are used and that changes may result in penalties.

3. Retrieve the memo heading and files **C7D-B1, C7D-M1,** and **C7D-E1.** Prepare the memo to Siu-Ki Kwok.

Heritage Productions

APPLICATION 7E *Heritage Productions*

In your last two assignments (see page 153), you accumulated material for a Malaysia cross-cultural training video project. In this assignment, you will use the information you have already collected and collect additional information if you need to do so. The information may come from a variety of sources— the Internet, electronic library resources, your school library, or a travel agency.

The companies agreed that the regular training guide would be developed. Ms. Mary Turnquist, manager of the Custom Products Department, has asked a team of employees to do the basic research for the training guide. The information produced by your team will be turned over to the Production Team to finalize the training guide. A comprehensive outline for the video has been developed. Each team member is responsible for collecting information about a portion of the outline. In addition, team members were asked to make a note of any country customs that they came across during their research.

You are responsible for the following topics:

Country Information
    People
        Ethnic groups
        Languages
        Religions
        Population
    Geography
        General location
        Capital
        Major cities
        Climate
    Government
        Type of government
        Political conditions
    Economy
        Major industries
            Manufacturing
            Agriculture
        Currency
  Customs
  (List any that you think should be on the list the team is compiling.)

Write one or two paragraphs about each of the four topics listed under the major heading *Country Information*. Use the subpoints under these topics as suggestions for information you might include. Make a list of the sources you used for the information.

COLLABORATIVE AND TEAM WRITING

Performance Goals

After you complete Chapter 8, you should be able to
- ❏ *Work with team members to reach consensus on issues and to write effective messages documenting the team work*
- ❏ *Edit communications more effectively*

OVERVIEW

Many organizations are team oriented. Rather than assigning a project to one individual, they assign the project to a team of individuals. The types of teams vary from organization to organization and even within organizations. In some cases, team members are from the same department or functional area. In other cases, cross-functional teams (members from different departments or functional areas) are used to obtain input from a variety of perspectives. Some teams have appointed team leaders while other teams have no formal leader. When leaders are not appointed, an informal leader usually emerges, and the leader may change when a new project is undertaken.

A key trend in organizations is to use teams extensively.

WORKING AS A TEAM

Working as a team is different than working as an individual. Different individuals bring different perspectives to a situation and may think the situation should be handled differently. The real benefit that organizations reap from team work is the different perspectives that are brought to bear on a situation. Teams make better decisions than individuals because they are more likely to consider a wider range of factors than any one individual would consider.

Since team members view situations from different perspectives, some disagreements about issues are inevitable. Disagreement on issues is not bad; in fact, disagreement can be very healthy. The way that you disagree is very important. Learn to disagree without being disagreeable. When team members respect the opinions of each other, they can approach a project with an open mind and work to reach the best possible solution.

Learning to work effectively with team members is a critical career skill.

Good problem-solving skills and good interpersonal skills are required to be an effective team member.

Problem-solving skills are important. Good problem solvers gain a clear understanding of a problem and all its components. They collect as much information as possible, and then they use that information objectively. They try to explore as many good alternatives as possible; then they look at the advantages and disadvantages of each alternative to determine the best course of action for all. This process cannot be accomplished without some "give and take." Being able to communicate ideas effectively is important. Some team members are able to present their ideas more persuasively than others. A caution to all team members is to make sure that the alternative selected is truly the best one—not an alternative that was not as good but was sold more effectively by the team member proposing it.

STRATEGIES FOR TEAM WRITING

Teams usually have to document their work in some fashion. The documents that teams write include letters, memos, and internal company documents, such as short and long reports, policies, procedures, proposals, and specialized documents of various types. Often the work done by the team must be submitted to a superior in the organization to be approved before it can be implemented.

The strategies used have to be adapted to the type of document that is written. The guides for effective planning that you studied in Chapter 2 apply to team writing as well. Once the team agrees on the information to be presented, then the team has to agree on the best way to present that information.

Reaching team consensus (agreement) prior to writing a message is important.

Team writing presents a special challenge because the document should not look like it was written by different people. The style should be consistent throughout the document. A reader should not be able to tell where one person stopped writing and another started writing.

Often the length of a document determines the strategy that is best to use for writing the document. On very short documents, the best strategy may be to have one person write the results and then have other team members edit the document to ensure that it represents the team's view. Team members may rotate the writing of documents so that one person does not always have to do it. However, if one team member has superior writing skills, that person may be selected to do the final writing, and other team members assume more of the other responsibilities to balance the workload.

Careful planning of content, stylistic elements, and format make documents written by teams look as though they were written by one person.

On long documents, the writing responsibility is often shared. When documents are written by more than one individual, care should be taken to ensure that each document is consistent in every respect. For example, if one writer uses an "em" dash and another uses two hyphens for a dash, it will be obvious that two people worked on the document. Or if one writer uses an acronym to refer to the company and another uses the full company name, it will be obvious that two different people wrote the document. Documents must be consistent in the use of tense, headings, writing style, and other attributes to avoid the appearance of being written by more than one person.

Group writing should be approached from both a content and a mechanical perspective. The best way to ensure that everything is included in the document and that content is not duplicated is to prepare a detailed outline. Once the outline has been developed, then the writing project can be divided into segments that can be handled by different team members.

CONTENT CONSISTENCY

Many issues must be discussed before a team writes a document.

- The level of detail is important. If several sections of a document are equivalent in importance, the amount of copy devoted to each should be similar.
- The style of writing should be similar. An active writing style usually works best. Team members also have to decide if the writing style is going to be objective or personal.
- Team members should ensure that sections fit together and flow smoothly. An effective way to ensure coherence is to open each section with a brief overview statement indicating what is covered in the section and to close each section with a very brief summary statement.

Team members should use a consistent pattern to present charts, graphs, tables, and other visuals. An effective way to accomplish this is to have each team member introduce a visual by its name or number prior to presenting it and follow up a visual with a statement about its content after it has been presented. Terminology used to refer to visuals should be the same. Teams should discuss options and make style decisions such as "Use *figure* for graphs, charts, and other illustrations and use *table* for information in tabular form."

Consistency is easier to achieve by planning for it than by editing an inconsistent document to make it consistent.

MECHANICAL CONSISTENCY

All parts of a document should have a consistent appearance. To ensure a consistent appearance, stylistic elements should be determined prior to writing, and all team members should follow the styles selected. Examples of stylistic elements that must be considered include

- font, font size, margins, and general layout
- type of headings and the style in which they are formatted
- use of italics or underlining for titles
- use of headers or footers
- pagination style

TECHNOLOGICAL CONNECTIONS

Effective group work depends heavily on the ability to share information easily. When people work together on a project, it is essential that they be able to brainstorm to generate ideas and to review and critique each other's work. Software is available today to facilitate the sharing of information. Two categories of software help to facilitate group work on documents.

GROUPWARE

Groupware offers many features, including scheduling, workflow automation, and document management. Document management enables the group to have access to documents and to send comments about the documents to a central point so that the entire group has access to all the comments from group members and can respond to them. A key advantage is that the group members can be in remote locations.

WORD PROCESSING SOFTWARE

Today's sophisticated word processing software also offers features to facilitate group work. Features called annotations, comments, redlining, or revisions are designed for documents that will be reviewed or edited by different people. These features allow you to mark through the original text and suggest changes. Each person editing or commenting on the document can use a different color or use their initials to indicate who made the suggested changes. These features allow the originator of the document to accept or to reject suggested changes. Note the illustrations on the next page.

INTERNET

THE SUPERHIGHWAY OF COMMUNICATIONS

Regular E-mail can be used to facilitate group work, but it does have some limitations. Normally, when groups use E-mail, they attach a document file to the E-mail message. The problem is that each team member makes comments on a different document rather than having all comments on the same document.

Software is now available for the Internet that helps to manage and track documents and revisions to those documents. The software lets users create directories for documents that the team can access.

MISCOMMUNICATIONS

Sign posted at the entrance of a building:

Part-time help wanted: Someone to sew buttons on the second floor.

Using [SHVH1] Word Processing Software [JMC2] [KMT3] for Collaborative Writing

This document illustrates the use of ~~modern~~ word processing software to facilitate a team's writing effort. Note that the original document remains the same until the revisions are either accepted or rejected. Different authors can use their initials or different colors to distinguish their comments. (In this case, Tom is using blue.) This document is also contained on your template disk. If you ~~L~~ook at it on screen, the color differences show up.-Only~~as well as~~ the initials show up on the printed version. (Note that words added are underlined and words deleted have a line through them.)

Team comments normally consist of changes in content as well as editorial corrections. In some cases, specific text is suggested for inclusion. In other cases, the comments are general suggestions about the content.

Communications are facilitated by transmitting documents electronically rather than ~~by paper~~ using paper documents. When documents are sent to all members of the team, all comments appear on the same master document. This is important because team members may make opposing suggestions. An example is included in this document.

Page: 1
[SHVH1] Don't you think we should make this apply to groupware as well as word processing software?
Page: 1
[JMC2] I think we should make this document apply only to word processing. If we want to deal with groupware, do it in a separate document.
Page: 1
[KMT3] I agree with Jane.

APPLICATION 8A *Review Guide 6:*
Use an Efficient, Action-Oriented Style

Rewrite the following sentences using an efficient, action-oriented style and using active voice unless it is awkward or inappropriate to do so.

1. The report was reviewed and studied carefully by the committee, but action on the findings was postponed until the next monthly meeting of the committee.

2. Checks in the amount of $100 were sent to the mayor of the city of Gilbert and to the governor of the state of Texas by the Action Council to assist in their campaigns for election to the same offices again.

3. Pat was encouraged by the staff to take several other options into consideration in addition to the proposals submitted by the three vendors.

4. Please make the announcement that in the event of a loss the team will return home at the conclusion of the game.

5. Terry was asked to repeat the information again with reference to the maximum earnings possible without loss of retirement benefits.

APPLICATION 8B *Editing and Language Arts Checkpoint*

Carefully read the document that follows; it is packed with errors. Use proofreader's marks to mark all errors in grammar, spelling, word usage, number usage, capitalization, and punctuation. Do not revise sentence or paragraph structure in this activity unless an error exists.

After you have marked all corrections directly on this document, access File 8B on your template disk and make the corrections you marked. If you do not have access to the template disk, key the document, making the corrections as you key.

After you have made all corrections, refer to page 238 in Appendix C for the solution and check to see that you corrected all errors. You may use on-line reference tools just as you would if you were doing this as part of your job. Save the file as 8B-sol.

Dear Dr. Krisman

The members of the University alumni association whom were present at our annual meeting truly benefited from you outstanding presentation, "Balancing Lifes Demands. Many member commented than the ideas you presented would help all of we not only to reduce stress, but also to live a fuller and more enriched life. Several members called and ask me to print your presentation in the *Alumni* News so that they could share it with friends and colleagues who was not fortunate enough to hear you.

May we share your ideas with the members of the University alumni association by include a three hundred-word abstract of your presentation in the next issue. Your article would be featured as the lead story with the report of the annual meeting. We would, of coarse, include your picture and brief biographical information about you with the article. In order to meet our press deadlines we would need to have all information in our office by the 20 day of this month.

Authors of articles in previous issues of the *Alumni News* have been quiet

pleased with the response them received form the readers. Many reported

renewing old friendships and making new friends. We know our readers

would enjoy and benefit from your excellent article.

Yours truly

After you have made all corrections, format the letter using the address for
Dr. Leslie Krisman located in the Address directory in Appendix A. Sign your
name and use the title Editor.

APPLICATION 8C *Team or Collaborative Writing*

Work with a team of four or five class members (called the HRM Team) to discuss each situation and reach consensus. If you need more information about the topic discussed, use on-line references or your school library to obtain additional information. Then write the memo required for each scenario. Address all memos to the Staff Development Committee of VanHuss Industries. In each scenario, try to involve at least two people in the actual writing of the memo. For example, one person may write the introductory section, and a second person may write the specific recommendations agreed on by the team. Individuals not involved in the writing should be responsible for editing and finalizing the documents.

1. Several members of your department have been complaining that meetings are not as effective as they should be. Discuss ways to make meetings effective, have the team reach a consensus, and write a memo summarizing your results.

2. Customers do not seem to like voice mail; some even have said that voice mail is abused. Your team has been asked to discuss the topic "Uses and Abuses of Voice Mail." Write a memo summarizing the key uses and abuses of voice mail.

3. While you were discussing voice mail, members of your team brought up the topic of improving telephone conversations. The team also decided to discuss the topic "Keys to Effective Telephone Calls." After consensus is reached, summarize the results in a memo.

4. Your team will be involved in presenting short, employee development segments in an orientation and training program. Since you will be using visuals for your presentations, the team decided to discuss guides for preparing effective visuals. After consensus is reached, summarize the results in a memo.

5. Your team has been asked to provide guides for managing time effectively. Discuss the topic, reach consensus, and write the memo.

APPLICATION 8D *Self-Assessment*

1. Use complete, grammatically correct sentences to answer each of the following items.

   a. Describe several different types of teams frequently used by organizations.

   b. What benefits do organizations gain by using teams?

   c. What skills are important for team members to develop in order to be effective members of a team?

   d. What strategies can be used to ensure that the content of a document written by a team is consistent?

   e. What mechanical strategies can be used to help make a team-written document consistent?

2. VanHuss Industries has divisions in foreign countries. Your team has been asked to discuss the possibility of using an international team with members from three foreign countries to work on a major customer service training program. Based on everything you have learned, what are the benefits and the problems of using an international team? How could you minimize some of the problems? Discuss the issues, reach consensus, and write a memo to the Staff Development Committee presenting your recommendations.

Heritage Productions

APPLICATION 8E *Heritage Productions*

You have completed your assignment in the Custom Products Department and have rotated to your new position, assistant manager in the Human Resources Management (HRM) Department. Mr. Gregory Garrison serves as manager of the department.

Heritage Productions has become more team oriented, and Mr. Garrison has asked you to work with a team of four or five HRM employees (from your class) to begin developing materials for training programs on team building. Mr. Garrison suggested that team members brainstorm and come up with a list of characteristics of an effective team; then check references on-line or in the library on the topic to see if any additional characteristics should be added to the list. He wants the team to discuss the combined list and agree on the ten most important characteristics. These ten characteristics should be summarized in a memo to him.

GOODWILL AND PERSONAL BUSINESS MESSAGES

Performance Goals

After you complete Chapter 9, you should be able to
- ❏ *Write effective goodwill and personal business letters and memos*
- ❏ *Edit communications more effectively*

OVERVIEW

All business letters and memos should be designed to build goodwill as well as to accomplish the specific purpose of the message. In addition, some messages are designed purely to build goodwill. As people conduct business, they establish relationships with customers, suppliers, vendors and other associates. Business relationships are, in effect, business friendships. Just as you would write congratulatory, thank you, and similar messages to friends, these types of messages are written to business "friends." This chapter focuses on suggestions for writing personal business letters and memos.

Nurturing business relationships is good business strategy.

TYPES OF PERSONAL BUSINESS MESSAGES

Commonly written personal business messages include the following categories:

- thank you messages
- congratulatory messages
- special occasion messages
- sympathy messages

The way personal business messages are written often depends on the relationship of the individuals involved. If the individuals have a very close relationship, the message is often quite personal. If the individuals just have a good business relationship, the message is usually warm and friendly but not overly personal.

Personal business messages are often just a product of good manners.

THANK YOU MESSAGES

Thank you notes probably are the most frequently written personal business messages. Many business situations provide an opportunity to build goodwill

Many people do not take the time to write thank you notes. Those who do build goodwill.

by writing a thank you note. Examples of situations in which you may want to write a thank you message are when you are

- being taken out for a meal.
- being granted an interview or being provided with a reference.
- receiving a gift, service, or large amount of business.
- having someone make a business contact or "open a door" for you.

Thank you notes should be short, specific, warm, and friendly. Personal business messages are always written in a personal style. They should be very specific about the reason for which they are written. They should not be excessive or gushy. An illustration of a thank you letter that was written after an interview is provided below.

Katherine R. Radakowich

432 Broad Street ■ Seattle, Washington 98121-8369 ■ (206) 555-0170

Current date

Mr. Mark Ferrante, Manager
Ferrante Financial Services
245 Washington Place
Pittsburgh, PA 15219-8037

Dear Mr. Ferrante

Thank you very much for giving me the opportunity to talk with you about a position as a financial analyst with Ferrante Financial Services. You were extremely helpful in providing information about the position, and I am now even more interested in it.

I especially enjoyed having lunch with several of the financial analysts in your company. They were very complimentary of the organization, their colleagues, and the working environment. They also seem to enjoy working as a team. I would like to be a part of that team.

Please let me hear from you soon. I hope you will give me the opportunity to demonstrate that I can be an effective financial analyst for Ferrante Financial Services.

Sincerely

Katherine R. Radakowich

ms

CONGRATULATORY MESSAGES

Congratulatory messages are written for both business and individual successes. Examples of business situations in which you may want to write a congratulatory message:

- A company receives a special award or citation.
- An individual receives an award or a promotion.
- A company, team, or individual wins a competition.
- A company expands its business.

Congratulatory messages should be short, specific, and sincere. They are written in personal style. An illustration of a congratulatory message written when a company received an award is presented below.

Most people do not expect congratulatory notes, but they appreciate them when they receive them.

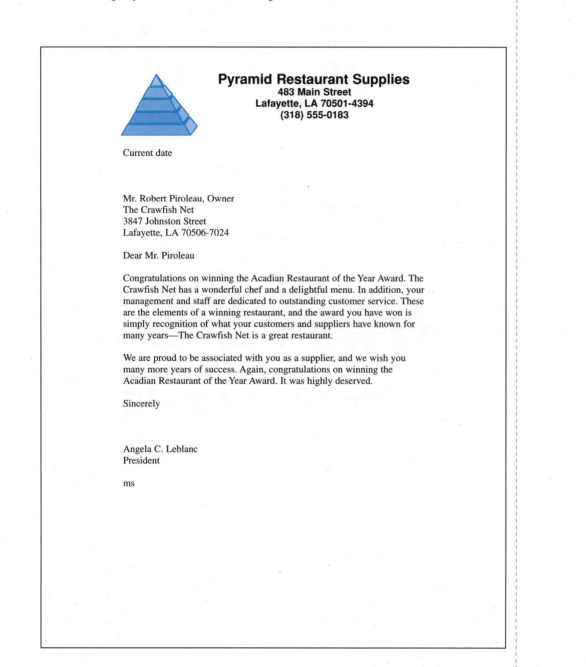

Pyramid Restaurant Supplies
483 Main Street
Lafayette, LA 70501-4394
(318) 555-0183

Current date

Mr. Robert Piroleau, Owner
The Crawfish Net
3847 Johnston Street
Lafayette, LA 70506-7024

Dear Mr. Piroleau

Congratulations on winning the Acadian Restaurant of the Year Award. The Crawfish Net has a wonderful chef and a delightful menu. In addition, your management and staff are dedicated to outstanding customer service. These are the elements of a winning restaurant, and the award you have won is simply recognition of what your customers and suppliers have known for many years—The Crawfish Net is a great restaurant.

We are proud to be associated with you as a supplier, and we wish you many more years of success. Again, congratulations on winning the Acadian Restaurant of the Year Award. It was highly deserved.

Sincerely

Angela C. Leblanc
President

ms

SPECIAL OCCASION MESSAGES

Special occasion messages are similar to congratulatory messages and are written for events that both businesses and individuals experience. Special occasions are often thought of as situations to share best wishes or greetings. Examples of special occasions on which you may want to write a greeting or best wishes message include

- holidays
- anniversaries
- company events, such as a merger or acquisition
- special days, such as Professional Secretaries Day

Best wishes messages are written in the same way that congratulatory messages are written. A special caution is necessary for holiday messages. Many holidays are religious rather than secular holidays. It is important not to offend by assuming that business associates celebrate the same holidays that you do. For example, businesses usually use a "Seasons Greetings" message for the Christmas holidays. This type of message is appropriate because almost everyone celebrates the season, but not everyone celebrates Christmas. Many businesses use greeting cards rather than personal messages for holiday greetings. Some businesses use the opportunity to thank customers for their business over the past year.

SYMPATHY MESSAGES

Sympathy messages are the most difficult type of message to write. Unless the business relationship is extremely close, most people purchase sympathy cards rather than try to write sympathy messages. If the relationship is close, a short handwritten note is added to the card.

TECHNOLOGICAL CONNECTIONS

Technology is often viewed as a cold and impersonal means of communicating; therefore, E-mail rarely is used for personal messages except within companies. If an employee receives an award or promotion, often other employees will send an E-mail message of congratulations. In fact, E-mail messages can be broadcast to a large group of people; therefore, companies often use E-mail to announce special recognitions to the entire organization.

One advantage of technology is the ability to use special fonts and clip art. Many people prefer to use a script font rather than a traditional font for personal messages. Invitations, congratulatory notes, thank you notes, and other personal messages are often written with a script font.

Clip art is used extensively for invitations, especially within companies for informal events. For more formal events, printed or engraved invitations are often sent. Clip art is also used extensively for announcements.

In some cases, announcements of and invitations to informal company events are posted rather than sent to all individuals. Posted announcements or invitations are normally prepared using large fonts and clip art. Clip art is used to attract attention and a large, bold font is used so that the copy can be read from a distance.

THE SUPER HIGHWAY OF COMMUNICATIONS

INTERNET

The Internet is rarely used for personal messages except for sending thank you or congratulatory messages by E-mail. As with domestic situations, E-mail is used more with internal communications than with external. Companies may use E-mail or intranets in much the same way that E-mail is used within the organization for thank you or congratulatory messages.

The Internet can be used to locate a listing of holidays for the countries in which you do business. Knowing the holidays and sending appropriate greetings can do much to build goodwill in an international setting. Knowing holidays of the countries in which you do business is also important in scheduling events.

MISCOMMUNICATIONS

For sale sign:

Antique desk suitable for lady with thick legs and large drawers.

APPLICATION 9A *Review Guide 7: Use Concrete Language*

Rewrite the following sentences using concrete language.

1. Marjorie will send a very large donation to the symphony in the near future.

2. You need to get a very big sweatshirt for Bill because he is very tall and heavy.

3. Pat put a lot of money in the savings account and earned a high rate of interest.

4. The team won a lot of games by a very small margin.

5. A large number of fans drove a long way to watch the team lose to a team with a much lower ranking.

APPLICATIONS

APPLICATION 9B *Editing and Language Arts Checkpoint*

Read carefully the document that follows; it is packed with errors. Use proof-reader's marks to mark all errors in grammar, spelling, word usage, number usage, capitalization, and punctuation. Do not revise sentence or paragraph structure in this activity unless an error exists.

After you have marked all corrections directly on this document, access File 9B on your template disk and make the corrections you marked. If you do not have access to the template disk, make the corrections as you key the document.

After you have made all corrections, refer to the document in Appendix C on page 239 for the solution and check to see that you corrected all errors. You may use on-line reference tools just as you would if you were doing this as part of your job. Save the file as 9B-sol.

The first quarter revenue figures for region iv was released today and you will be please to learn that once again the team exceeded it's 1st quarter revenue budget. Congratulations Each member of the team exceded the individual budget for the first quarter. We have consistent met both team goals for the passed three years but rarely has every member of the team exceed the budget plan. Its important that you review carefully the enclosed report that itemize the revenue generated for all targeted software products.

Of the six application software packages, the one that concerns me more is the project management software. Our project management software sales is far below the national average for the first quarter. In fact, not a single sales representative on our team meet the budget for project management software.

Would each of your analyze your territory carefully and give me an account by account projection of the project management sales for next quarter. I have asked Liz Jordan our technical support manager to come to our next regular scheduled team meeting and talk with us about ways we can increase our sales in this deficient area. Liz was very instrumental in helping the region iii team increase it's sales of project management software. I am sure she can help us improve our sales in this area.

During the next team meeting we will also view a new product release and begin planning for launching the sale of this product in our territory. You will be send a product release package prior to the meeting. Please review it careful so that we can use the meeting time effectively.

After you have made all corrections, format the memo to the sales staff from you. Use the current date and an appropriate subject line.

APPLICATION 9C *Writing Personal Business and Goodwill Messages*

Write the appropriate message for each of the following situations. Use the address file in Appendix A to obtain the addresses you need.

1. Your company, Viking Manufacturing Company, is a major supplier of GreenGate Industries. GreenGate Industries just received the National Manufacturing Quality Award as an outstanding manufacturing company. The award is given each year to five manufacturing companies nationally. The award is a major one coveted by many manufacturing companies. As a supplier, you had to submit information about GreenGate. Write a congratulatory letter to Ms. Marjorie Ducate, Chief Executive Officer, of GreenGate Manufacturing.

2. Your Office Management class completed a major unit on Office Furniture and Layout. Mr. Martin Rickenhouser, Marketing Manager of Diamond Modular Office Systems invited your class to visit the manufacturer's showrooms. The company hosted your class for:

   - A tour of the manufacturing plant
   - A tour of the showroom
   - A presentation by one of the major designers, Ms. Leigh James
   - Lunch

   Write Mr. Rickenhouser a thank you note on behalf of your class.

3. Roxanne Merriwether, an accountant in your Administration Division with VanHuss Industries, just received the Community Volunteer Award. One award each year is given by your community to the citizen who has made the most outstanding contribution. Roxanne is active in the United Way, Junior Achievement, the local Better Business Bureau, the Chamber of Commerce, and several charitable groups. VanHuss encourages employees to get involved in community activities; therefore, you want to publicly acknowledge this award to the entire company. Prepare a message that will be sent by e-mail to all employees of VanHuss Industries telling them of your colleague's award.

4. You have been asked to chair the annual VanHuss company picnic. Prepare the invitation that will be sent to all employees. The event is casual and very informal. It is held at the Lakefront Club. All employees and their families (or a guest) are invited to participate. Food, beverages, and a wide variety of recreational activities are provided. The event is scheduled for June 15. Activities begin at noon and end at 8 p.m. Write the memo inviting all employees. Use clip art to design an interesting invitation/announcement that can be posted on the bulletin boards throughout the company.

5. You asked Dr. Marshall Burge, one of your professors, to provide you with a reference for a summer position at Baytown Medical Supplies. He wrote an excellent letter that was instrumental in your being offered the summer job as an office assistant. Write Dr. Burge an appropriate thank you note.

6. Doug Smith, a maintenance supervisor with VanHuss Industries, celebrates his 25th year with the company on Monday of next week. Write a congratulatory message to Doug. He will be formally recognized with all employees celebrating anniversaries at the end of the year meeting, but you wanted to write a note on the day of his anniversary. Your company title is Manager of Human Resources.

Chapter 9

APPLICATION 9D *Self-Assessment*

Use complete, grammatically correct sentences to answer each of the following items.

1.a. Why is it important to write personal business messages?

1.b. Describe two or three types of personal business messages that are frequently written.

1.c. When would E-mail be appropriate for personal business messages?

1.d. Describe an appropriate strategy or writing style for congratulatory messages.

1.e. How is technology used to facilitate the preparation and distribution of personal business messages?

2. Mr. Carl G. Wentworth, Benefits Manager of VanHuss Industries, will retire in two weeks. He has 30 years of service with VanHuss and worked closely with all of the employees. You have been an employee of VanHuss for two years, and Mr. Wentworth was extremely helpful to you when you had surgery and missed work for three weeks. Write an appropriate personal business message to Mr. Wentworth.

Heritage Productions

APPLICATION 9E *Heritage Productions, Inc.*

You are continuing your assignment as Assistant Manager in the Human Resources Management (HRM) Department. Mr. Gregory Garrison serves as Manager of the department.

Heritage Productions currently has major projects in Germany, Japan, and Brazil. Mr. Garrison has asked you to put together a team to research these three countries because Heritage wants to be able to build good relationships with employees and customers in those countries He asked that you find out what holidays the countries celebrate, customs of doing business, and ways to build better relationships. You have asked several people to serve on three teams—each team will research one country. Determine which team you will serve on. Summarize the information you find in a memo to Mr. Garrison.

EMPLOYMENT COMMUNICATIONS

Performance Goals

After you complete Chapter 10, you should be able to
- ❑ *Write effective employment communications*
- ❑ *Edit communications more effectively*

OVERVIEW

Employment communications should be viewed from two different perspectives—the perspective of an employer trying to hire an effective employee and the perspective of an individual seeking employment in a suitable position. A variety of communications are often used in the employment process by both employers and prospective employees. Individuals seeking employment prepare:

- résumés
- letters of application
- thank you or follow-up letters
- requests for references
- requests for transcripts or other records
- acceptance letters and declination letters

    Employers prepare:

- position description statements
- letters scheduling interviews
- requests for references
- references for former employees
- job offers and rejection letters

The primary focus in this chapter is on preparing the résumé and letter of application. Only minor emphasis is placed on the other communications used in the employment process.

PLANNING THE EMPLOYMENT PROCESS

Employment communications are some of the most important and the most difficult communications you will ever write. They are important because they are instrumental in the type of position you obtain. The type of position you obtain, in turn, affects your entire life. They are difficult because most people

The key to success in the employment process for both the employer and prospective employee is matching the right person with the right position.

are not comfortable selling themselves and do not like to subject themselves to scrutiny. Condensing a lifetime of information into a one-page summary is not easy to do. Employment communications are especially difficult for young people who have not yet decided on a specific career.

The employment process has been further complicated by the trend toward electronic résumés. Today, many companies manage the employment process with on-line applicant tracking software. Writing employment communications to take advantage of electronically managed systems and, at the same time, to appeal to the final decision maker who probably will view the application in a traditional manner requires time, knowledge, and expertise. Both electronic tracking systems and electronic résumés are discussed on pages 202–203.

In many companies, applicants must first pass an electronic screening process before their applications are seen by decision makers.

DEVELOPING AN EMPLOYMENT STRATEGY

Strategy plays a key role in the employment process. Strategy is important to both employers and individuals seeking employment. Large organizations maintain departments that specialize in developing an effective strategy to ensure that the organization has the appropriate human resources ready and trained when they are needed. Employment strategy may be even more important in small organizations, even though they do not have a department responsible for the strategy. Small organizations cannot afford to make bad employment decisions.

Having a good job strategy may be even more important for individuals than for companies.

Strategy is just as important to individuals who are seeking employment as it is to organizations seeking employees. Individuals cannot afford to accept a job in which they are unlikely to be successful or in which they are likely to be dissatisfied. Therefore, developing an effective employment strategy can have a very positive outcome for an individual.

THE EMPLOYMENT PROCESS—EMPLOYER'S PERSPECTIVE

The first thing an employer must do to initiate the employment process is to determine exactly what needs to be done and what skills a prospective employee needs to have to accomplish the job in an effective manner. An accurate, up-to-date job description and a clear understanding of the job qualifications an individual needs to be able to perform the job provide the foundation for starting the hiring process.

Some companies underestimate the importance of having clear job specifications and an accurate, up-to-date job description.

THE EMPLOYMENT PROCESS—EMPLOYEE'S PERSPECTIVE

The first step in the employment process is self-analysis. You need to analyze yourself and know exactly what you have to offer and what you really want to do. You have to consider carefully the things you like to do and the things you do not like to do. The kind of environment in which you like to work is also important.

Objective self-analysis should be done before you start to look for a job. Ideally, self-analysis should begin early in the education process so that wise decisions can be made in selecting appropriate courses of study. Once you have examined your strengths and weaknesses as well as your likes and dislikes, you can begin to analyze jobs that might be appropriate for you.

An ideal match from the employee's perspective is a job in which your strengths are the major requirements of the job and your weaknesses are not

Few students know exactly what they want to do. Many wish for the proverbial crystal ball to help them make employment decisions.

very important in the job. Finding the perfect match may not be possible, but you should strive to get as close a match as possible.

THE JOB MARKET

Both organizations and individuals have many decisions to make about the job market. Organizations must determine where and how they will recruit potential employees. Individuals must determine where they will seek employment and the type of company or industry they will target. For some jobs, organizations must recruit locally; for other jobs, they recruit regionally or nationally.

Individuals have to make this same choice. They have to determine if they will limit their search to the local area or if they will consider other geographic areas. A key decision that individuals must make is whether they prefer to work in small or large companies. Both types of organizations have advantages and disadvantages. This decision should be considered early in the employment process because different markets have to be tapped depending on organizational size.

Finding a suitable employee or a suitable job requires careful planning and hard work. Some jobs are advertised in the open market. Notices may be placed in the classified ads of newspapers, or jobs may be listed with school placement departments, employment agencies, and/or governmental agencies. In these situations, the employment process for the applicant usually consists of making a telephone call or writing an application letter, sending a résumé, completing an application form, and participating in interviews.

Advertisements and placement agencies are not the only source of jobs, however. In fact, employment specialists estimate that only about one-third of all jobs are advertised in the newspaper or posted with agencies. Two-thirds of the jobs may be in what is often referred to as the hidden job market.

Primary sources for finding out about jobs on the hidden job market are knowledgeable individuals and specialized publications. Networking with these individuals is a key way to find out about some of the best jobs that are available. Well-informed people in a field will often know about jobs that are available in that field.

Many people have no idea how to go about networking for job information. A good way to start is to list people you know who might be able to provide you with information about jobs. Too many people try to be exclusive—on this list, the more names you have, the better your chances are of getting a contact. Your friends, your relatives, your parents' friends, instructors, business associates such as bankers, lawyers, doctors, association members, and any other contacts you can think of are all potential sources of job information. A nice, friendly letter letting them know you are in the job market and telling them you value their advice may be all you need for someone to suggest that you contact a particular company.

The individual who searches only advertised sources or agencies may miss out on the best opportunities. The individual who is willing to devote the time and energy necessary to search for the best possible job may create a number of desirable alternatives.

Strategic thinking and persistent effort are needed to find the right job.

Networking to discover jobs on the "hidden" job market may be the best career skill to learn.

Sometimes just asking friends and associates to review your résumé and application letter will produce suggestions of individuals you can contact about a position.

APPLICANT TRACKING SYSTEMS

Many companies use specialized technology to manage the employment process. The résumés they receive are scanned and maintained on-line. Then when the company has a position to fill, someone runs a keyword search to match the job requirements with the electronic résumés that are contained in the database.

Technology is changing the way companies manage the employment process.

Most large companies (companies with more than 1,000 employees) tend to own and manage their own applicant tracking systems. However, some large companies and many smaller companies contract with a company to maintain the database and track applicants for them. Human resource professionals estimate that about half of all companies use electronic applicant tracking. The trend today is to have a computer do the initial screening of employment communications rather than have employees decide which ones should be considered. Regardless of which approach is used—company owned or contracted service—résumés that will be read initially by computers need to be prepared differently than résumés that will be read only by human beings. These differences are described in the section on preparing résumés.

EMPLOYMENT COMMUNICATIONS

The employment process often involves numerous communications. In the early stages of the process, telephone calls, the résumé, and the application letter are the key ways in which job candidates communicate with prospective employers. The most important point to remember about these communications is that they are not designed to get you a job.

The primary goal of employment communications is to get an interview—do not expect to get a job from these communications.

Few, if any, companies would hire an individual on the basis of an application letter, a telephone conversation, or a résumé. Most companies insist on seeing and talking with an individual before they make a commitment to hire that person. Therefore, these preliminary communications should be designed to gain an employment interview.

TRADITIONAL RÉSUMÉ

The résumé is usually the first employment document that is prepared. It is an outgrowth of the self-analysis process. A résumé, sometimes called a data sheet or vita, is a summary of facts about you. Many people prepare one résumé; then they duplicate it and send it to multiple companies. Today, the capabilities of technology make it easy to store the résumé and customize or personalize it for each company.

A key decision in the employment process is whether to prepare a traditional résumé or an "electronic" résumé.

The style and content of résumés vary widely because they are designed to present the strengths of the individual in the most effective way. The design of a résumé is often determined by the amount and type of experience that an individual has had. A person who has had extensive experience should design a résumé that presents the results the individual accomplished in the work environment. As a manager, for example, you would illustrate your results by what you were able to get other people to achieve. A person with little or no experience should design a résumé that presents the skills that the individual has developed and the potential of the individual.

Human resource professionals screen résumés for results (usually reflected by action verbs); computers screen résumés for keywords that typically are nouns.

Résumés that report results are called chronological résumés. Generally, they are prepared in reverse chronological order because the most recent information is usually the most important. Résumés that present skills and abilities are usually called functional résumés. Both types of résumés present basically the same information; they simply organize and format it differently to emphasize strengths.

Résumés should be concise and should use action verbs liberally. They should also be error-free and formatted attractively. Statements are telescoped (shortened rather than written in complete sentences). The pronoun I is avoided because the entire résumé is written about the individual.

ELECTRONIC RÉSUMÉS

The advice to focus heavily on action verbs in a résumé works very well for traditional résumés that are screened by employees rather than a computer. However, that advice does not work well for electronic résumés that are tracked by computer. Tracking is usually done by keywords. As you know from searching for information on the Internet and other on-line references, keywords tend to be nouns. Therefore, the computer does not match many of the action verbs that are used extensively in résumés.

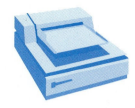

Scanners vary significantly in capability; use conservative assumptions in estimating what scanners can do.

The format of electronic résumés should be simple but attractive. Most scanning systems can handle bold print. Sans serif fonts scan better than serif fonts (letters with portions extended above or below the line). Avoid clip art and vertical lines because they present problems for many scanners. The first line of a résumé becomes the file name in many of the scanning systems; therefore, your name should be the only thing on the top line of the document.

This Arial font is a sans serif font.
This Times New Roman font is a serif font.

Some human resources professionals are recommending that a keyword section be included on your résumé. The keyword section is a list of keywords that describe your abilities and experience.

Other human resources professionals think that this approach is blatant and that it would be better to use the more subtle approach of including nouns in several sections of your résumé. An important consideration is that only the initial screening is done by computer. Once the résumé has been screened by the computer through a keyword matching process, the résumé is reviewed by individuals responsible for the vacant position. Since many résumés are ultimately read by both computers and employees, these professionals recommend that nouns be used extensively in the résumé rather than including a keywords section.

Keyword sections on résumés usually use the heading Keywords: *followed by a list of keywords that describe the applicant.*

Functional, reverse chronological, and electronic résumés usually contain the same types of information. The format and style vary somewhat.

Identifying information. The applicant's name is the most important piece of information and should be placed on the first line of the résumé. The address and telephone number should also be included in the identifying information. Many individuals include their E-mail addresses as well. Students often include both temporary addresses and telephone numbers at school and permanent home addresses and telephone numbers.

Always try to sequence and present information in a way that highlights your strengths and minimizes your weaknesses.

Career objective. The career objective is a statement specifying the type of position the applicant is seeking. Employment specialists often debate the value of including a career objective. Proponents believe that the career objective is important because it helps the recruiter match individuals with jobs that are available. It also shows the prospective employer that the individual has done some self-analysis and knows what he or she wants to do.

Opponents of the career objective point out that the career objective sets the tone for what the applicant wants, but employers are more interested in what the applicant has to offer the company. Opponents also point out that many applicants do not really know what they want to do so their career objective is often nebulous. Writing too narrow an objective can also be a limiting factor.

Most employment specialists advise students who have not yet had any job experience to include a career objective. A student's educational background could be applied in many different ways; therefore, it is helpful to let a prospective employer know what type of career is desired.

Summary of qualifications. The summary of qualifications provides a brief statement of what you believe are your most important qualifications. This section highlights what you believe are the key qualifications that match the job. Some employment specialists suggest that the summary of qualifications offers a good alternative to the career objective because it tells the employer what you have to offer rather than what you want.

This section may provide an opportunity to include nouns in the qualifications that would serve as keywords if the résumé is tracked electronically. In situations in which the résumé is in response to an ad or published job description, the qualification section can be tailored to show that you match the requirements of the job—regardless of whether the résumé is screened by the computer or an employee.

Most students feature education on the résumé because they have limited, if any, job experience.

Education. This section usually includes a listing of the diplomas and degrees earned, the schools attended, and the dates of attendance. The highest or most recent degree is listed first. Most employment specialists indicate that they like to see grade point averages listed when people are just out of school and have little experience. Many indicate that when students leave their grade point average off their résumés, the company assumes it was left off because the grades are not very good.

Experience. This section provides information about job positions previously held. The order of listing is from the most recent back to the initial experience. Usually job titles, employers, dates, and a brief description of each position are included. The position description should emphasize results rather than activities. At the same time, remember that nouns serve as keywords more than verbs do.

Honors and activities. Some résumés contain a special section for honors, hobbies, special interests, or activities. In other résumés, this information is integrated in the education or experience sections. Students with limited experience often use this section to show leadership potential. Many employment specialists recommend including interests because the information in this section can be used as an icebreaker in the interview. It gives the recruiter something easy to talk about that will put the applicant at ease.

Special skills. This section gives the applicant an opportunity to highlight special skills, such as computer skills, language skills, leadership skills, or some highly specialized skill. Many applicants prefer to integrate skills in other sections of the résumé.

References and personal data. Historically, these two sections were included on the résumé. Today, most employment specialists recommend that these sections be excluded from résumés. Personal data is excluded to avoid the appearance of providing discriminatory information. References normally are not checked in the initial employment stages; therefore, they are not necessary on the résumé. However, a typed list of references should be brought to every job interview so that you will have them if asked about references during the interview.

Two résumés are illustrated (below and on the next page). These résumés include nouns in case they are tracked electronically. The first résumé puts emphasis on education and qualifications. The second résumé puts emphasis on skills developed through experience.

Margaret C. Long

Temporary Address (Until June 1)
9385 Scanlan Avenue
Salina, KS 67401-3039
(913) 555-0142
E-mail: mlong@plains.ks.edu

Permanent Address
2847 Monroe Avenue
Boise, ID 83704-2531
(208) 555-0129

Career Objective

An entry-level desktop publishing position with an opportunity to advance to positions involving graphic design.

Qualifications and Special Skills

Desktop publishing skills. Key at 85 words per minute. In-depth knowledge of PublishWrite and DesignArt desktop publishing software as well as all major word processing, graphic, and presentation software.

General computer skills. Basic knowledge of spreadsheet, database, project management, and accounting software.

Interpersonal/communication skills. Excellent interpersonal skills. Work effectively as a team member. Experience and training in making presentations supported by computer visuals. Superior writing, editing, and design layout skills.

Education

Plains Junior College, Salina, Kansas, Associate in Arts degree, 1996. Majored in office systems and graphic design and earned a 3.5 grade point average on a 4.0 scale.

Midtown High School, Boise, Idaho, diploma, 1994. Graduated in top 5 percent of class.

Leadership Activities

President (1995–96) and vice president (1994–1995) of the Office Systems Association.

Active in the Midtown Honor Society and Cardinal Service Club. Editor of the Midtown News (1993–94).

Experience

Production manager of the Plains Reporter, 1995–96. Worked 25 hours per week. Responsible for layout and production of the Plains Reporter, published three times per week. Met every publishing deadline. Earned design award.

Assistant Production manager of the Plains Reporter, 1994–1995. Worked 20 hours per week assisting with layout and production. Supervised all desktop publishing activities.

Lynn D. Cochran
2746 Browndale Avenue
Minneapolis, MN 55424
(612) 555-0139

Career Objective

A sales management position with a medical technology company.

Work Experience

Medical Systems, Inc. Rochester, Minnesota.

Senior Account Manager. (1996–present) Manage 10 large hospital accounts and sell integrated medical systems solutions. Coordinate all sales activities of three account managers. Exceeded sales budget by at least 20 percent each quarter. Earned President's Club status.

Account Manager. (1994–1996) Sold integrated medical systems solutions to hospitals. Met and exceeded sales goals every quarter. Earned President's Club status.

Sales Trainee. (1993–1994) Sold medical systems to physicians. Coordinated training for users.

MedOffice, Inc. Rochester, Minnesota.

Technical Assistant. (1991–1993; worked 20 hours per week while in school) Installed medical office management software and provided technical assistance to customers. Trained users on software purchased.

Education

Medical Technology Institute, Rochester, Minnesota. Associate in Science degree, 1993, majored in medical technology.

Technical Training Seminars, Boston, Massachusetts.

Technical Selling Skills. Attended a six-week training program designed to teach technical representatives how to sell to physicians and office staff. May, 1993.

Management Development for Technical Sales Representatives. Attended a three-week training program designed to prepare account managers and sales representatives for management positions. September, 1996.

Community Service

Volunteer at Children's Hospital (10 hours per week)
Community Fund representative
Director of church outreach program
Coach, Peewee Soccer Team

APPLICATION LETTER

Letters that look like they are mass produced are not likely to be effective. Obtaining a name and writing to an individual is far more effective.

The main purpose of an application letter is to get an interview. As noted earlier, employers tend not to hire individuals on the basis of a letter or telephone call. Therefore, the focus of the application letter should be on convincing the employer to give you the opportunity to demonstrate why you should be hired.

TYPES OF APPLICATION LETTERS

Three types of application letters are written.

- One type is in response to an ad or a listing in a placement bureau. The employer has solicited letters of application. The applicant knows that the position is available and usually has specific information about the position. An example of this type of application letter is on page 209.

- Another type of letter is written at the suggestion of a networking contact who knows individuals in a company that has or may have positions available. An example letter is on page 210.
- The third type of letter is written so that it can be adapted to send to many different companies that may have positions available. You do not know a specific person to contact in the company. This letter corresponds to the cold call in sales. An example letter is on page 211.

WRITING STRATEGY

The following strategy with minor modifications can be used for all three types of application letters.

- Establish a point of contact.
- Specify the type of job you are seeking.
- Highlight your major qualifications.
- Refer to the résumé that you will enclose.
- Request an interview.

Note that the strategy for writing the application letter is very similar to the persuasive messages that you learned to write in Chapter 5. The emphasis in the letter of application is on persuading the employer to give you an interview. You are, in effect, trying to sell yourself as a qualified prospective employee who can meet the needs of the employer.

In Chapter 5, you learned that credibility, logical appeal, and psychological appeal can influence behavior. Remember that you are trying to influence the behavior of the prospective employer. To have credibility, the writer must be perceived by the reader to be knowledgeable, sincere, and in control. A message has logical appeal when the reader believes good reasons exist for doing what was asked. A message has psychological appeal when it stimulates the reader's emotions or when it relates to the reader's goals, values, or needs.

Presenting your qualifications effectively demonstrates that you are knowledgeable. The tone of your letter must be sincere. Showing that your qualifications match the requirements of the employer's job is the best logical appeal you can use. You can also use an emotional appeal by presenting your qualifications in a unique or interesting manner, such as providing an account of something special or extremely successful that you did on a previous job.

Point of contact. Establishing a point of contact lets the employer know how you found out about the job opportunity or about the company. People tend to trust individuals they know more than they trust strangers. Therefore, you can gain credibility by association with an individual whom the employer knows and respects. Networking goes farther than just locating an opportunity; it helps to gain favorable attention.

Establishing a point of contact is important even in *cold call* letters. You can always determine a name by calling the company and asking the person who answers the phone to give you the name of the Human Resources manager. You can use your business library or search the Internet for information about the company that can be used as a point of contact. Many libraries keep annual reports. Referring to something in the annual report's letter to stockholders can be used as a way of explaining why you selected a particular company. Articles in business newspapers and journals, such as the *Wall Street*

Establishing a point of contact demonstrates to an employer that you do your homework thoroughly—you network or you do research rather than write an impersonal letter.

*Create effective personal
letterhead to give your
application letter a
professional business
appearance.*

*Place your name on the first
line of the letterhead in case
the letter is scanned. Include
all contact information in the
letterhead rather than in the
body of the letter.*

Journal, Business Week, Fortune, Forbes, and many other publications, make excellent points of contact. All these publications have indexes that can be used to locate information on specific companies.

Applicants who make the effort to establish a reasonable point of contact demonstrate to employers that they have the initiative to do more than is required. That action builds credibility and appeals to employers.

Specify type of job. Specifying the type of job demonstrates to the employer that you have analyzed your qualifications and know what you can do well and what you like to do. A letter inquiring about "any job for which you may be qualified" makes a poor impression. It implies that you are desperate to get a job and will take anything. It also gives the impression that you do not know what you are qualified to do.

Highlight qualifications. The qualifications section of your letter should be action oriented. Most employers look for results-oriented employees. Therefore, you should write in a style that gives the employer the impression that you are accustomed to achieving good results. The important point to make is not just that you are qualified but that you are qualified for the specific job that the employer has available.

Refer to résumé. The résumé provides, in a factual style, information that is more detailed than can be presented in a letter. A simple reference to the résumé is all that is necessary. An effective approach is to make a statement about the résumé or to refer to specific information contained in the résumé. Simply telling an employer that a résumé is enclosed is not as effective.

Request an interview. Obtaining an interview is the purpose of writing the letter; therefore, the request for an interview should be stated positively and confidently. Self-confidence can be implied by asking when the person would like to interview you, rather than if the person would like to interview you. The last paragraph usually contains the request for the interview. As you learned in Chapter 2, the first and last paragraphs are the key emphasis positions in a document; therefore, the last paragraph is the most appropriate place to emphasize that you would like an interview.

The application letter should be prepared on personal letterhead stationery or on plain paper. Word processing software used with a laser printer makes it very easy to create a personal letterhead that can be used for application letters. Individuals who use the letterhead of their present company to apply for a different job demonstrate poor taste and make a bad impression.

The application letter should be edited carefully. An employment communication with errors may jeopardize your opportunity to obtain an interview. The employer may use the documents as an indication of your communication skills and of your attention to details. The best approach is to make the letter as nearly perfect as you can. A good way to think about the application letter is that it is the document that is used to transmit your résumé. It sets the tone for the way that your résumé will be read. Letters illustrating the three types of application letters discussed in this chapter are presented on pages 209–211. Note that with just a few minor modifications, the same letter can be used for all three types of application letters.

Lynn D. Cochran
2746 Browndale Avenue
Minneapolis, MN 55424
(612) 555-0139

Current date

Mr. Sven S. Sandberg
Vice President, Marketing
Medical Technologies, Inc.
1904 Hudson Road
St. Paul, MN 55119-3857

Dear Mr. Sandberg

Your advertisement in the *Medical Management Monthly* specifies
that only applicants with leadership ability, technical competence,
and a proven track record in medical sales should apply for the
position you have available for a sales manager. I can demonstrate
that I possess those three qualities; therefore, please consider me
an applicant for the position.

Management development training and my experience as a senior
account manager enabled me to develop the leadership skills you
desire. I attribute my successful sales record to technical competence
and to my ability to communicate technical information effectively to
nontechnical decision makers and users. The enclosed résumé
presents additional information showing you why I believe I am
qualified to be a sales manager for Medical Technologies, Inc.

May I come in and tell you about the plan I used to turn a sales
territory that was below budget for three years into a territory that
met President's Club requirements every single quarter? You will be
convinced, I am sure, that I can be equally successful as a sales
manager for Medical Technologies, Inc. Please let me know the date
and time that would be most convenient for an interview.

Sincerely

Lynn D. Cochran

Enclosure

Lynn D. Cochran
2746 Browndale Avenue
Minneapolis, MN 55424
(612) 555-0139

Current date

Mr. Sven S. Sandberg
Vice President, Marketing
Medical Technologies, Inc.
1904 Hudson Road
St. Paul, MN 55119-3857

Dear Mr. Sandberg

Randy Willis, a consultant who worked with me to automate the
volunteer schedules and records at Children's Hospital, indicated
that you may have a sales management position available. He
suggested that I contact you about that position.

Management development training and my experience as a senior
account manager enabled me to develop the leadership skills you
desire. I attribute my successful sales record to technical competence
and to my ability to communicate technical information effectively to
nontechnical decision makers and users. The enclosed résumé
presents additional information showing you why I believe I am
qualified to be a sales manager for Medical Technologies, Inc.

May I come in and tell you about the plan I used to turn a sales
territory that was below budget for three years into a territory that
met President's Club requirements every single quarter? You will be
convinced, I am sure, that I can be equally successful as a sales
manager for Medical Technologies, Inc. Please let me know the date
and time that would be most convenient for an interview.

Sincerely

Lynn D. Cochran

Enclosure

Lynn D. Cochran
2746 Browndale Avenue
Minneapolis, MN 55424
(612) 555-0139

Current date

Mr. Sven S. Sandberg
Vice President, Marketing
Medical Technologies, Inc.
1904 Hudson Road
St. Paul, MN 55119-3857

Dear Mr. Sandberg

Your Chief Executive Officer, Ms. Angela Peterson, wrote in this year's annual report that Medical Technologies, Inc., was positioned for long-term success because of its quality products, outstanding employees, and commitment to excellence in customer service. I share those ideals, and I would like to be one of those outstanding employees helping Ms. Peterson achieve those goals. Please consider me for a position in sales management if you have one available.

Management development training and my experience as a senior account manager enabled me to develop the leadership skills you desire. I attribute my successful sales record to technical competence and to my ability to communicate technical information effectively to nontechnical decision makers and users. The enclosed résumé presents additional information showing you why I believe I am qualified to be a sales manager for Medical Technologies, Inc.

May I come in and tell you about the plan I used to turn a sales territory that was below budget for three years into a territory that met President's Club requirements every single quarter? You will be convinced, I am sure, that I can be equally successful as a sales manager for Medical Technologies, Inc. Please let me know the date and time that would be most convenient for an interview.

Sincerely

Lynn D. Cochran

Enclosure

Always answer all questions on the application form honestly.

Prospective employers should provide honest previews of the job and prospective employees should use high standards of integrity in presenting information on their résumés.

APPLICATION FORM

Many companies require each job applicant to complete a standard application form. Much of the information that is requested on the application is similar to the information that is included in a résumé.

Even though the résumé provided by the applicant duplicates much of the information on the application, many companies prefer to have the information on a standard form. This is because standardizing the information facilitates comparison of the qualifications of the candidates. In addition, the company is assured of having all the information required to make a decision. On a résumé, the applicant chooses both the information to be included and the way that information is presented. Honesty and integrity are always important, and it is imperative that information provided on an application be factual and accurate. Inaccurate information provided on an application may result in the individual who was hired being fired on the basis of falsification of company records.

Always bring copies of your résumé and a list of references with you when you visit a company about employment. If you are asked to complete an application form, the well-organized information on the résumé will be extremely helpful.

If you are asked to provide references, you have the information available immediately. Common courtesy requires that an applicant request permission before listing an individual as a reference. Therefore, the prospective employer can be reasonably sure the individual listed is willing to provide information about the applicant.

TECHNOLOGICAL CONNECTIONS

Technology has almost revolutionized the employment process from the perspective of both the employer and the employee. From the employer's perspective, special software programs are used to analyze labor markets and determine the impact of hiring on issues such as discrimination. "Job computers" with scanners and specialized database software are used to track job applicants and manage the hiring process.

From the employee's perspective, technology makes it possible to custom design volumes of employment documents and make them look like they are professionally prepared, original documents. On-line references make it possible for applicants to do extensive research on companies in a timely manner. Software is available to lead prospective employees through the preparation of résumés and to data banks of employment data.

THE SUPERHIGHWAY OF COMMUNICATIONS

INTERNET

The Internet is a virtual gold mine of information about the employment process. Hundreds of documents on a variety of topics relating to employment were produced in a matter of minutes by using a search engine and keywords such as *employment* and *career*. These documents contained several different types of information including:

JOB LISTINGS

- Lists and descriptions of all types of government jobs available
- Lists and descriptions of jobs available in many different industries and in specific companies
- Lists and descriptions of jobs available in various geographic areas
- "Lists of lists" (indexes) of jobs, including where to find lists of jobs in specialized areas
- Web pages from college placement offices, headhunters, employment agencies, and companies listing employment opportunities currently available

INFORMATION ABOUT SPECIFIC POSITIONS AND CAREERS

- Profiles of various jobs that included information about the job, the requirements, career progression in the job, and demographics, such as percentage of males and females in the profession, working conditions and hours, salary levels at various stages of tenure, and reference information about the profession
- Information about careers from professional organizations representing the profession

INFORMATION ABOUT THE EMPLOYMENT PROCESS

- Results of surveys of recruiters, headhunters, and other employment specialists
- List of questions frequently asked in interviews
- Dos and Don'ts for writing résumés and application letters
- Lists of action or power verbs to use in résumés
- Guides for networking

INFORMATION USED IN RESEARCHING COMPANIES

- Articles on various companies from newspapers and journals
- Financial information on public companies
- Company web pages
- Stock reports
- Annual report information
- Directories, including addresses and telephone numbers

The real problem with using the Internet in the employment process is sorting through the masses of data and trying to find reliable, usable data. Caution is advised in using on-line resources. Always ensure that your sources are credible before using the information that is available on the Internet.

MISCOMMUNICATIONS

Sign at a restaurant:

> Open 7 days a week—excluding Sundays

APPLICATION 10A *Review Guide 8:*
Use Effective Sentence and Paragraph Structure

Rewrite the following sentences to improve their structure.

1. Please place the plant in the waiting room near the window.

2. If your arm has a cast on it, it will be removed in approximately six weeks.

3. Pat likes to shop in expensive stores, find good bargains, and decorating the house with those purchases.

Write the following paragraphs as instructed.

4. As part of your self-analysis in preparation for employment, you have been thinking about your strengths and weaknesses. Write a four- or five-sentence paragraph describing your strengths. Put parentheses around the topic sentence. Underline the linking or transitional words you used to make the paragraph coherent.

5. Write a four- or five-sentence paragraph about your weaknesses. Try to show how you have made progress improving on those weaknesses. Put parentheses around the topic sentence. Underline the linking or transitional words you used to make the paragraph coherent.

APPLICATION 10B *Editing and Language Arts Checkpoint*

Carefully read the document that follows; it is packed with errors. Use proofreader's marks to mark all errors in grammar, spelling, word usage, number usage, capitalization, and punctuation. Do not revise sentence or paragraph structure in this activity unless an error exists.

After you have marked all corrections directly on this document, access File 10B on your template disk and make the corrections you marked. If you do not have access to the template disk, key the document, making the corrections as you key.

After you have made all corrections, refer to page 240 in Appendix C for the solution and check to see that you corrected all errors. You may use on-line reference tools just as you would if you were doing this as part of your job. Save the file as 10B-sol.

Notice—Position Available for Network Manager

Applications for the new created position of network manager is now

being excepted in the Personal management department. Both internal an

external applicants must complete the standard application from. Forms for

internal applicants must contain the signature of the persons immediate super-

visor before they can be process. The deadline for applications are June 15th.

The new position is a Grade twelve position in the Administrative

Services Division. The new network manager will report direct to the manager

of Administrative Services. The principle reasons this new position was cre-

ated was to provide technical support and training to user of personnel com-

puters on the network and too have one person who will be totally responsible

for developing a comprehensive manual for user's and a network procedures

manual. These position requires a person with computer experience as well

as knowledge of computer operating systems and application software.

Network knowledge and supervisory experience is desirable but they are not required. The knew network manager will be sent to a 3-week training program in San Francisco. The training package was part of the contract for the new network.

The 1st responsibility when the new network manager returns is to develop and offer training courses for all employees who have excess to the network at this cite. The training will compliment the other computer training coarses that are available to employees. The Staff Counsel adviced us to make the courses mandatory for all new network users.

APPLICATION 10C *Writing Employment Messages*

Write the appropriate message for each of the following situations.

1. As part of the planning process for writing your résumé, you should complete the self-analysis you began earlier when you considered your strengths and weaknesses (Questions 4 and 5 in Application 10A). Use the following questions to help you think about the job objective you will use in your employment messages.

   a. Would you prefer to work in a small (fewer than 100 employees), a mid-size (101 to 500 employees) or a large (more than 500 employees) company? What are the advantages and disadvantages of working in each?

   b. What type of working environment do you prefer? Consider factors such as indoor vs. outdoor, formal vs. casual, working alone vs. working on a team, and so on.

   c. What geographic area appeals to you? Are you willing to move to other locations?

   d. What are your major job qualifications?

   e. What kind of salary can you realistically expect to earn on the job you seek?

   f. What is your job objective?

2. Look through the classified section of your local newspaper. Find an ad describing a position in which you would be interested and for which you are qualified.

3. Using your own factual information and the information you gleaned from your self-analysis, write a résumé that you can use to apply for the job you found in 10C-2.

4. Write a letter of application to send with the résumé. Select an appropriate name, title, and address if that information is not provided in the ad. Create a personal letterhead to use for the letter.

5. Your instructor told you that Mr. Jeff Rosenfield, owner of Midway Glass Company, is looking for an assistant this summer. He wants a bright individual with good communication skills and a good work ethic. No special skills are needed. Midway is located at 2736 Main Street. Use your city, state, and postal code. Write a letter applying for the job. Include a copy of your résumé.

6. Mr. Rosenfield interviewed you today. You spent a half hour with Mr. Rosenfield and then you spent about two hours with other employees. Then Mr. Rosenfield took you to lunch. Write an appropriate thank you letter. Confirm your interest in the position. (Refer to Chapter 9 if necessary.)

7. Select a company that might have positions similar to the one you desire. Find out as much as you can about the company. Write a letter inquiring about the availability of a position for which you would be qualified. Include a copy of your résumé.

Chapter 10

APPLICATION 10D *Self-Assessment*

1. Use complete, grammatically correct sentences to answer each of the following items.

   a. Describe ways to find out about jobs on the hidden job market.

   b. What is meant by an applicant tracking system?

   c. How does a traditional résumé differ from an electronic résumé?

   d. What factors should you consider in deciding whether to use a functional or a reverse chronological résumé?

   e. Describe the writing strategy that should be used for a job application letter.

2. Read the following job notices. Select the position for which you are best qualified and are most interested. Write a letter applying for the job.

OFFICE ASSISTANT

Great opportunity for person with excellent computer and communication skills. Prefer person with knowledge of word processing, spreadsheet, and database applications. Send letter and résumé to George Lee, General Manager, Lee and Associates, 213 Main Street, your city, state, and postal code.

MANAGEMENT TRAINEE

Excellent opportunity for bright person with limited experience. Six-month training program leading to management position. Must have good interpersonal skills, good communication skills, and good work ethic. Business background desirable but not required. Send letter and résumé to Joan D. Witt, Personnel Manager, Markson Company, 693 Main Street, your city, state, and postal code.

SALES TRAINEE

Leading office technology firm looking for a confident, aggressive sales trainee who has excellent communication and interpersonal skills. A business background is preferred but not required. Salary plus commission. Great opportunity for high earnings. Send letter and résumé to Richard Adamson, Productivity Systems, Inc., 294 Main Street, your city, state, postal code.

C A S E   S T U D Y

APPLICATION 10E *Heritage Productions*

You are continuing your assignment as asssistant manager in the Human Resources Management (HRM) Department. Mr. Gregory Garrison serves as manager of the department, and his responsibilities were recently expanded to include international job placement. Previously, all recruiting and employment activities were handled in the country in which the job opening was located. Mr. Garrison has asked you to explore how the HRM Department could use the Internet effectively with international recruiting and employment activities. Summarize the information you find in a memo to Mr. Garrison.

Heritage Productions

Address Directory

A

Ms. Elizabeth M. Addison, Director
of Product Development
Stonehedge Publishing Company, Ltd.
180 Piccadilly
London W1A 1 AZ   ENGLAND
Telephone: 071/836-582   FAX: 071/836-5317

A

American-Malaysian Chamber of Commerce
11.03 AMODA, 22, Jalan Imbi
Kuala Lumpur 551000, Malaysia

B

Ms. Carolyn Brandt
Manager Customer Service
Holiday Air, Inc.
PO Box 6958
Columbia, SC 29201-6958

B

Dr. Marshall Burge, Ph.D.
Professor, Business Administration
Central State University
Chattanooga, TN 37406-4829

D

Ms. Elizabeth Davis
Clearwater Industries
4938 Maple Walk Street
Humble, TX 77346-5802.

D

Ms. Yolanda DeShane
Human Resources Director
Hess Industries, Inc.
2948 Cloverdale Road
Gadsden, AL 35903-7184

D

Ms. Roseanne Desselles
12 Essex Street
Beverly, MA 01915-3867

D

Ms. Marjorie Ducate
Chief Executive Officer
GreenGate Industries
1283 Greystone Road
Waterbury, CT 06704-2248

E

The Embassy of Malaysia
2401 Massachusetts Avenue, NW
Washington, DC 20008-2888

H

Ms. Martha Henderson
Henderson & Henderson
3862 Taft Avenue
Oshkosh, WI 54900-4762

H

Heritage Productions, Inc.
390 East Pearson Street
Chicago, IL 60611-9374
(312) 555-0188 [4] 555-0190
Fax: (312) 555-0108 [4] 555-0146

J

Dr. Evelyn Jervey
Jervey and Associates
P.O. Box 2847
Hopkins, SC 29061-2847

K

Mr. William Kerry
Kerry Container Company
PO Box 3857
Milwaukee, WI 53201-3857

K

Dr. Leslie Krisman
4392 Hunter Boulevard, S.
Seattle, WA 98144-3847

M

Ms. Renee Marks
Sales Manager
Resort Wear Boutique
6400 East Camelback Road
Scottsdale, AZ 85251-6973

M

Mr. Robert Mendoza
5938 Blossom Road
Rochester, NY 14610-4298

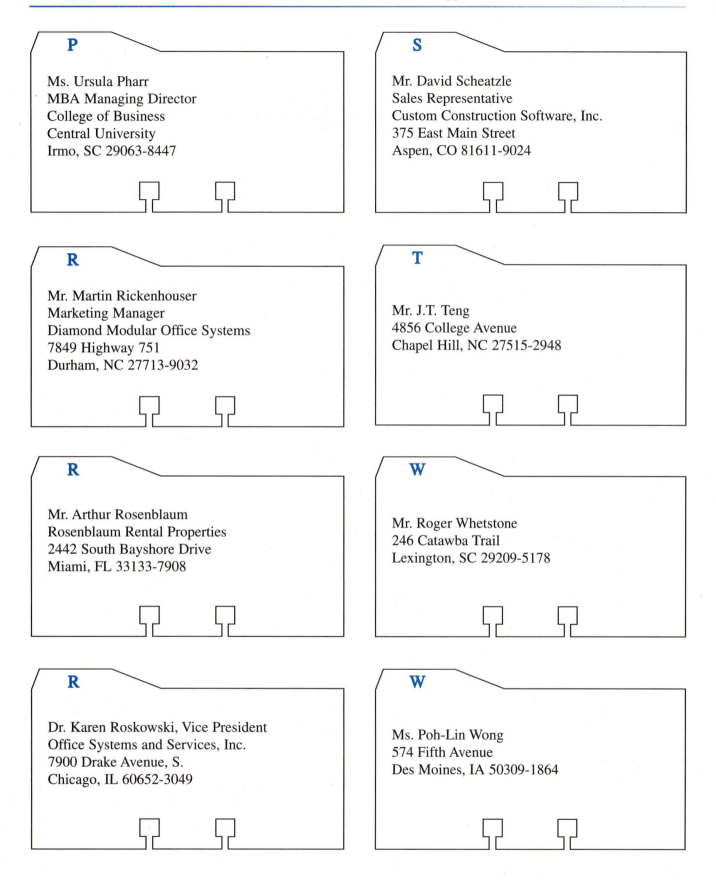

P

Ms. Ursula Pharr
MBA Managing Director
College of Business
Central University
Irmo, SC 29063-8447

R

Mr. Martin Rickenhouser
Marketing Manager
Diamond Modular Office Systems
7849 Highway 751
Durham, NC 27713-9032

R

Mr. Arthur Rosenblaum
Rosenblaum Rental Properties
2442 South Bayshore Drive
Miami, FL 33133-7908

R

Dr. Karen Roskowski, Vice President
Office Systems and Services, Inc.
7900 Drake Avenue, S.
Chicago, IL 60652-3049

S

Mr. David Scheatzle
Sales Representative
Custom Construction Software, Inc.
375 East Main Street
Aspen, CO 81611-9024

T

Mr. J.T. Teng
4856 College Avenue
Chapel Hill, NC 27515-2948

W

Mr. Roger Whetstone
246 Catawba Trail
Lexington, SC 29209-5178

W

Ms. Poh-Lin Wong
574 Fifth Avenue
Des Moines, IA 50309-1864

Editing and Language Arts Checkpoint Guides

Cluster	Description
C	**Capitalization Cluster**
C.1	Capitalize nouns which identify persons, places, things, or trade names, and the pronoun *I*; do not capitalize common nouns.
C.2	Capitalize the first word of a sentence; also capitalize the first word of complete sentences in quotation marks or following a colon.
C.3	Capitalize days of the week, months of the year, and holidays.
C.4	Capitalize titles within an address and those that precede a proper name; generally do not capitalize job titles that stand alone or that follow a name unless they are titles of extreme distinction.
C.5	Capitalize specific department, board, committee, or division names; do not capitalize organizational terms that stand alone.
C.6	Capitalize names of geographic regions or districts; do not capitalize compass directions or general locations.
C.7	Capitalize specific course names and main words in titles of articles and books; do not capitalize general course names.
C.8	Capitalize nouns which precede numbers and letters except page, paragraph, and line references.
G	**Grammar Usage Cluster**
G.1	**Grammar usage—subjects/verbs**
G.1-1	Use complete sentences; i.e., sentences with both a subject and a verb.
G.1-2	Ensure that subjects and verbs agree in person and number; use nouns and objects appropriately.
G.1-3	Use the appropriate tense of a verb to express time.
G.2	**Grammar usage—pronouns**
G.2-1	Ensure that a pronoun agrees with its antecedent in person, number, and gender.
G.2-2	Use the nominative case of pronouns for subject and predicate nouns, the objective case as direct and indirect objects, the possessive case to denote ownership.
G.2-3	Who, whom, which, and that are often confusing. Use who and whom to refer to people. Use who as the subject of a verb; use whom as the object of a verb. Use which and that to refer to things. Use that in restrictive clauses (provide essential information); use which in nonrestrictive clauses (provide additional non-essential information).
G.3	**Grammar usage—adjectives**
G.3-1	Use adjectives to modify nouns or pronouns.
G.3-2	Use positive degree of comparison for equal or no comparison; use comparative degree for comparison of two unequal items; use superlative degree for comparison of three or more items.
G.4	**Adverbs**
G.4-1	Use adverbs to modify verbs, adjectives, and other adverbs.
G.4-2	Use appropriate comparison for adverbs.
G.5	**Grammar usage—prepositions and conjunctions**

Cluster	Description
G.5-1	Use conjunctions appropriately to show connecting relationships.
G.5-2	Use prepositions appropriately to show the relationship between a noun or pronoun and other words in a sentence.
G.6	**Grammar usage—possessives**
G.6-1	Use apostrophe s to form possessive of singular and plural nouns not ending in s.
G.6-2	Use apostrophe to form possessive of plural nouns ending in s.
G.6-3	Use possessive pronouns appropriately.
G.6-4	Add apostrophes to the last owner's name to show joint ownership; use apostrophe s to each owner's name to show separate ownership.
N	**Number Usage For Business Writing Cluster**
N.1	**Number Usage—general conventions**
N.1-1	Spell out numbers one to ten; use numerals for numbers larger than ten.
N.1-2	Spell out numbers that begin sentences.
N.1-3	Use words for approximate or large round numbers (1-2 words); use numbers for round numbers in millions or higher with word modifier.
N.1-4	When two numbers are adjacent, use figures for one and words for the other.
N.1-5	Use figures for page numbers.
N.1-6	Use figures for units of measure and with symbols.
N.2	**Number Usage—dates and time**
N.2-1	Use figures with a.m. and p.m.; use words with o'clock.
N.2-2	Use figures for days following months; use ordinals (th, d, st) only when number precedes the month or is used alone.
N.3	**Number Usage—percentages, fractions, money**
N.3-1	Use figures with percentages (except infrequent use in text if 1-2 words).
N.3-2	Use figures when expressing money.
N.3-3	Do not add zeros to even sums of money; add zeros for mixed sums; do not write numbers in figures then in words except for legal use.
N.3-4	Spell out fractions unless they are in a combination with whole numbers.
N.4	**Number Usage—addresses**
N.4-1	Use words for street names one to ten; figures for numbers above ten.
N.4-2	Use figures for highways.
N.4-3	Use figures for house numbers and post office boxes except for the number one.
P	**Punctuation Cluster**
P.1	**Punctuation—comma**

Cluster	Description
P.1-1	Use a comma to set off introductory words, long introductory phrases, and introductory dependent clauses.
P.1-2	Use a comma to set off independent clauses joined by a coordinating conjunction; do not use a comma to separate a compound verb
P.1-3	Use a comma to separate three or more items in a series (the comma before a conjunction is optional)
P.1-4	Use a comma to set off a nonrestrictive clause or phrase; do not use a comma with a restrictive clause or phrase.
P.1-5	Use a comma to set off nonessential or interrupting elements in a sentence.
P.1-6	Use a comma to set off words of direct address.
P.1-7	Use a comma to separate the day from the year or date and the city from the state.
P.1-8	Use a comma to introduce a quotation.
P.1-9	Use a comma to set off contrasting phrases and clauses and for transitional words.
P.1-10	Use a comma to set off two or more parallel adjectives (*and* could substitute for the comma).
P.2	**Punctuation—colon, semicolon**
P.2-1	Use a colon to introduce enumerations, lists, or a long, formal quote and between hours, minutes, and seconds when figures are used.
P.2-2	Use a semicolon to separate independent clauses when the conjunction is omitted.
P.2-3	Use a semicolon to separate independent clauses linked by conjunctive adverbs, transitional words, or phrases.
P.2-4	Use a semicolon between items in a series when the items contain commas.
P.3	**Punctuation—period, question mark, exclamation point**
P.3-1	Use a period after a complete sentence, indirect question, or courteous request.
P.3-2	Use a question mark after a direct question or a series of questions.
P.3-3	Use an exclamation point after emotional words, phrases, or exclamatory statements.
P.4	**Punctuation—hyphen, apostrophe, quotation marks**
P.4-1	Use a hyphen to join a compound adjective that forms a single unit preceding the noun it modifies; do not use a hyphen if the first word is an adverb ending in *ly*.
P.4-2	Use a hyphen to join compound numbers between 21 and 99 and fractions when they are spelled out and used as a modifier.
P.4-3	Use a hyphen with the prefixes *ex*, *self*, and between a prefix and a capitalized word.
P.4-4	Use an apostrophe with contractions, to show omissions, and as a symbol for feet and minutes.
P.4-5	Use quotation marks to enclose titles and direct quotations; long quotations that are indented do not require quotation marks.
T	**Titles of Works**
T.1	Italicize title of books, newspapers, magazines, movies, and plays.
T.2	Put quotation marks around parts of a larger work, such as the title of an article or column in a newspaper.
T.3	Put quotation marks around titles of radio and television shows.

Cluster	Description	
W	**Word Usage / Spell Check Challenge Cluster**	
W.1	a	article used before words beginning with a consonant
	an	article used before words beginning with a vowel
W.2	accept	(v.) receive or take; agree to
	except	(prep.) leave out; other than; (v.) omit; exclude
W.3	advice	(n.) recommendation
	advise	(v.) give counsel
W.4	affect	(v.) change or influence
	effect	(n.) outcome or result; (n.) to cause or bring about
W.5	appraise	(v.) establish value
	apprise	(v.) notify or inform
W.6	capital	(n.) wealth or net worth; city that is seat of government
	capitol	(n.) chief building of a government; state house
W.7	cite	(v.) quote or summon
	sight	(n.) vision; worth seeing
	site	(n.) location or place
W.8	coarse	(adj.) rough texture or finish
	course	(n.) line of motion; series of lectures; place to play golf; method
W.9	complement	(v.) to complete or fill
	compliment	(n.) praise; present with gift
W.10	council	(n.) an appointed or elected group of advisers
	counsel	(n.) advice; (v.) advise
W.11	eminent	(adj.) distinguished; famous
	imminent	(adj.) threatening; about to happen
W.12	form	(n.) shape, standard document
	from	(prep.) separation; away
W.13	knew	(v.) past tense of know
	new	(adj.) recently made; unused
W.14	loose	(adj.) not restrained or secured
	lose	(v.) suffer a loss; not know where to find
W.15	peace	(n.) calm; tranquil
	piece	(n.) portion of; quantity
W.16	personal	(adj.) private; individual
	personnel	(n.) staff; employees
W.17	exceed	(vb.) go beyond
	precede	(v.t.) come before
	proceed	(v.i.) continue; go forward
W.18	principal	(adj. or n.) head of school; main; chief; sum of money
	principle	(n.) basic truth; rule of conduct
W.19	quiet	(adj.) still; noiseless
	quite	(adv.) completely; very
W.20	stationary	(adj.) fixed; not moving
	stationery	(n.) writing paper
W.21	perspective	(n.) mental view
	prospective	(adj.) likely to happen
W.22	access	(n.) able to obtain or make use of
	excess	(adj.) more than the usual or specified

Application 2B—Solution Document

TO: Department Managers

FROM: Your Name

DATE: May 20, 19—

SUBJECT: Technology Changes

    The **Executive Committee** plans to **meet** on **Tuesday**, June **6,** 1997, at **two**
C.5   G.1-3   C.3   P.1-7   N.2-1
o'clock to develop a strategic plan for implementing technology changes. At **its** meeting
G.6-3
last **March 15,** the **members** of the committee discussed our current technology status
N.2-2   C.1
with Ashley **Price,** a leading **consultant** with Central Technology **Services,** and asked for
P.1-5   C.4   C.1
her **advice. She** agreed to **appraise** our **situation and** to report back to us.
W.3   G.2-2   W.5   P.1-2
    Ashley called **Rick,** our **personnel** manager, this **past** week and **said, "May I**
P.1-5   W.16   G.3-2   P.1-8 C.2
interview **five managers** and about **twenty experienced,** knowledgeable computer **users?**
N.1-1 C.4   N.1-3   P.1-10   P.3-2
If it is possible, Rick, please schedule the interviews during the **first** part of next **week."**
N.1-1   P.4-5
Rick **is** scheduling **three-fourths** hour slots for **managers'** interviews **and a half-hour**
G.1-2   N.3-4   G.6-2   W.1   P.4-2
slot for each computer **users** interview. All managers should do **their** best to
G.6-1   G.2-1
accommodate **this request** (or **these requests**) **from** Rick for staff and managerial time.
G.2-1   W.12
If you are unable to schedule an interview early next **week,** please call me **immediately**
P.1-1   G.4-1
so that I can **choose** someone else **who** can participate.
G.1-2   G.2-3
    Please report **to Conference Room A** in our **new** facility on Highway **10** on the
G.5-2 C.8   W.13   N.4-2
south side of town for your interview. This **site** is **more** convenient for staff than the
C.6   W.7   G.4-2
building at **One Main Street,** and it is very quiet. **Reminder!** Allow 15 minutes to get
N.4-3   P.1-2   W.19   P.3-3
there in plenty of time for your interview. **Also,** please read the 12-page report that is
G.4-1   P.1-1
attached. The information on **page 5** about our mainframe **computer will be of**
C.8   N.1-5   G.1-1
(**computer may be of,** or **computer is of**) particular interest.   **━━━▶**

As our **consultant** points out in the report, personal **computers, not mainframe**
C.4   P.1-9
computers, are the wave of the future. About **75 percent** of our computing is handled by
P.1-9   N.3-1
our mainframe. **Two hundred** personal computers handle the other **25 percent** of our
N.1-2   N.3-1
computing. Of the **200, fifty** (or **of the two-hundred, 50**) are 386 processors. Our
N.1-4
consultant **counsels** us that the **computers with 386 processors** need to be replaced at
W.10   P.1-4
one time rather **than** in a **piecemeal** fashion. We also need to install **a network, upgrade**
G.5-1   W.15   P.1-3
software, and add (or **upgrade software and add**) more storage capability. If we

accept our **consultant's advice,** our **Long-Range** Budget **Committee** will, of **course,**
W.2   G.6-1   W.3   P.4-1   C-5   W.8
have to determine the **effect** replacing **these** computers will have on our **capital** budget
W.4   G.2-1   W.6
before we **proceed** with this action.
W.17
          The predicted cost is **$2 million which** is **significantly higher** than our current
C.2   N.1-3   G.2-3   P.4-1
budget for computer hardware and **software; consequently,** we will have to act very
P.2-3   P.1-9
cautiously. I estimate it will cost **$2,400** to replace each 386 **computer; the** (or
G.4-2   N.3-3   P.2-2
computer. The) software will be an additional **$500.** We only owe **$5,000** on the
N.3-2   N.3-3
principal of the loan on the mainframe **computer;** therefore, we will probably keep it.
W.18   P.2-2
          It's imminent that our technology will be **upgraded; we** (or **upgraded. We**)
P.4-4 W.11   P.2-2
must **complement** our investment in hardware with an investment in our **personnel.** We
W.9   W.16
have explored both **self-paced** training and the new course, **Arntson Computer-Based**
P.4-3   C.7
Training for Windows. We will report on all of these developments at the **June** meeting.
C.3

Application 3B—Solution Document

TO: Jan Marks, Training Manager

FROM: Student's Name

DATE: June 8, 19—

SUBJECT: Effective Team Building Training Materials

Thank you for giving me **an** opprtunity to review the *Effective Team Building* training
_{W.1}
materials. I **examined** the training package **from** both the **perspective** of the trainer and our
_{G.1-3}   _{W.12}   _{W.21}
personnel who would take the **course**. I also tried to **appraise** the value relative to **its** cost.
_{W.16}   _{W.8}   _{W.5}   _{G.6}
From the **trainer's** perspective, the materials **are** comprehensive. The package **includes**
_{G.6-1}   _{G.1-2}   _{G.1-2}
an **outline,** a trainee manual, audio and video **tapes,** slides, and an assessment. The content is
_{P.1-3}   _{P.1-3}
relevant and is **written** in a **clear,** concise way. Very little reinforcement is **provided, however**.
_{G.1-3}   _{P.1-10}   _{P.1-9}
From the **learner's** perspective, the material has only one major **flaw**. The learner is not
_{G.6-1}   _{G.2-1}
required to participate **actively**. Overall **though,** the program is **quite** good.
_{G.4-1}   _{P.1-1}   _{W.19}
The complete program with materials for **75** trainees is **priced** at **$6,000** or about **$80**
_{N.1-1}   _{G.1-3}   _{N.3-3}   _{N.3-2}
per trainee. Additional training packets are **$60 each,** which will make the per employee cost
_{N.3-2} _{P.1-4}
slightly lower if we train all **those** employees **who** work in a team environment. This program
_{G.4-1}   _{G.2-2}   _{G.2-3}
is the **most** expensive of the **three** programs that we have evaluated. These costs do **not, of**
_{G.3-2}   _{N.1-1}   _{P.1-5}
course, include the time of our employees.
_{P.1-5}
Since one additional training program is scheduled to arrive for review on June **15**, I
_{N.2-2}
recommend that the decision be **postponed** to see if that program is more cost **effective than**
_{G.1-3}   _{W.4}   _{G.5-1}
this one. I plan to be at the Highway **12** Training Center on the **16th** of **June,** and I will be
_{N.4-2}   _{N.2-2}   _{P.1-2}
happy to review the materials while I am **there** if you would like me to do so.
_{G.4-1}

Application 4B—Solution Document

The Board of Directors of the Economic Alliance **has** scheduled a meeting with Robert
_{C.2}   _{G.1-2}
West, Mayor of Horrell **Hill;** Judy Ledbetter, President of County **Council;** and Wayne
                                          _{P.2-4}   _{W.10} _{P.2-4}
Roxbury, Secretary of **Commerce;** at **1:45** on **Tuesday,** March 26. The primary purpose of the
_{P.1-4}   _{P.2-4} _{P.2-1}   _{P.1-7}
meeting is to identify two **pieces** of land **north** of Highway **10** that have **100** acres per **site** and
                          _{W.15}   _{C.6}   _{N.4-2}   _{N.1-6}   _{W.7}
take **initial** steps to obtain options to purchase this land. **This** step is critical so that we will not
      _{G.3-1}   _{G.1-2}
lose out on economic development prospects again because of our inability to locate suitable
_{W.14}
sites for manufacturing plants immediately.
_{W.7}

The Economic Alliance will also review Bob **Smith and Tom Graham's** proposal to
                                                                              _{G.6-4}
upgrade the conference room and shift **from** portable projection equipment to a **stationary**
                                              _{W.12}   _{W.20}
multimedia platform for presentations to visiting prospects. The funds are available for the

project; permission is **needed** to build a base platform that is **12** feet long, **6** feet deep, and
_{P.2-2}   _{G.1-3}   _{N.1-6}   _{N.1-6}
10 inches high. The multimedia podium will be mounted on this base platform.
_{N.1-6}

The last item **proposed** is a plan to beautify Rosewood Boulevard between **First** Street
                          _{G.4-2}   _{N.4-1}
and **Ninth** Street. This area is the gateway to our city and **needs** to be enhanced with
      _{N.4-1}   _{G.1-2}
landscaping, benches, and appropriate lighting to create a positive first impression for visitors

to the city. The landscape architect with **whom** we have consulted has provided a cost estimate
                                          _{G.2-3}
for the project. **An** architectural drawing of the area will be on display at the meeting.
                  _{W.1 and C.2}   _{P.1-1}
The Board **welcomes** your comments or suggestions on these topics prior to the
              _{G.1-2}
meeting. Please send them to me as early as possible.

Application 5B—Solution Document

Thank you for giving me the opportunity to review the Productivity Improvement and Cost Reduction proposal **Christopher** McBride **submitted** to you and to give my assessment of
C.1　　　　　　　　　　　　　G.1-3
it. I analyzed the proposal **carefully,** and I have a number of **reservations** about it even though
　　　　　　　　　　G.4-2　　P.1-2　　　　　　　　　　　G.1-2
Christopher McBride is an **eminent** consultant.
　　　　　　　　　　　　　　　W.11

My **principal** concern is that the approach Christopher proposed is **a** standard industrial
　　　　W.18　　　　　　　　　　　　　　　　　　　　　　　　　W.1
engineering approach. **Its** major emphasis is on efficiency rather than on **effectiveness.** The
　　　　　　　　　　G.6-3　　　　　　　　　　　　　　　　　　W.4
industrial engineering approach works reasonably **well** for some factory and routine clerical
　　　　　　　　　　　　　　　　　　　　　　　G.4-1
operations; however, it generally does not produce good results in a work setting involving
　　P.2-3　　　　　P.1-9
professionals. My second concern **is** the cost quoted. The first phase cost of **$25,000** is about
　　　　　　　　　　　　　　　　　G.1-2　　　　　　　　　　　　　　N.3-3
20 percent too high.
N.3-1　　　　G.4-1

As we discussed earlier, most of your **personnel** are professional employees—many of
　　　　　　　　　　　　　　　　　W.16
whom are doing routine work that could be **delegated** to support staff. Delegating **effectively**
G.2-3　　　　　　　　　　　　　　　　　G.1-3　　　　　　　　　　　　W.4
would reduce **costs** and enhance the positions of your support staff **substantially**. **Christopher's**
　　　　　　G.6-1　　　　　　　　　　　　　　　　　　　　　G.4-1　　　　G.6-1
proposal **does** not address this issue at all.
　　　　G.1-2

My **advice** to you is to try to obtain a proposal that **focuses** on effectiveness and that is
　　　W.3　　　　　　　　　　　　　　　　　　　G.1-2
designed for professional employees. I have a meeting in your building on **Monday, March 14,**
　　　　　　　　　　　　　　　　　　　　　　　　C.3　　　　P.1-7　　　　　P.1-7
from 2:15 to 3:15 in **Conference Room C** and could meet with you about the proposal at 3:30.
W.12　　P.2-1　　　P.2-1　　　C.1
Just **let** me know if you want to meet at that time.
　　　G.1-2

Application 6B—Solution Document

Data from the Outsourcing Printing Report clearly showed that the cost of printing could be reduced **substantially** (G.4-1) by discontinuing the outsourcing of many of VanHuss Industries printing jobs. Therefore, a **second** (N.1-1) phase of the report **was authorized** (G.1-2 G.1-3) to determine the feasibility of setting up an in-house electronic publishing system.

Problem

The primary purpose of **this** (G.2-1) phase of the project **was** (G.1-2) to determine the percentage and type of work **that** (G.2-3) could be **handled** (G.1-3) internally. This information can then be **used** (G.1-3) to determine the best and most cost **effective** (W.4) system **to** (G.5-2) meet the needs of VanHuss Industries.

Supporting Data

All of the request **forms** (W.12) for outside printing for the **past** (G.4-1) year were collected and analyzed to determine the type and volume of printing. In many cases, job samples **had** (G.1-3) to be obtained and were analyzed by the printing production team **who** (G.2-3) determined whether or not the job could be handled internally. Four electronic printing system proposals from local vendors were analyzed to determine capabilities and prices.

Data Analysis

The **analysis** (G.1-2) of the request forms for outside printing showed that during the past year about **90** (N.3-1) percent of the black and white printing and about **40** (N.3-1) percent of the color printing could have been done **internally** (G.4-1) on an electronic publishing **system** (G.1-2). All four of the systems that **were** (G.1-2) demonstrated to the evaluation team could have handled **those** (G.2-2) jobs that were identified as internal jobs.

All four **systems** (G.2-1) include **high-resolution** (P.4-1) laser printers with the capability of handling color as well as black and white copy. The proposals **from** (W.12) all four vendors **include software,** (G.1-2) **scanners, and two** (P.1-3 N.1-1) workstations with **two**-page (N.1-1) display monitors. The Hess system **uses** (G.1-2) two separate printers—one for color printing and the other for black and white printing. The cost of the Hess system is **$41,750** (N.3-3). This cost is **$2,000** (N.3-2) more **than** (G.5-1) the other **systems; however,** (P.2-3 P.1-9) the system **has** (G.1-2) advanced features that make it feasible to do additional jobs internally.

Specifications for the four systems and a complete cost analysis are attached. ➡

Conclusion

The conclusion of the Outsourcing Printing Report indicated that an in-house system could be

justified at a cost of **$80,000** if at least **40** percent of the printing volume could be shifted
                    N.3-2   N.3-1
internally. The volume of printing that could be shifted internally **far** exceeds the minimum
                                                                   G.4-1
requirements, and all systems evaluated meet the cost restrictions. The Hess electronic
       P.1-2
publishing system meets the needs of VanHuss Industries **better** than the other three systems.
                                                         G.4-2
Recommendation

The Hess system should be purchased and installed within the next **six** weeks. This time frame
                                                                N.1-1
allows time **for personnel** in the Printing Center to be adequately trained before the
            G.5-2 W.16
outsourcing contract non-renewal notice must be given.

Application 7B—Solution Document

PRESENTATION TO SELECTED STAFF—NOVEMBER 15, 19—

Would you like to have **12** extra hours a week to devote to the responsibilities you think
are the **most** important of everything you do in your **job?** Dr. Ashu **Sopios,** an **eminent expert,**
completed a communications audit for our company. His conclusion **was** that staff members in the
Business Services Department and the Claims Department could save an average of 12 hours per
week if the company **developed** an extensive file of **form** documents for situations that **lend**
themselves to form applications.

As a way of **proceeding** with this task, **Dr.** Sopios suggested that we first identify
situations in **which** form letters could be used **effectively**. The **second** step is to determine the
type of form that would be best for each situation. Then form letters can be drafted by a team of
employees **who** are knowledgeable in the area. A **cross-functional** team will review the letters
before approving **them**.

Ten supervisors identified about **fifty** situations in which form letters would save a
significant amount of time. To qualify as a situation requiring a form letter, an average of five
letters a week must be written to customers to solve that situation. Variable forms or form
paragraphs could be used **effectively** in most of the situations. Because complete forms are
impersonal and guide forms are inefficient, the supervisors recommended that neither complete
forms **nor** guide forms be used.

Supervisors plan to name **five** teams this week to develop the first draft of the form letters.
Each team will be asked to prepare ten form letters. After all letters have been **drafted,** the **cross-**
functional team will review the letters and either approve them or suggest revisions. Employees
who **draft** correspondence in these two areas will be provided with a list and a brief description of
all form letters as well as with a disk containing the form **letters.**

Application 8B—Solution Document

Current date

Dr. Leslie Krisman
4392 Hunter Boulevard S.
Seattle, WA 98144-3847

Dear Dr. Krisman

    The members of the University **Alumni Association who** were present at our annual
                         C.1   G.2-3
meeting truly benefited from **your** outstanding presentation, "Balancing **Life's Demands."** Many
                         G.6-3   G.6-1   P.4-5
members commented **that** the ideas you presented would help all of **us** not only to reduce stress,
G.2-1   G.2-3   G.2-2
but also to live a fuller and more enriched life. Several members called and **asked** me to print
                                                                  G.1-3
your presentation in the *Alumni News* so that they could share it with friends and colleagues who
                                T.1
were not fortunate enough to hear you.
G.1-2
    May we share your ideas with the members of the University **Alumni Association** by
                                                   C.1
including a **300**-word abstract of your presentation in the next **issue?** Your article would be
G.2-2   N.1-1   P.3-2
featured as the lead story with the report of the annual meeting. We would, of **course,** include your
                                                      W.8
picture and brief biographical information about you with the article. In order to meet our press

deadlines, we would need to have all information in our office by the **20th** day of this month.
      P.1-1   N.2-2
    Authors of articles in previous issues of the *Alumni News* have been **quite** pleased with
                                                        W.19
the response **they** received **from** the readers. Many reported renewing old friendships and
           G.2-2   W.12
making new friends. We know our readers would enjoy and benefit from your excellent article.

Yours truly

Student's Name
Editor

ms

Application 9B—Solution Document

TO: Sales Staff

FROM: Student's Name

DATE: Current date

SUBJECT: First Quarter Sales Report

The first quarter revenue figures for **Region IV were** released **today,** and you will be
$\quad\quad\quad\quad\quad\quad\quad\quad\quad\quad\quad\quad\quad\quad\quad$ C.6 $\quad\quad\quad\quad$ G.1-2 $\quad\quad\quad\quad\quad$ P.1-2
pleased to learn that once again the team exceeded **its first** quarter revenue budget.
G.1-3 $\quad\quad\quad\quad\quad\quad\quad\quad\quad\quad\quad\quad\quad\quad$ G.2-2 N.1-1
Congratulations! Each member of the team **exceeded** the individual budget for the first quarter.
$\quad\quad\quad\quad\quad$ P.3-3 $\quad\quad\quad\quad\quad\quad\quad\quad\quad$ W.17
We have **consistently** met both team goals for the **past** three **years,** but rarely has every member
$\quad\quad\quad$ G.4-1 $\quad\quad\quad\quad\quad\quad\quad\quad\quad\quad\quad\quad$ G.1-3 $\quad\quad\quad$ P.1-9
of the team **exceeded** the budget plan. **It's** important that you review carefully the enclosed
$\quad\quad\quad\quad$ G.1-3 $\quad\quad\quad\quad\quad\quad$ P.4-4
report that **itemizes** the revenue generated for all targeted software products.
$\quad\quad\quad$ G.1-2

Of the six application software packages, the one that concerns me **most** is the project
$\quad\quad\quad\quad\quad\quad\quad\quad\quad\quad\quad\quad\quad\quad\quad\quad\quad\quad\quad\quad\quad$ G.4-2
management software. Our project management software sales **are** far below the national average
$\quad\quad\quad\quad\quad\quad\quad\quad\quad\quad\quad\quad\quad\quad\quad\quad$ G.1-2
for the first quarter. In fact, not a single sales representative on our team **met** the budget for
$\quad\quad\quad\quad\quad\quad\quad\quad\quad\quad\quad\quad\quad\quad\quad\quad\quad\quad$ G.1-3
project management software.

Would each of **you** analyze your territory carefully and give me an **account-by-account**
$\quad\quad\quad\quad\quad\quad$ G.2-2 $\quad\quad\quad\quad\quad\quad\quad\quad\quad\quad\quad\quad\quad$ P.4-1
projection of the project management sales for next **quarter?** I have asked Liz **Jordan,** our
$\quad\quad\quad\quad\quad\quad\quad\quad\quad\quad\quad\quad\quad$ P.3-2 $\quad\quad\quad\quad\quad\quad$ P.1-5
technical support **manager,** to come to our next **regularly** scheduled team meeting and talk with
$\quad\quad\quad\quad$ P.1-5 $\quad\quad\quad\quad\quad\quad$ G.4-1
us about ways we can increase our sales in this deficient area. Liz was very instrumental in
helping the **Region III** team increase **its** sales of project management software. I am sure she
$\quad\quad\quad$ C.6 $\quad\quad\quad\quad\quad\quad\quad$ G.2-2
can help us improve our sales in this area.

During the next team **meeting,** we will also view a new product release and begin planning
$\quad\quad\quad\quad\quad\quad\quad$ P.1-1
for launching the sale of this product in our territory. You will be **sent** a product release package
$\quad\quad\quad\quad\quad\quad\quad\quad\quad\quad\quad\quad\quad\quad\quad\quad$ G.1-3
prior to the meeting. Please review it **carefully** so that we can use the meeting time effectively.
$\quad\quad\quad\quad$ G.4-1
Enclosure

Application 10B—Solution Document

Notice—Position Available for Network Manager

Applications for the **newly** created position of network manager **are** now being **accepted** in
G.4-1 G.1-2 W.2
the **Personnel Management Department**. Both internal **and** external applicants must complete the
W.16 C.5 G.5-1
standard application **form**. Forms for internal applicants must contain the signature of the **person's**
W.12 G.6-1
immediate supervisor before they can be **processed**. The deadline for applications **is** June **15**.
G.1-3 G.1-2 N.2-2
The new position is a Grade **12** position in the Administrative Services Division. The new
N.1-1
network manager will report **directly** to the manager of Administrative Services. The **principal**
G.4-1 W.18
reasons this new position was created **were** to provide technical support and training to **users** of
G.1-2 G.1-2
personal computers on the network and **to** have one person who will be totally responsible for
W.16 G.5-2
developing a comprehensive manual for **users** and a network procedures manual. **This** position
G.6-1 G.2-1
requires a person with computer experience as well as knowledge of computer operating systems

and application software. Network knowledge and supervisory experience **are desirable,** but they
G.1-2 P.1-2
are not required. The **new** network manager will be sent to a **three**-week training program in San
W.13 N.1-1
Francisco. The training package was part of the contract for the new network.

The **first** responsibility when the new network manager returns is to develop and offer
N.1-1
training courses for all employees who have **access** to the network at this **site**. The training will
W.22 W.7
complement the other computer training **courses** that are available to employees. The Staff
W.9 W.8
Council advised us to make the courses mandatory for all new network users.
W.10 W.3

Evaluation Guide

✓ Assess Each Communication

1 Does the communication accomplish its objective?

A message is effective if it meet the needs of both the reader and the writer and is appropriate for the situation.

2 Is the communication objective and logical?

A communication should be factual, and decisions should be based on sound, logical reasons. The message should present adequate information to support the decisions made.

3 Is the tone positive and confident?

The message should convey the impression that the writer is knowledgeable and credible. It should build goodwill and focus on what can be done rather than on what cannot be done.

4 Is the communication the right length?

Only those ideas essential to conveying the message completely and effectively and to ensuring courtesy and building goodwill should be included. Ideas should be conveyed in a concise, but courteous manner.

5 Is the message clear and easy to understand?

A message is clear if the reader understands the message without having to reread any part of it. Sentences and paragraphs are reasonably short, and vocabulary is appropriate. Tables, illustrations, and graphic aids are used when appropriate to simplify content.

6 Is the message coherent?

The words, sentences, and paragraphs should be sequenced logically and flow smoothly. They should fit together to convey a message. Appropriate transitional words should be used to link ideas.

7 Are important ideas emphasized?

The reader should be able to discern which ideas the writer considers more important and which are less important than others.

8 Does the communication have unity?

The message should have a sense of wholeness; that is, the reader should be able to discern a beginning, middle, and end. All ideas in a paragraph should be related to one topic.

9 Is the writing style effective?

The message should be interesting and free of clichés, platitudes, and outdated expressions. It should convey a considerate, pleasant, and helpful tone that is appropriate for the situation.

10 Does the message create a good image?

The format and physical appearance should support the message, be consistent, and create a favorable impression.